GOD'S
MYSTERIOUS
WAYS

GOD'S
MYSTERIOUS
WAYS

SUFFERING, GRACE, and GOD'S PLAN
for JOSEPH

GARY INRIG

Discovery House.
from Our Daily Bread Ministries

God's Mysterious Ways: Suffering, Grace, and God's Plan for Joseph

© 2016 by Gary Inrig
All rights reserved.

Discovery House is affiliated with Our Daily Bread Ministries, Grand Rapids, Michigan.

Requests for permission to quote from this book should be directed to: Permissions Department, Discovery House, P.O. Box 3566, Grand Rapids, MI 49501, or contact us by e-mail at permissionsdept@dhp.org.

ISBN: 978-1-62707-527-5

Printed in the United States of America
First printing in 2016

To the memory of our beloved daughter Janice,
and in honor of her wonderful children Morgan and Connor,
with tested confidence in our never-failing, always faithful God.

The steadfast love of the LORD never ceases;
his mercies never come to an end;
they are new every morning;
great is your faithfulness.
"The LORD is my portion," says my soul,
"therefore I will hope in Him."
Lamentations 3:22–24

CONTENTS

PREFACE

It was all very puzzling. In a time before cellphones made such a thing far easier, someone had worked hard to track me down and give me an urgent message. I was to call a specific police officer as soon as possible, but I was assured that the situation had nothing to do with my own family. As soon as I spoke with the officer, I understood what was so important: a member of our congregation had been murdered while on business in a distant city. Police there had asked our local police to inform the widow; in turn, our city police wanted me, as the family's pastor, to break the news to this unsuspecting woman.

Instantly, I felt overwhelmed, unqualified to carry out such a duty. But it had to be done, and quickly. Calling on the Lord for strength and wisdom, I set out, knowing the news would devastate that young mother. Nothing would ever be the same for her or her children. In an instant, everything was different.

Thankfully, life-transforming moments are not always so devastating. But sudden, unexpected, shocking moments are far from uncommon.

A young student-athlete, one day before going to university, suffers a freak accident while frolicking on a children's slippery slide. A broken neck leaves him paralyzed, creating a totally unexpected future for him and his entire family.

A person in a position of great trust and responsibility is exposed for a secret life. The news unleashes a tidal wave of pain and shame on a widening circle of people, who not only feel betrayed and angry but have to deal with the wreckage from another's sin.

The birth of an anxiously awaited baby is closely followed by the discovery that that she has a serious genetic anomaly, which abruptly redefines a family's expectations and responsibilities.

A doctor's diagnosis of a serious malignancy or the report of a serious accident plunges both the recipient and those closest to him into the valley of the shadow of death.

An economic downturn, a market slowdown, or simple bad management causes the collapse of a once-thriving company, throwing faithful employees out of work in an area where good jobs are few and far between.

The list could be extended indefinitely. Such is life in a fallen world.

Sometimes, these hard moments are the consequence of our own bad choices or behavior. Just as often, they come unheralded and undeserved, forever changing the fabric and pattern of our lives. They demolish our cherished hopes and dreams.

But life-changing moments aren't always for the worst. Some things suddenly and dramatically change life for the better. Sometimes they come serendipitously, as apparently "chance" events produce wonderful results: an unplanned meeting turns into a romance, leading to a happy lifelong marriage; a casual introduction leads to a job or the beginning of a new professional relationship; a businessperson stumbles onto a remarkable opportunity; a researcher happens on a finding that has great practical benefits, as well as major economic significance. Other positive life-changers we anticipate, plan on, and prepare for: a wedding, the birth of a child, an educational program, a career in a new city. With all of these blessings come new challenges and demands, though they are ones we prefer immeasurably over the negative kind.

Perhaps you've seen the television commercial depicting two large white boards, each covered with yellow and blue magnets. An investment company spokesman explains that the yellow magnets are for good things, while the blue magnets represent negative life events. The first board is for events in peoples' past; the second for their expectations of the future. After people place their magnets, the spokesman wryly points out that colors on the "past board" are remarkably balanced—an almost even mixture of blue and yellow. But the "future" board is overwhelmingly yellow. Quite naturally, people want to anticipate good, encouraging events, choosing not to dwell on those traumas and tragedies that, deep down in our hearts, we know life will bring.

Researchers call such a response "optimism bias." We look to the future expecting good things. Who wants to focus on fears about the future? Yet we humans are curiously ambivalent. Studies show that when people are asked about the collective future of society, a large majority expresses pessimism—especially about their country's direction or the capability of its political leaders. When asked about their personal future, though, those same people are remarkably optimistic. Bad things may happen to other people; we feel confident they won't happen to us.

When we're honest with ourselves, we know our future won't be "trauma-lite." Reality forces us to recognize the inevitability of pain and loss in a broken world. Some things will make life easier and better, but others will make it far harder and more challenging. That is commonsense realism; it is also enduring biblical wisdom. Ready or not, hard times will come.

That is what makes the story of Joseph so compelling. Few people in Scripture experienced such deep, soul-crushing betrayal and injustice, for such a prolonged period. His lows were deep, devastating, and enduring. And then, within hours, he was elevated from the dungeon to a pinnacle of unimaginable power, wealth, and luxury, a lifestyle almost unequaled in his world.

But these events weren't simply cruel fate or good fortune. At every stage, Joseph's life was within the providence of his good and gracious God, who was as present in the hard times as in the good times. The enduring contribution of Joseph's story is not what it tells us about him, but what it teaches us about the ways of God—his God and ours. Those ways, as we will see, are often deeply mysterious. Still, they are unfailingly good.

My own family has found itself in one of those unexpected, overwhelming situations that change life forever. In the matter of moments, we realized that the future would no longer be like anything we had anticipated. Lessons we learned from the life of Joseph have taken on new significance for us, and, like him, we have experienced our Lord's grace and faithfulness in new ways.

Because of our Lord Jesus Christ, it is right for His people to live with a God-trusting "optimism bias" even in the harsh reality of life's worst moments. Here is the Lord's promise: "After you have suffered a little while, the God of all grace, who has called you to his eternal glory in Christ, will himself restore, confirm, strengthen, and establish you" (1 Peter 5:10).

William Cowper, whose great hymn "God Moves in a Mysterious Way" is obviously reflected in the title of this book, mulled the providence of God with these words:

Deep in unfathomable mines
Of never failing skill
He treasures up His bright designs
And works His sov'reign will.
Ye fearful saints, fresh courage take;
The clouds ye so much dread
Are big with mercy and shall break
In blessings on your head.

This is a book written out of hard, often dark times in our lives. Yet the Lord's blessings have overflowed throughout, and we as a family have learned the truth of David's familiar words: "Even though I walk through the valley of the shadow of death, I will fear no evil, for you are with me; your rod and your staff, they comfort me" (Psalm 23:4).

It is wonderful to know that the Lord walks with us through the valley, but it is also wonderful to have others who do as well. I am beyond grateful to my precious wife, Elizabeth, our special grandkids, Morgan and Connor, our son, Stephen, and our daughter Heather, as well as their spouses and our other wonderful grandchildren. Together, we walked with my daughter Janice on her journey to her eternal home.

And to many family and friends who will read this book, we say a very inadequate thank you: you have loved us, prayed with and for us, encouraged us, and helped us in a multitude of ways. "God is not unjust so as to overlook your work and the love that you have shown for his name in serving the saints, as you still do" (Hebrews 6:10).

ONE

GOD'S TAPESTRY

I can scarcely imagine a worse way to welcome a new year.

Our oldest daughter had been complaining about strong headaches and a general lack of well-being throughout the Christmas season. She finally agreed to follow our urging to seek medical help when, driving to her job one morning, she had to pull over to the side of the road because the headaches were causing her to vomit.

Around noon, Janice, a divorced single parent with two delightful children, went with her mother to the local urgent care facility while I stayed with the children. Preliminary tests led to Janice being referred to the community hospital across the street for further evaluation. When those results revealed an ominous mass in her head, she was transferred by ambulance to the regional hospital. It was New Year's Eve, and the larger facility would have more equipment and specialists for diagnosing her condition more precisely and then carrying out the necessary treatments.

Elizabeth and I traded responsibilities, and I followed the ambulance to the hospital, accompanying Janice through the inevitable admitting rituals. As the old year passed into history, the experience was surreal. What kind of way was this for us to celebrate a new year?

By now Janice had been given medicine to relieve her pain. She was actually feeling better and more cheerful than she had in days. But the wait for the doctor seemed interminable. When he finally arrived, he gave us news with kindness and clarity: the tests, preliminary as they were, showed evidence of a significant tumor on Janice's brain. Only exploratory surgery could reveal its exact nature, so Janice would need to be admitted immediately. The news was almost too much to digest.

There is no way to prepare specifically for an event like that. I'm old enough to recognize that my body is wearing out, but my daughter, healthy and strong in her early forties? She was my firstborn—I remembered so well anxiously awaiting her arrival. She had opened doors to rooms of love in my heart that I hadn't even known existed. Then she had gifted us with two delightful grandchildren who had enriched our lives in so many ways. I couldn't help but ache for those children, asleep at our home under my wife's care, completely unaware that their world was completely and irrevocably changing.

Elizabeth and I already knew that 2013 was going to bring significant challenges. Within a few months we would both be stepping down from two decades of ministry in a church we deeply loved. But nothing like this had been on our horizon! How would my beautiful daughter, who had already faced so many difficulties and challenges in her short life, handle all the losses and changes that were now about to cascade upon her?

Remarkably, there was a peace even in the midst of the shock. Janice was strangely calm, perhaps because of the medication but more, I am convinced, because of the Lord's presence. The threat was real, fear was appropriate, and the next fifteen months would find us navigating places we never would have chosen to visit. A few days later, surgery would reveal that her tumor was a *glioblastoma multiforme*, the most aggressive form of primary brain cancer. It has no known cause and a very bleak prognosis.

But Janice was in her forties, and doctors assured us that her relative youth might make a difference toward a positive outcome. Through all that followed, our daughter showed remarkable courage and determination as well as a resilient faith in her Lord, though she was not without times of deep distress. We journeyed with her through seemingly endless doctor visits, chemotherapy and radiation, research about other treatment possibilities, and the irritating and wearying processes of dealing with medical and governmental bureaucracies.

Janice was a fighter. She was determined to go back to work and provide for her children, and she fought to regain the strength to do so, aided by the compassionate response of her fellow workers. She also determined to travel, returning to her Canadian roots to share with her children the people and places that had shaped her in the years before they were born. By this time, Janice and her children had moved from their home into ours, and family life took on new forms. But she longed for the opportunity to move her family back into their own home.

Sadly, the cancer was relentless. About six months after her radiation ended, it became evident that, while the disease had been delayed, it hadn't been defeated. Janice was forced to leave work. Then, as her pain and inability to cope increased, doctors advised that only a much more radical surgery could prolong her life.

A week before Christmas, she had the surgery—but while it diminished the size of the tumor, it also left her with very little use of her right arm or leg. Now she was dependent, unable to walk unaided or even to feed herself. She spent that Christmas and New Year's Day recovering in the intensive care unit.

A few weeks later, after about a month in the hospital and a rehab facility, Janice was able to come home with us, to spend her last weeks surrounded by people who loved her—including two parents who would have done anything to change places with her. Those were precious days, especially for Elizabeth and me, but hard days for Janice and her children. Exactly one month before Easter, on the first day of spring, she graduated into the presence of her risen Lord, in whose presence there is fullness of life and joy.

There are times when life hurts more than we can even say. Whether it's due to an accident, a medical diagnosis, our own foolish choices, or the sinful actions of others, everything changes, and not for the better. Times like that bring a deep groaning in our spirit.

A wise person once observed that if we are untroubled by the pain, suffering, and evil of our world, we suffer either from hardening of the heart or softening of the brain. At many points in our lives, the suffering in our world seems almost theoretical—we are enjoying good things, and misery is something that happens mostly to other people in other places. But then suffering gets up close and personal, barging into our lives unannounced, uninvited, and unwelcome, taking over everything. At such times, life comes fast and hard, squeezing cries from us: "Why?" "Why me?" "Why this?" "Why now?" Where, we wonder, is God in the midst of all this? If He truly loves me, why doesn't He stop the trouble or deliver me from it?

But even when life seems good, we know it won't always be that way. Sooner or later, we know that we will find ourselves facing the results of living in a sinful, fallen world. When his family was facing totally unexpected challenges, a friend of mine wisely said, "You don't get to choose your trials!" There are, of course, self-inflicted hardships, but for the most part, he was exactly right. In tough times we find ourselves grasping for something reliable to hold onto, a solid place to plant our feet. Only then are we able to live with hope and confidence, even joy, in the midst of inescapable pain and hurt.

We live in one of the most privileged times of human history. Technology has enabled us to live lives of well-being unimagined by people before us. We take for granted medical advances, creature comforts, and communication devices that enrich our lives in endless ways. Ironically, almost all of those good things also have a dark side. Our pursuit of creature comforts, personal security, or peak experiences too often leads us into lifestyles that distort and devastate family life, leaving us sad and alone in times of trouble.

Medical advances may prolong the length of our lives, but they often don't improve the quality of our living. When our daughter was in the rehab hospital, staffers would often comment on our consistent presence, pointing out that many were almost never visited by anyone.

In times of suffering, I have learned most from fellow-sufferers. It isn't usually their words that help me, but the examples they provide. It isn't often, in the midst of our journey through life's hard and dark places, that we get clear answers.

And, most likely, such an answer wouldn't really help us. The doctors could provide no reason why Janice had acquired the kind of cancer she had. Even if they could have, it wouldn't have changed the grief she felt, the loss her children were undergoing, and the choices we needed to make. It wasn't explanations we needed as much as enablement to live through what we were enduring—and the encouragement to trust in the Lord who knew what He was doing, even when we didn't.

In an important way, what happens *in* us at such times is more important than what happens *to* us. I can't control most of what happens to me, but I can, by God's grace, nurture what happens in me.

Over the years, the story of Joseph has continued to prove helpful and important to me. He may have lived long ago and far away, yet his life mirrors our own in so many ways. In highly dramatic forms, Joseph underwent some of life's worst experiences—bereavement, hatred, betrayal, attempted murder, enslavement, false accusation and injustice, wrongful imprisonment, and ingratitude. On the other hand, his was the ultimate rags-to-riches story, one of sudden elevation to power, prominence, and prosperity.

Joseph could have used his new privileges to take revenge on those who had oppressed him, yet he chose not to. In the midst of both the good and the bad, God was mysteriously working for His own glory, for the good of Joseph, and for the very people who had caused Joseph so much pain. Woven deeply into the fabric of the story is a life-giving and hope-sustaining truth: As believers in Christ, we can live with the confidence that *our covenant-keeping God is persistently at work for the good of His people, in the darkest of times and in the most unlikely of ways.*

There is a story, probably apocryphal, about a shipwreck in which only one man survived. He managed to gather some materials, piece together a raft, and eventually land on a desert island. He scraped together a shelter and scrabbled to find food and water to keep himself alive, all the while hoping that someday he could catch the attention of a passing ship. From time to time, he would see vessels in the distance, but none noticed his efforts to hail them.

Then a ship came closer than one ever had before. Desperately, the man tried to wave it down, and even lit a signal fire. But the ship kept on sailing. To make things even worse, when the ship was well past, sparks from the fire set the thatched roof of the man's shelter ablaze. He could only stand and watch as everything he needed to survive burned up. His last hope was gone.

Full of despair, the man didn't notice that the ship slowly began to turn and make its way toward his little island. But looking up, he watched with increasing excitement as it drew closer and closer. Finally, it came to a stop, a lifeboat was put over the side, and a party was dispatched to rescue him. Once on board, all the man could do was repeat his gratitude over and over again. Finally, though, curiosity got the best of him—he asked the crew why they had turned around so long after they had sailed past. "Why, we saw the signal fire you made when you set your shelter on fire!" the captain answered. The very thing that looked like it had destroyed him had, in fact, saved him. The fire that seemed to consume his hope was the means of preserving his life.

Joseph was a man whose hope seemed to be utterly consumed by the evil of others. Time and again, he appeared the helpless victim of people and circumstances. But chance wasn't ruling his life, God was. And when things finally did change, remarkably, the cause wasn't the "fickle finger of fate" but the gracious hand of his good and sovereign Lord. As he would say to his brothers decades later, in one of the great statements of Scripture, "You meant evil against me, but God meant it for good" (Genesis 50:20).

For thousands of years, the story of Joseph has captured the imagination of those who heard it. It was told around the campfires of the ancient Israelites as they traveled through the desert out of Egypt, to children in Sunday school entranced with the story of a "coat of many colors," even to modern musical theater audiences in the form of *Joseph and the Amazing Technicolor Dreamcoat*. But Joseph's story is not intended to stand alone, simply to acquaint us with a man worthy of imitation, enabled by God to rise above terrible circumstances. No, it comes as part of a larger story, of God's work that ultimately includes us, through the work of the Lord Jesus Christ.

So before we engage the Joseph story directly, it is extremely helpful to see it against a larger background. The most important insight we can start with is that the hero of the story isn't Joseph, but Joseph's God—the God who has revealed himself fully in our Lord Jesus Christ.

The Real Hero

The account of Joseph takes up more space in the book of Genesis than the story of any other person with the exception of Abraham, who is given almost the same amount. We are told more about Joseph than we are about Adam, Noah, Isaac, or Jacob. Yet this isn't simply the story of one's man's remarkable life and achievements, although there is much about his life to admire.

Joseph stands in contrast to many of the Bible's major figures in his lack of glaring flaws and personal failures. He was, of course, a sinful person, just as we all are, and he certainly had his moments of doubt, despair, and failure. But the Holy Spirit graciously chose to draw a veil over those as He recounted Joseph's story.

Still, God himself is the hero of Joseph's story, as He is of the entire Bible. The theme of Joseph's life is the providential, gracious care of our faithful, triune God who carries out His purposes and fulfills His promises for His people. God works not only through the faithfulness of Joseph but also through the sins of Joseph's brothers, through the seduction of an immoral woman and through the schemes of a pagan king. We will only read the Joseph story properly if we see it as part of the much larger story of who God is and what He is doing in the world.

The same thing is true in our lives. It's unlikely that any of us will be called to play the kind of strategic role in God's program that Joseph was. But our lives are part of the tapestry that God is weaving through history. Our sovereign God has a purpose for each of His children, and no part of our lives is outside of that purpose. That is why the apostle Paul can say with such assurance that "we know that for those who love God all things work together for good, for those who are called according to his purpose" (Romans 8:28).

Central to this declaration is the truth that we matter to God, not because of our merit or achievement, but because of His mysterious grace that called us to salvation through faith in the Lord Jesus. We are in the hands of a personal, loving God who is "for us" (Romans 8:31). We "know" the truth of Romans 8:28, not because we always feel it, but because God has declared it. And the One who promises to work "the good" is the one who controls "all things," not just some. We are not part of a random universe, in the hands of random fate, chance, or karma. A sovereign, gracious God is mysteriously at work in our lives, even in the midst of our pain, pleasure, and perplexity.

This bedrock conviction makes a world of difference. We may live in a fallen, frustrated, decaying world where terrible things happen even to God's people. Yet even though God does not cause those terrible things, He works in and through them. Even sinful things can't short-circuit the purpose of God in our lives to work everything for our good.

(I do wish to note, however, that what Paul identifies as the "good" is not necessarily our present peace or prosperity, or what makes us look or feel good. The good of Romans 8:28 is the ultimate good, realized, as Romans 8:29 goes on to tell us, when salvation is complete, and we are fully "conformed to the image of [God's] Son.")

God's Greater Story

Joseph's story is found in Genesis, an enormously important book that sets out the basic pattern of all that God is doing in human history. The story of Genesis is, in fact, the story of the Bible itself—God's plan to redeem and restore the world and humanity. The ancient world was full of creation stories, usually involving battles between various gods. But Genesis reminds us, in the brief but powerful description of its first chapter, that the one true God is Creator of everything, including human beings, the pinnacle of His creation. And all that He made was very good.

But the entrance of sin by the rebellion of the first couple means that they, and we, came to live in a fallen world where evil and death run rampant. The first eleven chapters of Genesis—covering the events leading up to the great flood of Noah's time and the scattering of humanity from Babel—reveal the tragic consequences of humanity's arrogant desire to deify itself and live in rebellion against God. But, in an amazing example of grace, God refused to turn His back on the humans He had created. Instead, He purposed to redeem all of creation, through a family of His choosing. He would bless the lineage of Abraham, through whom He would then bless the nations.

God's plan would reach its consummation when a Man born into the line of Abraham, Isaac, and Jacob would come as the great Redeemer and Restorer. This would be none other than the God-man, Jesus Christ, the Son of God who took on a human body to redeem the fallen world through His substitutionary death on the Cross, His victorious resurrection over death, and His triumphant return in glory to reign as King of Kings and Lord of Lords.

It is always tempting to read parts of the Bible in isolation from this great arc of God's purposes, to see Scripture as a series of individual stories. So we should constantly remind ourselves that Joseph's intriguing life in Genesis only finds its full meaning against the larger canvas of God's Word.

Moses wrote the book of Genesis to a group of refugees, connected by lineage to their ancestors Abraham, Isaac, and Jacob—Joseph's great-grandfather, grandfather, and father, respectively. Under Moses's leadership, and through God's delivering hand, the people had just escaped centuries of oppression in Egypt. Now, headed for the Promised Land and on the verge of becoming "a great nation" (Genesis 12:2), they needed to know who they really were as a people. They also needed to understand their destiny—they weren't just any people, but God's special people.

So Genesis should be read from the perspective of Mount Sinai, where God entered into a specific covenant with the people (as exemplified by the Ten Commandments) and called them to be His "holy nation" (Exodus 19:6). That Exodus moment wasn't the beginning of Israel's existence—it was the fulfillment of the even greater promise God had made with Abraham, the "Abrahamic covenant" that declared God's ultimate intention to bring salvation and renewal to the world through the gift of His own Son. After centuries of existence in Egypt, a land full of false gods, the Israelites needed to know the attributes and purposes of the one true God they had been called to know and serve.

We too are part of that people and that program. Although most of us are not Israelites by heritage, we have been joined to God's people by grace through faith in Christ. So the story of Israel becomes our story. As a part of the church of our Lord Jesus Christ, we have a distinctive place in God's program—a program that is rooted in God's dealing with the family of Abraham, Isaac, and Jacob.

Through His human agent Joseph, God saved the Israelites from extinction by starvation (or assimilation) in Canaan, because through them He intended to bless the world through the incarnation of His Son. In light of that great purpose, all that happens in the Joseph story shines with a brighter significance.

A Defining Moment

Let's look even more closely at Joseph's place in the unfolding story of God's purposes. We have noted that God's intention to redeem His fallen world put the focus directly on one man, Abraham, the most important person who ever lived after Jesus Christ and Adam. *God had a plan to bless the nations through Abraham's family.*

Abraham had been part of a moon-worshipping family in the great ancient city of Ur, in southern Mesopotamia in modern-day Iraq (see Joshua 24:2). But God sovereignly broke into his life with an astonishing promise:

> "Go from your country and your kindred and your father's house to the land that I will show you. And I will make of you a great nation, and I will bless you and make your name great, so that you will be a blessing. I will bless those who bless you, and him who dishonors you I will curse, and in you all the families of the earth shall be blessed."

> Genesis 12:1–3

Those words, repeated in various forms throughout Genesis, contain the heart of the Abrahamic covenant. It is the unilateral promise of a sovereign and gracious God to a man who was, astonishingly, seventy-five years old and still without children. There are three essential parts of this covenant. The first is *personal*: Abraham will have a family and

22

it will grow into a great people. The second part is *national*: Abraham's descendants will not just be a people, but a nation, implying that they will have a land of their own. This promise is given explicit definition in the events that follow. The third part is *global*: this Abrahamic family will become a source of blessing to all the families of the earth. Joseph's own life will become a vivid example of how God blesses not only the family of Abraham, but other peoples as well. Through Joseph, much of the ancient world will be saved from starvation. Through the greater Joseph, the Lord Jesus, the blessing of eternal salvation will extend to a "people for God from every tribe and language and people and nation" (Revelation 5:9).

We learn another important fact as the story of Genesis unfolds: *God always had a plan to send His people into Egypt.* One of the greatest moments in Abraham's life is recorded in Genesis 15. Feeling the days of his life running out, but still childless after years in the land of Canaan, Abraham complained that the Lord had given him no heirs of his own. In response, the Lord told Abraham to look into the night sky and number the stars if he could. "So shall your offspring be," God said. Humbled by this amazing promise, Abraham "believed the LORD; and he counted it to him as righteousness" (Genesis 15:5–6).

That divine declaration not only sealed Abraham's standing before God as a righteous man. It also became the foundational truth of God's gift of salvation, showing that we, as sinful people, are saved through faith in Christ, apart from any merit of our own. The Lord then commanded Abraham to prepare a ritual, strange to us but common in the ancient world, by which He would ratify a formal commitment. By a covenant, God bound himself to unfailingly keep His promise to give Abraham abundant offspring who would bring blessing to the world. And God specified the geographical boundaries of the land He intended to give Abraham and his heirs (Genesis 15:18).

God also mentioned an important detail that directly impacts the Joseph story: "Know for certain that for four hundred years your descendants will be strangers in a country not their own and that they will be enslaved and mistreated there. But I will punish the nation they serve as slaves, and afterward they will come out with great possessions" (Genesis 15:13–14 NIV). Though the Lord did not identify Egypt as that country, that fact was painfully clear by the time the book of Genesis was written. The setting of Joseph's story was foreseen and foretold by God centuries before it happened. The Israelites' sojourn in Egypt, painful as it was, was not a detour—it was firmly within the wise purposes of God.

A third fact emerges from this: *God will use Egypt for the good of His people.* This circumstance is a step forward, not backward, in the plan of God. Being a landless people must have seemed like a tragedy as the centuries in Egypt wore on. But in the light of God's plan and purpose, it was a necessary step, a fact that could be seen only by trusting God's Word. So when Jacob wondered whether he should move his family from the Promised Land to join his son Joseph in Egypt, he was told by the Lord: "I am God, the God of your father. Do not be afraid to go down to Egypt, for there I will make you into a great nation. I myself will go down with you to Egypt, and I will also bring you up again" (Genesis 46:3–4).

Surely this is counterintuitive. Why would God choose Egypt as the place to build His people rather than the Promised Land? Why grow them into a "great nation" through oppression and slavery in a foreign country and not through freedom and prosperity in their own homeland? The answer is probably that the Israelites risked losing their God-intended identity in Canaan. They were being assimilated by marriage into the local people and seduced by their immorality and idolatry.

In the decade or so that followed Jacob's return to the Promised Land after his lengthy stay with his uncle and father-in-law Laban in Haran, his sons were becoming more and more Canaanite. The story is a sordid one. One son, Reuben, committed incest with Jacob's concubine Bilhah (Genesis 35:22). Two other sons, Simeon and Levi, used the God-given covenant sign of circumcision to get revenge on the Canaanites who had raped their sister. Their anger at the men's sin was justified; the atrocity they committed was nothing less than mass murder (Genesis 34). The murderous hatred of Jacob's sons toward their own brother (Genesis 37) and Judah's casual involvement with intermarriage, cultic prostitution, and paganism (Genesis 38) make it clear that this was not a family capable of bringing blessing to the world. They were becoming more and more like the Canaanites and less and less like the people God had called them to be.

Canaan was certainly a threat, but so was Egypt. It was the superpower of the region, an advanced urban civilization capable of building the pyramids—an immense contrast to the primitive, rural culture of Canaan. At this time in their history, Egyptians held a deeply engrained prejudice against foreigners. Combined with a profound sense of their own superiority, they created a kind of apartheid which, evil as it may have been, actually protected the Israelites. So we read that when Joseph's brothers came to Egypt, "They served [Joseph] by himself, the brothers by themselves, and the Egyptians who ate with him by themselves, because Egyptians could not eat with Hebrews, for that is detestable to Egyptians" (Genesis 43:32 NIV).

When Jacob's family later arrived in Egypt with their sheep and livestock, Joseph insisted they tell the nation's officials that they were herdsman: "Then you will be allowed to settle in the region of Goshen, for all shepherds are detestable to the Egyptians" (Genesis 46:34 NIV). God would use this arrogant, sinful racism to further His purposes for His people. The Egyptians' contempt for outsiders would insulate the people of Israel, allowing them space to begin to become the great nation God intended them to be. He would use the Israelites' enemies for the Israelites' good.

One of the intriguing features of the Joseph story is how rarely God intrudes directly into the action, in contrast to the experience of his forebears, Abraham, Isaac, and Jacob. On at least five occasions, Jacob was given a direct visionary encounter with the Lord, as well as the remarkable experience of physically wrestling with God himself (Genesis 32:22–32). Joseph had no such experiences—no voice from heaven, no vision of a ladder reaching to heaven, no visit from an angel, no meeting with God "face to face" (Genesis 32:30). Nevertheless, the God of Abraham, Isaac, and Jacob is everywhere present, behind the seen and the scenes, even as sinful people carry out their selfish and sinful actions.

Much of the time, Joseph must have wondered how the unjust sufferings he was experiencing bore any relation to the sense of destiny God had given him in the dreams he had experienced as a teenage boy. But, looking back, he was finally able to see the hand of God at work.

One of the decorations my mother had placed in our family room was a framed needlepoint of a poem by an unknown author.[1] On the one hand, I don't remember paying it much deliberate attention. On the other, it was there for years and apparently etched itself on my youthful heart. My mind has often gone back to that poem, especially as I have visited weavers' shops in the Middle East and seen women working at the shuttle as people have for centuries. The poem's style is quaint, but its truth is enduring:

My life is but a weaving
Between my Lord and me.
I cannot choose the colors
He worketh steadily.

Oft times He weaveth sorrow
And I, in foolish pride,
Forget He sees the upper
And I the under side.

Not 'til the loom is silent,
And the shuttles cease to fly,
Shall God unroll the canvas
And explain the reason why.

The dark threads are as needful
In the Weaver's skillful hand,
As the threads of gold and silver
In the pattern He has planned.

There are plenty of dark threads in Joseph's life. Yet when we see the tapestry of his life, there is an unmistakable beauty. So it is with all of us. No one is exempt from the dark threads, and some are so unimaginably dark that we think they will destroy the design entirely. Any pattern seems to have vanished. But that's not true.

Looking back, we—just like Joseph—can occasionally see the hand of God. This side of heaven, it will probably remain a mystery to me why my daughter died at the time and in the way she did, and why at this point in our lives my wife and I would be entrusted to play such a significant role in raising her children. But we know, as the apostle Paul did, that nothing can separate her, or us, or our grandchildren from the love of God which is in Christ Jesus our Lord (Romans 8:39).

Each of us is a work in progress, and the Lord over all knows exactly what He is doing. As John tells us, "Beloved, we are God's children now, and what we will be has not yet appeared; but we know that when he appears we shall be like him, because we shall see him as he is" (1 John 3:2). Armed with that confidence, we now turn to trace the Weaver's work in the life of Joseph.

TWO

FAMILY MATTERS

The twenty-first century is not proving to be kind to the family. The massive social experiment launched by the sexual revolution of the 1960s has transformed the cultural landscape to such an extent that it seems, at times, that intact nuclear families may soon qualify for the endangered species list.

In my youth, children were typically raised by their biological parents, with extended family nearby. Such families are now a minority. Divorce, remarriage, cohabitation, soaring out-of-wedlock birthrates with the corresponding epidemic of fatherlessness, changing moral and sexual standards, even the redefinition of gender and marriage themselves have all combined to transform the social landscape. As one observer has noted, "Researchers who study the structure and evolution of the American family express unsullied astonishment at how rapidly the family has changed in recent years, the transformations often exceeding or capsizing those same experts' predictions of just a few articles ago."[1]

Families are the indispensable building block of society, an essential component of human flourishing, established as so by God himself at creation. Family was also one of the first victims of the entrance of sin into our world, so that, since the fall, there has never been a golden age of family life. Nevertheless, there have been tested and tried models, which, although they are far from perfect, embody God-given truths. The past few decades have witnessed an ongoing assault on such models, an assault which has focused the "culture wars" primarily on matters related to marriage, family, and sexuality.

The US Supreme Court decision of 2015 which remarkably found a right to same-sex marriage in the Constitution serves as a critical benchmark of how far the dismantling of millennia-old concepts of marriage, morality, and family have gone. The lighting of the White House in rainbow colors to celebrate that decision only served to reinforce the tectonic shift in our cultural values. But that moment was hardly the end of the change. In the months since, there has continued to be a mounting pressure to normalize almost any conceivable expression of sexuality, all in the name of what has been termed "expressive individualism."

In such a climate, those who cherish values they believe are rooted in God's creation and God's Word are readily dismissed either as hopelessly prejudiced or as fossil-like remnants of a past age. The new wisdom calls us to jettison the idea of family as a group of people linked by birth, marriage, or adoption for more flexible and accommodating understandings. Now "family" describes a group of people with whom one shares values and resources, at least for the present moment. Since love alone is said to be what defines family, we are left with a bewildering array of options—serial parenting, distance parenting, nonresidential parenting, surrogate parenting, homosexual partner parenting, transsexual parenting, and a multitude of other forms that seem to grow weekly.

Sadly, children are the primary losers in such arrangements. As youth specialist Chap Clark observes, "The effect has been powerfully destructive. Allowing for the definition of family to be reshaped to line up with almost any casual encounter between two or more people is to deny thousands of years of societal history. The [children are] left to discern how to handle the multi-conflicting messages related to home, stable relationships and internal security."[2]

This hurt is evident in a multitude of ways, not least in the troubles that cripple our school systems and in the criminal gang activity among rootless youth, social problems that will only be resolved by addressing them primarily at the family level. Even a superficial analysis makes it clear that fractured families produce fractured lives. Those, in turn, lead to fractured communities, producing a downward spiral that will be ultimately reversed only if and when God, in grace, intervenes.

The Bible is not romantic or sentimental about the challenges of family life. The same book that establishes family as the center of God's intention and provision for humans also makes it clear that marriage (and thus the family) was the first casualty of the entrance of sin. Adam and Eve's rebellion against God caused them to hide from and blame one another. Family was the setting for the first murder, as Cain killed his own brother, Abel. Even the life of Abraham, the great father of the faith, displayed the effects of sin. Twice he betrayed the God-given sanctity of marriage by using his very attractive wife, Sarah, as a bargaining chip to protect his own life and promote his own interests.[3] He also found himself the target of his nephew Lot's greed, a feud in which he modeled a grace-filled response.[4]

While God's Word realistically portrays the challenges of family life, it insistently points us to the family as God's gift for human flourishing. It is the place where lives are formed, truth is taught, values are learned, faith is cultivated, security and love are experienced, and God's love and grace should be experienced and shared.

We don't get to choose the times we live in, but we do get to choose how we live in those times. We may wish that we lived in an era that nostalgia deceives us into believing was almost entirely "family-friendly." But we don't. So, because families matter, whenever and wherever we live, we need to live in God-honoring ways that promote family health.

A Broken, Dysfunctional Family

Joseph was not raised in a healthy family. After Scripture's brief notice of his long-awaited birth (Genesis 30:22–24), we meet Joseph as a seventeen-year-old, enmeshed in a family that epitomizes dysfunctionality. His father's choices had produced a chaotic disarray of wives, concubines, and children, all competing for their place in the complicated family system.

It was a system in which the now-motherless teenager had to make his own way. His mother, Rachel, had died giving birth to his younger brother, Benjamin, and that lack of a protective mother made Joseph a convenient and unprotected target for his brothers' festering resentment.

> These are the generations of Jacob. Joseph, being seventeen years old, was pasturing the flock with his brothers. He was a boy with the sons of Bilhah and Zilpah, his father's wives. And Joseph brought a bad report of them to their father.
> Now Israel loved Joseph more than any other of his sons, because he was the son of his old age. And he made him a robe of many colors. But when his brothers saw that their father loved him more than all his brothers, they hated him and could not speak peacefully to him.
>
> Genesis 37:2–4

Joseph's family history was one of chaos and confusion. As a young man, his father had fled Canaan to escape the wrath of his older twin, Esau—Jacob had deceived and cheated him to get the family birthright. Jacob's parents were already wanting him to leave, concerned that he would marry a local Canaanite girl as Esau had. Jacob traveled hundreds of miles to his mother's family home in Paddam-aram, an area of modern Syria.

When he arrived, Jacob his heart was instantly captivated by his beautiful cousin Rachel, whom he determined to marry.[5] However, his shrewd and unprincipled uncle Laban saw other possibilities. Laban deceived Jacob into first marrying Rachel's older sister Leah, and then maneuvered a marriage with Rachel—at the cost of fourteen years of servitude.

That enough was a terrible way to begin married life. But the inevitable polygamous tension was only compounded by Leah's abundant fertility and Rachel's inability to conceive. Rachel's shame at her own failure and her envy of her sister led to the desperate act of giving her servant girl Bilhah to Jacob as a kind of substitute. Perhaps Bilhah, as a surrogate, could provide sons for her husband.

The plan seemed to succeed. But when Bilhah conceived, Leah countered by giving Jacob her servant girl, Zilpah. With three fertile women conceiving children, the family grew—and so did Rachel's pain. The agony of her inability to bear a son for her husband is revealed in her plaintive words when the longed-for child finally arrived: She said, "God has taken away my reproach," calling the boy Joseph and begging, "May the LORD add to me another son!" (Genesis 30:23–24). The Hebrew words translated "taken away" and "add to" sound very much like the Hebrew name she gave her son: Joseph. He was Jacob's eleventh son, but his arrival as the long-awaited firstborn of the beloved Rachel instantly made him the favored one. The other women and their sons could only see Joseph as a threat to their hard-won status. But this divided family found a new kind of unity: they had no use for Joseph.

We can only imagine what life was like in that polygamous rat's nest of relationships. But I got a clearer idea while reading the autobiography of a highly respected professor of World Christianity at Yale, a Roman Catholic scholar named Lamin Sanneh. He had been born and raised in a polygamous Muslim family in an impoverished village in the West African country of Gambia. The story of his encounter with and conversion to Christianity is a remarkable one, as is the account of his journey from that out-of-the-way village to the heights of academia.

For our present purpose, I'm interested in Sanneh's account of growing up in a polygamous home. He was the oldest son of his father's second wife, and by the time he was ten, there were eight children by the two women. As he writes about his and other polygamous families, Sanneh describes the relationship between the wives and their husband:

> A husband of many wives may pretend to be above the fray, but in truth the male ego is no match for the jealousy of women unsheathed for battle. The jealousy of co-wives is impregnable to the thunder of a husband intent on exercising his authority. The male temper is a mere tempest in the household teacup. . . . Individually or in concert the co-wives are the prime movers in the domestic sphere, with the man bobbing in and out of his wives' lives on a rotation dictated by the women's natural cycles.[6]

Inevitably, the inherent jealousy between wives will be manifested and magnified in the relationships among the children. Children identify with their mothers far more than with their fathers. As Sanneh observes,

Sibling rivalry is rife among children of the same father, whereas children of the same mother observe a uterine pact that prescribes collaboration and mutual bonding. . . . Children by the same paternity are born to strife and to abiding distrust, while, to make for a viable household, children on the maternal side are like peas in a pod.[7]

He speaks of "the peculiar complexity of polygamy," with its competing factions and shifting alliances. "Children make their way in that world by weaving and dodging among complex patterns of maternal assurance."[8]

That was the kind of family into which Joseph was born. Growing up would have been a challenge, even had his mother survived. But that was not to be, as she died giving birth to Joseph's brother Benjamin (Genesis 35:16–19). So, by the age of seventeen, Joseph was without a mother to fend for him, and he also needed to protect a younger brother against the family dynamics. Still, he was the firstborn son of his father's cherished wife, a position that gave Joseph a special place in his father's heart—and first place on his brothers' "most-hated" list.

Given the family dynamics, Joseph's troubles with his brothers were almost inevitable. But two situations combined to make a bad thing worse. First, we are told, Joseph was assigned to shepherd the family flocks with some of his brothers—specifically the sons of his father's concubines Zilpah and Bilhah. On his return, he "brought a bad report of them to their father" (Genesis 37:2).

It is hard to be sure exactly what is going on here. It is possible that this "bad report" was an invention of Joseph, though it could have been factually true. From all that we know of the brothers, they would have given Joseph plenty of ammunition for such a report. If the report was true, what might have been Joseph's motivation? Was this information that Jacob really needed to know? Or was it simply the action of a spoiled child, trying to put his brothers in the worst possible light? Whatever his motives, the outcome was the same: Joseph further alienated his already jealous brothers. He made it clear that he wasn't going to go along with them, just to fit in. That gave his offended brothers even more reason to hate him.

The second issue was to prove far more troublesome. Joseph's father, Jacob, had himself experienced the damage of favoritism in his own upbringing—his parents' preference for one son over another had driven wedges between mother and father and between Jacob and Esau. Of all people, Jacob should have known better. But his grief-filled love for Rachel caused him to love her long-awaited son, "the son of his old age," in an openly preferential way. Oblivious to the feelings of his other sons, Jacob chose a symbol almost guaranteed to inflame his sons' simmering envy: "a robe of many colors."

This rendering is so familiar that it is hard to think of this garment in any other way. But it is likely that this translation is misleading.[9] Probably, the Hebrew expression doesn't refer to the color of the coat, but to the fact that it had long sleeves. Combined with special ornamentation, it would mark its wearer as a person of elite, even royal, status. This coat singled Joseph out, making it clear that he was the preferred one, the son with a special status, the "princely one" destined to inherit leadership in the family. It is as if a father were to give his older sons mountain bikes and the youngest the most expensive sports car.

Jacob's actions screamed favoritism, and he was pouring lighter fluid on a smoldering fire. Ironically, the ensuing explosion would damage the favored son most of all.

"When his brothers saw that their father loved him more than all his brothers, they hated him and could not speak peacefully to him" (Genesis 37:4). This brotherly hatred now becomes the theme of the chapter: "they hated him even more" (37:5); "so they hated him even more" (37:8); "his brothers were jealous of him" (37:11). The family had become a cauldron of anger, jealousy, and hatred, feelings that would have been more properly directed at the father who was playing favorites. Joseph, however, was an easier target. Meanwhile, Jacob seemed determined not to see the growing animosity.

This is the family through whom God said He would bless the world! Clearly, before He could ever use Jacob's heirs in that way, He would have to fundamentally transform them. And that would require bringing these men to a place of heart-changing repentance.

For Joseph, the favored son and hated brother, the journey to usefulness would send him through the refiner's fire. Any arrogance and sense of personal superiority in his life needed to be purged. Only after experiencing bitter suffering and harsh injustice would Joseph be prepared for the remarkable purposes the Lord had for him. But before that long, hard journey began, God planted a special sense of destiny deep in Joseph's heart. It was a forecast of divine plans for and through Joseph, plans far beyond his capacity to imagine.

There is a warning in this sad portrait of a broken, dysfunctional family. From all we can tell, Jacob was a talented and wealthy man, able to provide for his family's physical needs at a level far beyond the average for the people of his time. But he was largely a failure in his most important assignment—as a model of a godly man showing self-sacrificing love for his children's well-being. His sons were fully responsible for their sinful choices, but Jacob's partialities made it easier, not harder, for them to do the wrong thing. His is an example that should cause every parent to engage in some thorough, even painful, self-evaluation.

God's Dream, Not Joseph's

> Now Joseph had a dream, and when he told it to his brothers they hated him even more. He said to them, "Hear this dream that I have dreamed: Behold, we were binding sheaves in the field, and behold, my sheaf arose and stood upright. And behold, your sheaves gathered around it and bowed down to my sheaf." His brothers said to him, "Are you indeed to reign over us? Or are you indeed to rule over us?" So they hated him even more for his dreams and for his words.
>
> Then he dreamed another dream and told it to his brothers and said, "Behold, I have dreamed another dream. Behold, the sun, the moon, and eleven stars were bowing down to me." But when he told it to his father and to his brothers, his father rebuked him and said to him, "What is this dream that you have dreamed? Shall I and your mother and your brothers indeed come to bow ourselves to the ground before you?" And his brothers were jealous of him, but his father kept the saying in mind.
>
> Genesis 37:5–11

Joseph was God's man in his generation, the one who would shape the future of his entire family. Privileged as he would ultimately be, he would not have the same remarkable experiences with God that his forefathers Abraham, Isaac, and Jacob had. They received visions and direct messages from God, encountered angels, and had mysterious occasions when God himself had appeared to them. Joseph would not have such moments in his life. The Lord is always the same, "yesterday and today and forever" (Hebrews 13:8), but He doesn't always do things the same way!

On the other hand, the Lord did reveal himself in Joseph's life through dreams, as He had done with others earlier in the book of Genesis.[10] Four of those dreams were experienced by others, and Joseph was given God's help to interpret them. But the two dreams of Genesis 37, given to a seventeen-year-old boy, were to shape the rest of his life. They were not the products of a repressed psyche or the overactive imagination of a teen-aged boy; the context makes it clear that these are God-sent dreams, divine revelations of Joseph's and his family's destiny.

His brothers viewed the dreams very differently. When Joseph related the first dream, "They hated him even more." The brothers felt no need to call for someone to interpret what they were hearing. When Joseph spoke of seeing their sheaves bowing down before his, which remained upright, it could only represent his preeminence over them and their submission to him. They couldn't (and didn't) miss the implication: "Are you indeed to reign over us? Or are you indeed to rule over us?" (Genesis 37:8).

In the brothers' eyes, this was the dream of an arrogant, self-promoting, spoiled adolescent. Joseph could have responded, "That's not my plan—it's God's!" But he made no attempt to analyze his dream. He let it speak for itself, and his brothers hated him. Though he must have understood that the dream indicated his coming lordship over his brothers, he had no way to know how costly and difficult the dream's fulfillment would be.

What are we to make of Joseph here? It seems certain that he believed the dream had come from God himself. (He would later say of the Egyptian king's dreams, "The dreams of Pharaoh are one; God has revealed what he is about to do"—so he clearly viewed such dreams as coming from God.) But why did Joseph feel it necessary to tell his brothers?

He must have known that they would be less than enthusiastic about this remarkable revelation! Was he simply naive, wanting to share something that was significant to him? Perhaps, but he could have kept the dream to himself—the brothers had no need to know it and Joseph could just leave its outcome in God's hand. Or maybe it was sheer arrogance, the gloating of a young man tired of bullying. Perhaps it was a desire to get revenge for their animosity He was, after all, only seventeen years old, not an age when wisdom and discretion flourish!

Whatever Joseph's reason, the result was both immediate and predictable: "They hated him even more for his dreams and for his words" (37:8). They had hated Joseph for his place in their father's heart; now they hated him even more for his place in God's purposes.

Not long after, Joseph had another very similar dream. Intriguingly, in the Joseph story, dreams always come in pairs—Joseph's two, those of Pharaoh's cupbearer and baker in prison (Genesis 40), and Pharaoh's (Genesis 41). This was not an accident; as Joseph would explain to Pharaoh, "The doubling of Pharaoh's dream means that the thing is fixed by God, and God will shortly bring it about" (Genesis 41:32). That is probably the reason for the repetition here.

Again, the meaning of this dream was transparent: the sun, moon, and eleven stars bowing down "to me" represented Joseph's elevation above all of his family members. He was in the place of unquestionable supremacy, a supremacy that included even his parents, the obvious interpretation of the sun and moon.[11] It was one thing to suggest that a younger brother would be elevated above his brothers; such things can happen, as they had with Jacob and Esau. But in the patriarchal society of the ancient world, it would be startling to have a son exalted above his parents. Joseph wasn't being represented simply as the channel of Abrahamic blessing in his own generation; the dream said he would have precedence over even his father.

Joseph felt compelled to recount this dream to his brothers as well, and once again when his father was present. Like his sons before him, Jacob instantly recognized the implication—he, the father, would bow in submission before his son. He angrily protested the idea, yet was so intrigued that he could not dismiss what he'd heard: he "kept the saying in mind" (37:11). Jacob intuitively realized that he should not dismiss these dreams as the imaginings of an immature and spoiled son. Neither could the brothers dismiss them as youthful foolishness. Scripture says they "were jealous of him," implying that they wanted for themselves what the dreams said Joseph would get. The dreams stuck in their minds, an irritating presence deepening their hatred and anger and producing a growing desire to rid themselves of "this dreamer" (37:19). With plans to kill him, they said, "We will see what will become of his dreams" (37:20).

It is important to reinforce a simple but significant fact: Joseph's dreams were God's dreams. They didn't represent Joseph's personal ambitions in life, a projecting of his own desires.

In too many cases, when people discuss this passage, the moral of the story is transformed into something like this: "Everyone has a dream, a desire to make a difference with his or her life. Like you, Joseph had a dream—to be a great leader in his family. He refused to let it die, even though so many things conspired against him. Be a Joseph! Dream big, and don't let anyone steal it away!" There may be value in having a personal "dream," a dominating life goal, provided that it is carefully evaluated in the light of Scripture, honest prayer, and godly counsel. It is not necessarily wrong to pursue such dreams. But no matter how valuable goals and hard work may be, this interpretation bears no resemblance to what this passage is about.

Joseph is not dealing with some self-generated dream. This is a declaration of his future, given in dream form, by God himself. It is a form of prophecy. We must not reduce this story to a moralistic vignette about the value of positive thinking in our lives.

We have no idea what Joseph's life ambition may have been at this point. We do know what God's plan and purpose were, a plan that He would sovereignly and surprisingly make reality. As it turned out, in the short term, Joseph's dreams became nightmares. His brothers didn't bow down before him: they threw him into an empty cistern in preparation for killing him, then decided to sell him into slavery. Joseph's dreams would take him through dark valleys of slavery and unjust imprisonment.

Contrary to all appearances, though, the Lord was working in and through all things to put Joseph in just the right place at just the right time to deliver his family. A time would come when his brothers *would* bow before him, and he would be in a position to save the ones who had hated him so deeply. At present, however, those God-sent dreams only inflamed the jealousy and hatred his brothers already felt. The revelation of Joseph's destiny was like waving a red flag in front of a bull already snorting in anger.

Joseph never sought to fulfill these dreams on his own. He had no power to do that. All he could do was trust the God who had given the dreams, staying faithful to Him even in the hardest experiences. In doing so, Joseph points us to a great certainty: *Both the Lord's promises to us and His purposes for us will be accomplished in and for us, whatever the circumstances of life.* That does not remove our responsibility to live in God-honoring ways. Rather, it deepens our confidence that "He who began a good work in [us] will bring it to completion at the day of Jesus Christ" (Philippians 1:6).

Our lives may not be broken in the same places as Joseph's. Our battles may not be those that come from a tumultuous home life, though for some they may be. Whatever the case, battles and hardships will come. We are given no exemption from hardship; what we are given are God's great promises.

My daughter, my wife, and I have all heard a doctor tell us that we were dealing with a cancer in our bodies. Our daughter's was obviously the most traumatic, because of its severity, her age, and her status as a mother of young children. But I can also vividly recall the anxious, sleepless nights after my wife was diagnosed with an advanced breast cancer in her mid-forties. Still, in all those moments, we found ourselves breathing the oxygen of God's sure promises. We needed and loved life- and hope-sustaining words like, "If God is for us, who can be against us? He who did not spare his own Son but gave him up for us all, how will he not also with him graciously give us all things?" (Romans 8:31–32). In and through the brokenness and evils of life, as well as our own failures and shortcomings, our God is for us—not against us. He is constantly working to accomplish His purposes, to keep His promises, and to bring deliverance and blessing to us. Then He uses us to bless others.

Joseph's story shows that the Lord will use us—but before He can fully do that, He will work to refine and transform us progressively into the people He desires us to be. The pampered and immature "daddy's boy," the seventeen-year-old who brought his father a bad report against his brothers and paraded both his coat and his dreams before them, is a far cry from the seasoned, wise, compassionate, and tested leader who would become an agent of blessing to his family and the nations of his world.

Through the school of suffering, with the seemingly "chance" circumstances of life as tests, God's deliverer would begin to emerge in Joseph. The very things that threatened to destroy him would actually prepare him for God's purposes. Through Joseph, his hate-filled, hardhearted brothers would be brought to a repentance that changed them and the future of their entire family.

Strikingly, God is never mentioned in the events of Genesis 37. But He is far from absent. His fingerprints are everywhere—in Jacob's family history, with all its brokenness, which God had superintended; in the family destiny, with its roots in the calling of Abraham; in the family dynamics, where the brothers' hatred would lead them to sell Joseph to the very place God desired him to be; to the dream, in which God revealed what only the unfolding years would make plain. He is behind the scene and the seen, using even the sinful actions of people to praise Him.

And so it is in our lives. God promises "'I will never leave you nor forsake you.' So we can confidently say, 'The Lord is my helper; I will not fear; what can man do to me?'" (Hebrews 13:5–6).

THREE

WHEN EVIL WINS

There are times when it is almost painful to watch the news. We witness terrorists kidnapping young girls, forcing them to convert to Islam, and selling them as wives or sex slaves; beheading innocent victims, all the while taunting their political enemies; attacking people praying in a synagogue, eating in a restaurant, or attending a concert. We see vicious criminals stuffing vans and boats with refugees desperately seeking a place to raise their families free of warfare and terrorists; too many of these innocent people die without reaching their goal. We observe prominent celebrities and powerful businesspeople, widely praised for their achievements but using their position and prestige to abuse others.

The list goes on—obviously guilty criminals getting off on legal technicalities; immense corporations bending the law to their own gain; racists flouting their prejudices; top-level executives lining their pockets with bonuses and stock options while cutting lower-level workers and destroying the value of investments; dictators exploiting destitute citizens while secreting billions of dollars out of their nations; corrupt politicians gaming the system to their advantage; television preachers enjoying lifestyles of the rich and famous while exploiting the trust of pensioners; parents inflicting abuse on the very children God has given them to nurture and protect. No wonder the poet James Russell Lowell wrote of "Truth forever on the scaffold, Wrong forever on the throne."

Still, the most painful times for most of us take place far from the attention of the media, in the private, unpublicized happenings of our personal lives. Few experiences in life are as bitter as betrayal—and the closer the betrayer, the more bitter the taste:

- The "friend" whose social media posts are intentionally cruel, intensely personal, or maliciously out of context.
- The employer who fires a faithful employee without true cause or promotes a less qualified person out of dishonorable motives.
- The employee or advisor on whom you relied, who breaks your trust and steals your money, your customers, or your reputation.
- The spouse who abandons you to find "greener grass," leaving you to try to pick up the pieces.
- The parent who deserts you, the prodigal who breaks your heart, the supposed protector who instead abuses you emotionally, physically, or sexually.

To compound the trauma, many of the perpetrators seem to sail through life while their victims struggle to reconnect the broken pieces of their lives. It seems the abusers reap nothing negative from their evil, often harvesting more than their share of life's good things.

Where is God at such times? Why does He seem so silent or far away? In a fallen and broken world where the wrong people too often win, God can feel entirely absent. No wonder the psalmist declared, "I was envious of the arrogant when I saw the prosperity of the wicked" (Psalm 73:3), and the prophet cried out, "Why does the way of the wicked prosper? Why do all who are treacherous thrive?" (Jeremiah 12:1).

As we come to the next stage in Joseph's story, that may be our response as well. The wicked have their way, and Joseph is turned into a helpless, seemingly hopeless, victim. God's direct actions are never seen; what is seen is the apparent triumph of appalling evil.

But what is visible does not tell us the whole story. God is never absent, especially in His care for His people. Behind the scene, He is at work, in and through a multitude of seemingly chance events as well as people's deliberately evil choices and actions. Through it all, God is carrying forward His plans for salvation and blessing. Perhaps, as we see God's mysterious providence in the life of Joseph, we will better recognize that the same God is perpetually and mysteriously at work in our own lives—for His glory and for our highest good.

A Good Walk Spoiled

> Now his brothers went to pasture their father's flock near Shechem. And Israel said to Joseph, "Are not your brothers pasturing the flock at Shechem? Come, I will send you to them." And he said to him, "Here I am." So he said to him, "Go now, see if it is well with your brothers and with the flock, and bring me word." So he sent him from the Valley of Hebron, and he came to Shechem. And a man found him wandering in the fields. And the man asked him, "What are you seeking?" "I am seeking my brothers," he said. "Tell me, please, where they are pasturing the flock." And the man said, "They have gone away, for I heard them say, 'Let us go to Dothan.'" So Joseph went after his brothers and found them at Dothan.
>
> Genesis 37:12–17

Fifty years is a long time to be married. Lord willing, by the time this book is in your hands, my wife and I will have reached that milestone. The Lord has been very gracious to me. Elizabeth and I met at university. I hadn't dated much in my first year and a half, but she ignited my interest—so I fought off my reticence and asked her out. Self-centeredly (and rather foolishly), I asked her to accompany me to a church service at which I was preaching, and then to have coffee afterwards. What kind of woman could resist such an enticing invitation?

Elizabeth responded very politely to that glorious opportunity: "I'm very sorry, but I can't. I have other plans." I wasn't terribly smart, but I was pretty sure I was hearing a brush-off. I was disappointed, but decided I'd get over it. The Lord would have someone else, I trusted.

The two of us studied in the same part of the university library, and a few days later, I saw her ahead of me, going down the stairs to her next class. I also noticed her bracelet slip off her wrist and fall to the ground. I picked it up, rushed after her, and returned it. As we walked together, she told me how disappointed she'd been that she hadn't been able to accept my invitation. So there was hope! It didn't take me long to ask her out again. And that was it—neither of us ever dated anyone else.

In the ensuing years, Elizabeth made up for missing that sermon of mine thousands of times over. Amazingly, she claims that she still enjoys listening to me preach! She has been a wonderful person to go through life with, and I've often wondered what would have happened if that bracelet had stayed on her wrist. Would I really have been so stupid as to not pursue a second chance?

Elizabeth insists that the bracelet's clasp was unreliable—she did not drop it on my account. It really was an accident. But I'm convinced that it wasn't a *random* accident. Behind the seen was the unseen hand of a gracious God, looking out for one of his foolish sons.

One of the Bible's great truths is that we have a sovereign God who works all things according to the counsel of His own will. He isn't a remote, deistic god who wound up the watch of creation and then sat back to let things take their own course. As He says of himself, "My counsel shall stand, and I will accomplish all my purpose" (Isaiah 46:10).

We as humans may have a hard time believing that. We see life at the ground level, with all of its seemingly chaotic chances and accidents. We see people making choices, often sinful ones, and wonder where God is in the midst of it all. But He is there, even if we cannot see Him.

The Bible makes this assertion in many places. For example, we read in Psalm 135:6, "Whatever the LORD pleases, he does, in heaven and on earth, in the seas and all deeps." Daniel 4:35 tells us, "He does according to his will among the host of heaven and among the inhabitants of the earth; and none can stay his hand or say to him, 'What have you done?'" We are told of the Lord Jesus that "in him all things hold together" (Colossians 1:17) and that "he upholds the universe by the word of his power" (Hebrews 1:3).

Our Savior taught that our heavenly Father's concern for us extends even to the minutiae of our lives: "Are not two sparrows sold for a penny? And not one of them will fall to the ground apart from your Father. But even the hairs of your head are all numbered. Fear not, therefore; you are of more value than many sparrows" (Matthew

10:29–31). Our triune God is sovereign not only over the movements of stars and galaxies, but also subatomic particles. He knows and cares about both the monumental and the trivial in the lives of His children. He is Lord over all, and He carries out that lordship with infinite variety and creativity—most often unseen and unrecognized by us. But all the time, He is there.

———————◾———————

God's mysterious providential care is most certainly at work even during the most tragic events of Joseph's life, recorded in the last half of Genesis 37. God's name never occurs in the narrative; chance and coincidence seem to rule. Yet the passage of time will reveal exactly the opposite. God is at work, getting Joseph exactly where God wants him to be.

- The brothers "just happened" to pasture at Shechem, where Jacob "just happened" to have good reason to be concerned about their safety (vv. 12–13).
- Joseph "just happened" to wander in a field where he met a man who had "just happened" to overhear his brothers' plans (v. 17).
- The brothers "just happened" to move to Dothan, which was on a main caravan route to Egypt (v. 17).
- Joseph "just happened" to meet them while he was wearing the special robe that symbolized his brothers' grievances and inflamed their hatred (v. 23).
- An Ishmaelite caravan on its way to Egypt "just happened" to pass by that particular place at that particular time (v. 25).
- Reuben "just happened" to be away when the sale of Joseph was made (v. 29).
- The Ishmaelites "just happened" to sell Joseph to one of Pharaoh's high officials (v. 36)

It was not chance, however, but the sovereign Lord invisibly arranging all those apparent accidents of life, using both the routine circumstances of life and the evil deeds of sinful people for His own ends.

This story begins with the rather bland observation that Joseph's brothers had gone to pasture the family's sheep at Shechem, an area about fifty miles north of the family home in Hebron. The herd was obviously sizable if it required the presence of ten of the brothers to tend it. And fifty miles is a long way to herd sheep! The patriarchs had chosen Hebron as their home base because of its good pastureland; there must have been some significant reasons, unknown to us, for the brothers to undertake such a demanding journey.

Another fact made their destination even more surprising. Shechem was the very area where, just two years earlier, the brothers Simeon and Levi had carried out an atrocity against the local residents (Genesis 34:25–30). Their outrageous actions had endangered their entire family, and Jacob quickly relocated them. The Shechemites' pain and anger would still be fresh, and their hunger for revenge unsatisfied. That alone made Shechem a dangerous place for any one member of Jacob's family to go, never mind ten of them.

No wonder Jacob was worried about the well-being of his sons! We are not told why Joseph had stayed home—was this another act of fatherly favoritism, sparing the "chosen one" from potential danger? Did the special coat show that his father considered Joseph above such duties as shepherding? Did the brothers simply not want him along? We cannot know. Whatever the case, Jacob's anxiety about the other brothers reached the point that he decided he should send his special son to discover whether things were "well" with them.

The word rendered "well" is the Hebrew word *shalom*, which means "peace." It probably betrays Jacob's fear that either the brothers or the Shechemites might resort to violence once again. So his assignment for Joseph was, on the one hand, entirely understandable. On the other, it showed that Jacob was remarkably oblivious to his own family's interpersonal dynamics. Seemingly clueless about what was going on between his older sons and Joseph, he failed to recognize that the real danger to his family wasn't external but internal. Never in his wildest imaginings could Jacob have envisioned events turning out as they did.

Joseph seems equally unaware. He raised no objection to his father's directions, dutifully setting out immediately, never conceiving it would be twenty-two long and often painful years before he would see his father again. He made the long, solitary trek to Shechem only to be frustrated. The brothers were no longer there, and there was no way to determine where they might have gone.

But as he was "wandering in the fields," Joseph "just happened" to encounter a stranger, who "just happened" to engage him in conversation. In the ensuing discussion, this man revealed that he had "just happened" to overhear the brothers say to one another, "Let us go to Dothan" (37:17). This was a town about twelve miles northwest of Shechem, in a valley that separates the hills from the coastal mountains. There was nothing unusual about shepherds in the dry season seeking more adequate pasture, and Dothan was nearer the coast. Yet the presence of this stranger at just the right moment seemed so remarkable to later rabbis that many of them suggested that he was, in fact, an angel sent by God. Although he was not an angel, he clearly was an agent of God's special providence.

Armed with this new information, determined to carry out his father's assignment, Joseph set out for Dothan, a place which "just happened" to be near the main trade route linking Egypt and the fertile and populous regions that stretched eastward into Mesopotamia. This was an area outside the territory familiar to Jacob and his family, so information about what happened there would be more likely stay there, rather than leaking back to Jacob, sixty-five miles away in Hebron.

It is amazing that, as Joseph traveled, he chose to wear his special robe rather than normal working clothes. Such an elegant coat was entirely inappropriate for the mission he was on. Was he oblivious to the effect it would have on his brothers, or was he deliberately provoking them? The former seems more likely to me, but wearing that robe was guaranteed to provoke a powerful reaction.

The Brothers' Conspiracy

They saw him from afar, and before he came near to them they conspired against him to kill him. They said to one another, "Here comes this dreamer. Come now, let us kill him and throw him into one of the pits. Then we will say that a fierce animal has devoured him, and we will see what will become of his dreams." But when Reuben heard it, he rescued him out of their hands, saying, "Let us not take his life."

And Reuben said to them, "Shed no blood; throw him into this pit here in the wilderness, but do not lay a hand on him"—that he might rescue him out of their hand to restore him to his father. So when Joseph came to his brothers, they stripped him of his robe, the robe of many colors that he wore. And they took him and threw him into a pit. The pit was empty; there was no water in it.

Then they sat down to eat. And looking up they saw a caravan of Ishmaelites coming from Gilead, with their camels bearing gum, balm, and myrrh, on their way to carry it down to Egypt. Then Judah said to his brothers, "What profit is it if we kill our brother and conceal his blood? Come, let us sell him to the Ishmaelites, and let not our hand be upon him, for he is our brother, our own flesh." And his brothers listened to him. Then Midianite traders passed by. And they drew Joseph up and lifted him out of the pit, and sold him to the Ishmaelites for twenty shekels of silver. They took Joseph to Egypt.

Genesis 37:18–28

The brothers' first response to the sight of Joseph, alone and vulnerable, wearing "that coat," is telling: "Here comes this dreamer!" (37:19). Their contempt is evident. They have distanced themselves from him; he is not "Joseph" or "our brother" but "that dreamer." I suspect that a significant number of their conversations on this "business trip" had been about their obnoxious younger brother Joseph. What turned long-standing irritation to hot anger was the memory of those dreams he had narrated, dreams that seemed so arrogant and self-promoting. Now, enraged by his mere presence and the sight of that coat, they quickly formulated their response: "Let us kill him . . . and we will see what will become of his dreams" (37:20).

It is not hard to imagine a gang of hot-headed street kids coming to such an impetuous decision. But these were grown men, most of them in their twenties. You would hope that someone would have the maturity to make allowances for this younger brother, calling the others to consider the boy's grief over the loss of his mother, or pointing out the role their own father had played by his blatant favoritism. That was not to be. Caught up in their own selfishness, damaged by their father's favoritism, nurtured in sibling rivalry, twisted by jealousy, and fearful that the dreams might indeed be true, they set their minds on the unthinkable: Joseph must be murdered in cold blood!

No matter how annoying Joseph might have been, nothing could excuse that kind of response. Yet, without hesitation, the older brothers agreed to a heinous murder to end both the dreams and the dreamer. But they failed to recognize that in fighting the dreams, they were fighting God himself, and that was a battle they could not win. In fact, their resistance would only further the ultimate fulfillment of those hated dreams.

When Reuben, the oldest brother, heard about the murder plot, he knew he had a responsibility to stop the others. His instincts were right, but he lacked the strength to oppose them directly. His father would later describe him as "unstable as water" (Genesis 49:4), a penetrating insight into Reuben's lack of moral fiber.

Instead of robustly challenging the evil plan, Reuben attempted to distract and delay his brothers, suggesting an intermediate step: "Shed no blood; throw him into this pit here in the wilderness" (37:22). Although his motivation isn't entirely clear, Reuben probably felt responsible as the oldest son to be his father's stand-in. His intention to return and rescue Joseph was honorable—he was the only one to offer even token resistance to the blood fever that had seized the mob—but his lack of courage was deplorable. In the end, he stood by passively as the others abused Joseph.

Quickly, ruthlessly, the brothers carried out Reuben's alternate plan. Overpowered by sheer numbers, probably taken completely by surprise, Joseph was helpless to defend himself. Within moments, he was brutalized—seized, stripped of his robe, and thrown into an empty cistern. Such pits were common, designed to collect water during the wet season. Usually about ten feet deep, they had a narrow opening at the top and a widening base; hewn from rock or dug into the ground, they were plastered to hold water. This was the dry season, however; there was no water in the pit. A person inside had no way to escape without help from the surface. Abandoned, such a person would inevitably die.

The hardhearted brothers, like a pack of animals, then sat down to enjoy their meal, closing their ears to their brother's desperate pleas echoing out of the pit. Twenty-two years later they would remember that moment with shame: "We saw the distress of his soul, when he begged us and we did not listen" (Genesis 42:21). Joseph's cries may not have moved their hearts, but the sound never left their consciences.

Soon after, a Bedouin caravan[1] "just happened by." At this time, the brothers were very near the main trade route leading to Egypt, and this particular group had chosen this particular route at this particular time. Bedouin caravans don't run by formal timetables and, in the normal course of affairs, a person might go days without encountering one. But God's providence has its own schedule! This seemingly chance appearance led Judah to suggest an alternate plan, one that would avoid the blood guilt they would incur by actually killing their brother[2]: "Let us sell him to the Ishmaelites" (37:27).

Judah's leadership at this moment will prove significant in later years. He stepped into a leadership gap, but his motivation was greed, not pity. Judah's new plan would seemingly accomplish the desired result: Joseph would be permanently removed from the family, and the brothers could make some money in the process: "What profit is it if we kill our brother and conceal his blood? Come, let us sell him to the Ishmaelites, and let not our hand be upon him, for he is our brother, our own flesh" (37:26–27).

There was no brotherly love in this suggestion; it was a hardhearted, pragmatic attempt to get rid of Joseph while avoiding blood guilt and the possible vengeance of God. It was certainly "the lesser of two evils," but still unspeakably evil. Kidnapping, followed by slave trading, was a capital offense in the laws of the ancient Near East (see for example Exodus 21:16 and Deuteronomy 24:7). It was, by any measurement, an atrocious choice.

Judah's proposal did, however, spare Joseph's life. It was both less sordid and more shrewd than murder. The twenty shekels of silver the brothers received for Joseph may not have been a fortune, but at a time when working shepherds earned perhaps eight shekels a year, it wasn't trivial.[3] It also carries an ominous foreboding of a time when One far greater than Joseph would be sold by another Judah (*Judas* is the Greek form of the name *Judah*) for thirty pieces of silver (Matthew 26:14–16).

Judah's brothers apparently shared the same compunction about cold-blooded murder, so they readily agreed to his proposal. Retrieving Joseph from the pit, they quickly struck a deal with the passing traders, bidding farewell to the hated dreamer and his dreams. They had disposed of Joseph once and for all—or so it would seem for the next twenty-two years, until the terrible secret they hid from their father would be revealed in the most unexpected of ways.

Covering Up

When Reuben returned to the pit and saw that Joseph was not in the pit, he tore his clothes and returned to his brothers and said, "The boy is gone, and I, where shall I go?" Then they took Joseph's robe and slaughtered a goat and dipped the robe in the blood. And they sent the robe of many colors and brought it to their father and said, "This we have found; please identify whether it is your son's robe or not." And he identified it and said, "It is my son's robe. A fierce animal has devoured him. Joseph is without doubt torn to pieces." Then Jacob tore his garments and put sackcloth on his loins and mourned for his son many days. All his sons and all his daughters rose up to comfort him, but he refused to be comforted and said, "No, I shall go down to Sheol to my son, mourning." Thus his father wept for him.

Meanwhile the Midianites had sold him in Egypt to Potiphar, an officer of Pharaoh, the captain of the guard.

Genesis 37:29–36

Reuben had been away on some unknown duty, probably related to the care of the sheep. He returned to discover that Joseph was gone, sold into slavery. When he had the opportunity, Reuben had not stood up to his brothers' evil plans. Now it was too late. In his absence, the secret plan to rescue Joseph had turned into disaster.

Reuben's role in this matter was the least despicable, but even now he made no effort to pursue the traders and try to retrieve Joseph. He simply poured out his dismay in purely selfish terms: "And I, where shall I go?" (37:30). The last place he wanted to go was home, where—as the oldest brother—he would have to take the lead with their father, Jacob. Somehow, Reuben would have to account for Joseph's absence. That was the true source of his pain, not the thought of what was likely to happen to his younger brother, now on his way toward slavery in Egypt.

But the other brothers were more resourceful. Since they could not let their father know what they had done, the old man must be deceived. While they hadn't shied away from the idea of killing or selling their brother, it struck them as wrong to explicitly lie to their father. So they would instead maneuver him into drawing his own conclusion that Joseph had been killed by a wild animal.

The brothers turned Joseph's hated robe into a weapon against their father. Dipping it in a goat's blood and strategically tearing it, they returned the robe to their father. And they made no attempt to soften the blow they knew would break his heart: "This we have found; please identify whether it is your son's robe or not" (37:32). The request itself and the impersonal "your son's" show the utter callousness of their hearts. Of course it was Joseph's—there was no other coat like it. So Jacob drew the inevitable conclusion: the bloody robe was proof of a violent death. "It is my son's robe," Jacob said. "A fierce animal has devoured him. Joseph is without doubt torn to pieces" (37:33). So was Jacob's heart.

There is grim irony in the fact that the brothers killed a goat to deceive their father. Years earlier Jacob himself, along with his mother, had used a goat's hide to deceive his own virtually blind father (Genesis 27). It never entered Jacob's once-deceitful mind that his own sons could be complicit in an atrocity.

No one ever really gets over the death of a child, and Jacob certainly didn't. For the next twenty-two years he would live with the wound of that moment, which he refused to allow to heal: "No, I shall go down to Sheol to my son, mourning" (37:35).[4] For Jacob, this wasn't just the death of a son: Joseph wasn't *a* son, he was *the* son. If Jacob had dreams—of the personal, aspirational kind—his had all centered on Joseph. With Joseph gone, Jacob's hopes and dreams vanished.

Carrying out their role in this fictional funeral, the brothers crowded around Jacob, wearing deceitful expressions and speaking hypocritical words of comfort to their unsuspecting father. They cried crocodile tears, feigning concern at the very moment they deceived their father in a way that broke his heart.

At the end of Genesis 37, we see a father entering into lifelong, inconsolable grief. He had been victimized by his own sons, who feigned concern as they joined their sisters in an attempt to console him. But Jacob could not and would not be comforted. For the rest of his life, there would be a Joseph-sized hole in his heart.

Paradoxically, the brothers had not really put Joseph out of their lives. His absence was the ever-present reality of their family life. Jacob's grief for Joseph left a deep impression on the brothers, as would become evident years later. And they carried their own guilt, as events would ultimately expose.

As for Joseph, he had seemingly been carried into oblivion. Sold as a slave into the home of an Egyptian military officer, Joseph had no apparent future and almost no reason to hope. The memory of his dreams served only to mock him, as he tried to survive as a stranger in a strange land.

As a young man, his future had just days before seemed bright with promise. But overnight, those prospects had come to a sudden and brutal end. By all appearances, Joseph was a helpless victim, betrayed by family and abandoned by God, a prime candidate for bitterness and despair. Yet remarkably, he was exactly where God wanted him to be.

We, of course, have an advantage that Joseph didn't have: we know how his story ends. We can see the providential hand of God where Joseph could see only the clenched fist of evil.

Most of us have had the experience of going through a maze, as our family did once on a vacation. My ten-year old grandson Connor could hardly maintain his excitement when we arrived, and he immediately challenged me to a race—which of course he won. Connor then made the trip three more times, challenging anyone he could find. Those kinds of mazes are fun. But the maze of life's harsh reality is very different. At ground level, we are confronted with bewildering obstacles that seem to block any hope of getting through to the other side.

When Joseph began his trip to meet with his brothers, he had no idea that he was entering a labyrinth that would take him two decades to navigate. We can look down at Joseph's life from God's perspective and see the maze leading to the exact ending God intended. But Joseph had to go through his maze one step at a time, just like we do. None of us can be sure where the next turn will take us.

We can learn an important truth from Joseph's life, a truth played out over and over in the pages of Scripture: *God is often most present when He seems most absent.* That becomes apparent in Genesis 39, where we are told four times that the Lord was with Joseph (vv. 2, 3, 21, 23). Christ-followers have God's unbreakable promise when we enter life's darkest moments: "I am with you always, to the end of the age" (Matthew 28:20). Or, as the book of Hebrews puts it, "'I will never leave you nor forsake you.' So we can confidently say, 'The Lord is my helper; I will not fear'" (13:5–6). In my own journey through "the valley of the shadow of death," the familiar words of Psalm 23 have taken on a deep resonance: "I will fear no evil, for you are with me" (v. 4).

A second great truth that emerges from this traumatic period of Joseph's life is also of great comfort: *God uses the very things that seem to kill the dream to advance it.* God's purposes for Joseph, plans that involved him being in Egypt, in no way excuse the evil behavior of his brothers. They were unspeakably evil, and they would suffer consequences—though for a time they seemed to have succeeded in their schemes. But a time would come when Joseph would realize that his brothers' sinfulness had put him in the very place God intended, to bring deliverance to His people and blessing to the nations, just as His covenant with Abraham had promised. Joseph was a God-sent, not a God-abandoned, man. The evils that affected Joseph, harsh as they were, were not random or accidental but Father-filtered, part of a larger good. So it is for every one of God's children.

Twenty-two years after a terrified, traumatized teenager tried to fall asleep the first night in his new master's home, he would stand before his brothers as the second most powerful man in the world. And he would say to them, "You sold me here, [but] God sent me before you to preserve life" (Genesis 45:5). That good result came at a high cost, especially for Joseph and Jacob. Old Testament scholar Iain Duguid says it well:

> God's sovereign plan left Joseph stripped naked and thrown into a pit. His sovereign plan for the good of his family left Jacob inconsolably

bereaved, in a state of sorrow and dark emptiness that would mark his life for the next twenty years or so. Jacob's and Joseph's dreams were completely shattered and broken, and there was no voice from heaven telling them it would all work out well in the end. They were left with nothing to fall back on, other than their faith in God and His promises.[5]

It is unlikely that our own situation will ever be as dramatic as either Joseph's or Jacob's. Yet the outworking of God's plan in our lives might find us in places almost as dark as theirs, with nothing to fall back on except God and His promises. But what a backup plan that is!

We are actually in a much better position than Jacob and Joseph were. Our knowledge of our God's person and promises is infinitely richer than theirs, because of the coming of our Lord Jesus Christ. We also have God's written Word and the confirmation of His faithfulness down through the ages. Most of all, our internal resources are deeper, since we have the blessing of God's indwelling Spirit.

We conclude this chapter with an even greater truth: *Joseph's rejection by his brothers is paradoxically their means of salvation.* His rejection will lead to his family's physical salvation from famine. It will save his family nationally, since Joseph's presence in Egypt will prevent their slide into Canaanite lifestyles and ultimate assimilation. Most importantly, Joseph's suffering will bring him to a robust faith in his Lord that will lead in turn to his brothers' repentance.

This pattern of salvation by rejection portrays the ultimate Savior and Deliverer, the One whose rejection by the sinners who crucified Him on a cross paradoxically becomes our means of salvation.

FOUR

THE WHEELCHAIR VIEW

My daughter's first surgery took place a few days after that momentous New Year's Day. It involved taking biopsies and debulking the tumor in her left temporal lobe. The surgeon said the tumor was too large to remove entirely, and it was too entangled with critical brain functions related to speech and sight to attempt any more. A few days later the pathology report revealed the severity of the cancer, although, as we were to realize, the doctors attempted to put the most positive spin possible on the implications.

Although church and ministry responsibilities remained, our lives were now organized around Janice's recovery. We walked with her through a rigorous course of chemotherapy and radiation that drained all of us, especially Janice. She and her two children moved into our home, and we began to walk together through the next stages of this totally unexpected journey.

Our other children and our friends rallied around to give us all the love and support they could. Janice's children were a constant source of delight, even in the midst of their concern and grieving for their mother. And Janice herself constantly surprised us with the depth of her resolve and resilience, as she endured physically demanding treatments, numerous doctor's visits, and the undesirable side effects of her medications. Of course, there were moments when the reality of what she was facing was almost overwhelming.

Radiation itself is a scary proposition. Janice was fitted with a mask, so the rays could be directed to precisely the right place in her brain. Elizabeth agonized, as only a mother can, when Janice needed to go by herself to be evaluated and fitted. Her mother's heart yearned to share that moment, to be whatever peaceful presence she could be to her daughter.

As Elizabeth sat in the waiting room, she realized that the small band of people occupying that space were all facing very similar challenges. They too had unexpectedly found themselves in the society of the suffering—their faces and, to some extent, their stories became familiar in the weeks that followed.

We took turns driving Janice to her appointments, and she was unfailingly brave. Each time she was called in for treatment, we longed to walk in with her, but it was a place she had to enter alone.

Though the technicians were always kind and gentle, she was suffering and we suffered with her. Still, we knew that as Janice faced much of this process by herself, she was never out of God's care and protection.

After the treatments, her strength gradually returned. She insisted on returning to work, both to provide for her children and to demonstrate her determination to overcome the cancer. The doctors agreed that this was both possible and wise. Janice's company, a foster and adoption agency, graciously altered her caseload to make her return feasible. Spending her days serving others was wonderfully therapeutic, and Janice battled the fatigue and weakness caused by her treatments to head out the door each morning.

Life was more normal, but it would never be the same again. Questions about Janice's future, and ours, though rarely spoken, were never far from our minds. In fact, our lives had already changed dramatically when we stepped out of our church ministries at the end of June.

Janice was now longing to take her children from their birthplace in California back to her childhood home in Canada. The children had never been there, and she wanted to share with them people and places that were special to her, as well as see family and friends for her own sake.

By midsummer, she was able to make such a trip, and the five of us set off on a driving tour that would cover more than thirty-five hundred miles.

It was a very special journey, full of wonderful moments as well as the challenges any family experiences when they spend that much time together in a car! But the friction was minor compared to the opportunity to reunite with relatives in Vancouver, many of whom Janice's children had never met. It also gave Elizabeth an opportunity to spend time with her brother David, a missionary for more than fifty years in Chile, who had just been admitted to hospice care in his own battle with cancer. He was aware that his home-going was close at hand, and his radiant trust in the Lord was a gift to us all. By the time we returned home, he had entered his heavenly home.

We went on to Calgary, where we had lived seventeen years, and reunited with many special friends who had been part of our church family. These were people who had known and loved Janice as a child, and now, at a very difficult period, came alongside us with love and encouragement. Their compassion and good works were like oxygen to our spiritual lungs at a time when we deeply needed it.

The beginning of the school year brought us into our "new normal." But within a couple of months, Janice's behavior was becoming increasingly erratic. We began to see evidence of the tumor's growing presence, as she had more frequent memory lapses, headaches, unpredictable behaviors, and increasing fatigue. Brain scans showed that the mass had grown significantly, and it became necessary for Janice to stop working. The doctors recommended surgery.

Because of her relative youth, the medical team suggested a radical procedure, one that held more hope of prolonging her life. We were prayerful and hopeful as the surgery took place a few days before Christmas 2013. But when Janice awoke, there were discouraging signs: her speech was clear, but she struggled to move her right arm and leg even slightly. We hoped this would be temporary, but that was not to be. Despite intensive therapy, Janice's right hand and arm regained only limited mobility and her right leg could no longer support her. My little girl now required a wheelchair.

For the next two months, first in a rehabilitation hospital and then at our home, she used the wheelchair. Both her mother and I found ourselves doing things for Janice that we had done when she was very small. I loved to do whatever I could to aid her, though her dependence on me was heart-wrenching. We spent a lot of time helping Janice in and out of her wheelchair, taking her for walks, and attending to her needs and desires. Those days were hard but precious, and far too short.

My daughter had never really enjoyed being a "pastor's kid." She loved me, but she found it hard to feel singled out for special scrutiny, and she developed a highly-tuned hypocrisy detector. Janice often struggled with church and certain kinds of church people though she always declared a deep faith in Jesus. Now, in the wheelchair, that faith became even more evident.

Psalm 121, with its repeated declarations that the Lord is the helper and keeper of His people, had always been her favorite. As she looked at her own mountain of cancer, she relied on the Lord to keep her fears under control. She didn't, I think, fear death itself, so much as the terrible reality that she wouldn't be there to watch and help her precious children, Morgan and Connor, grow up and make their way through life. That sad fact she needed to entrust to the Lord, her helper.

All too soon, from our perspective, those wheelchair days were gone, followed by Janice's confinement to bed. Then, on March 20, 2014, she graduated into the presence of her Lord and Savior.

I've written our story at some length, probably because it does me good to recall it, but also because I want to make a simple point. There is a vast difference between an armchair view of suffering and a wheelchair experience of it. Suffering is one of the great realities of human existence in a fallen world, and there are times when we can sit at a distance and think about it. But then it comes "up close and personal," in our own experience or the life of someone we love.

As it happened, I had intended to begin 2013 with a sermon series entitled "Great Questions." I asked my congregation to submit questions on which they wanted a biblical perspective. After four decades of pastoring, I was pretty confident I knew what most of them would be.

I was all but certain that people would raise questions related to suffering. After all, that is our universal experience. Over my years as a pastor, I had thought a great deal about suffering, prayed about it, taught about it, and wrestled with it in my own life. And, of course, I had been given the privilege and responsibility of walking with sufferers as they sought understanding, counsel, companionship, and comfort while going through some of life's deepest waters. As a result, I was fairly sure how I would approach the question.

Then came New Year's Day of 2013. Janice's brain cancer forced me not just to look at the question, but to live it. Now it wasn't just something I was going to preach about. The theoretical problem of suffering looks very different than the actual experience of it.

I don't know to what extent Joseph had ever thought about suffering. He had certainly felt it, when his mother had died giving birth to his brother Benjamin. He had experienced it as the victim of his brothers' jealousy and hatred, culminating in their stunning brutality at Dothan, when his life was spared only because they could sell him into slavery in Egypt. Now, as we see Joseph in Egypt, almost every precious thing in his life has been forcibly stripped from him. He has become a virtual poster child not just for suffering, but for undeserved suffering. Where, he must have wondered, was God in all this? What about the promises of those dreams?

The Lord's Mysterious Ways

Now Joseph had been brought down to Egypt, and Potiphar, an officer of Pharaoh, the captain of the guard, an Egyptian, had bought him from the Ishmaelites who had brought him down there.

The LORD was with Joseph, and he became a successful man, and he was in the house of his Egyptian master. His master saw that the LORD was with him and that the LORD caused all that he did to succeed in his hands. So Joseph found favor in his sight and attended him, and he made him overseer of his house and put him in charge of all that he had. From the time that he made him overseer in his house and over all that he had, the LORD blessed the Egyptian's house for Joseph's sake; the blessing of the LORD was on all that he had, in house and field. So he left all that he had in Joseph's charge, and because of him he had no concern about anything but the food he ate.

Genesis 39:1–6

Some time ago I required cataract surgery. I have been nearsighted for most of my life, and needed glasses to drive and function in daily life. With the encouragement of my ophthalmologist, I decided to have a lens implant that would make me farsighted—able to see clearly at a distance. By God's grace, the surgery was successful. Ironically, things that had been cloudy without glasses were now clear, while things that were once clear up close were now blurry. Before, I would take off my glasses to read; now I have to find and put them on to read! It all reminded me of 1 Corinthians 13:12: "Now we see in a mirror dimly, but then face to face."

One of the things we see very dimly now is the way the Lord is working in our lives. This is particularly so when we go through times of great difficulty and hardship that seem unjust. We may not like suffering consequences for our actions or choices, but at least we realize that, to some degree, we deserve them. But what about cases where there seems to be little or no connection between what we've done and what we're experiencing? Undeserved suffering—when bad things happen not only to good people but to God's people—is one of the great challenges in life.

The Bible faces that question not by giving us philosophical discourses but by telling stories of God's mysterious work in the lives of His people. That is certainly the case with Joseph. Abandoned by his family, he must have wondered whether he had also been abandoned by God. He had emerged from the pit of his brothers' hatred only to find himself in the fire of slavery in a foreign land. What of those dreams now? Cut off from all that was familiar, any reasonable hope for the future had vanished. He would be easy prey for self-pity, bitterness, or festering anger.

The land in which Joseph found himself stood in almost complete contrast to everything he had known before. The Promised Land had, as its center, a hilly spine running its length—plains to the west reached to the Mediterranean, while the eastern side fell off dramatically to the Jordan Valley and the Dead Sea, the lowest place on earth. Egypt, on the other hand, was centered on the one of the world's great rivers, the Nile. It flooded each year, providing abundant water for irrigation and leaving behind rich, fertile soil.

Canaan was underpopulated and underdeveloped, with a number of small tribal groups competing with one another for prominence. In contrast, Egypt was an ancient kingdom, centered on the Pharaoh, who was not merely ruler but a kind of god on earth. He was seen as the Egyptians' intermediary with the heavenly gods. Canaan was a land of villages and small city-states; Egypt had large, impressive cities.

The Egyptians worshiped local deities, as the Canaanites did, but they also had nature gods such as Ra (the sun god) and Osiris (the god of vegetation). Ra was embodied in his living representative, the Pharaoh. Such cultural and theological differences must have been overwhelming and bewildering to the young Hebrew.

And Joseph's life circumstances had changed drastically. He had apparently been forced to stand at auction in a slave market, a piece of merchandise to be inspected and bid on by potential buyers. He became the property of an influential Egyptian named Potiphar, a man devoted to Pharaoh and the Egyptian gods, as his name suggests—it means "he whom the sun-god Ra has given." Potiphar held high military office, and he was wealthy enough to have a household full of slaves catering to his needs and desires.

While Potiphar's specific responsibilities as "an officer of Pharaoh, a captain of the guard" (Genesis 39:1) aren't entirely clear, he was certainly a significant individual with military responsibilities and political connections. He was a man of prominence and power, before whom Joseph was a helpless slave, without status or identity. Joseph was a complete outsider, with no one nearby who spoke his language, no one to whom to appeal for help, and no one who cared about his well-being or future.

We do not know how long Joseph served as a slave in Potiphar's house, or how long he endured his imprisonment in an Egyptian jail. We do know that he was seventeen when he had the dreams that led his brothers to sell him (Genesis 37:2), and we also know that he was thirty when he was suddenly elevated by Pharaoh (Genesis 41:46). The thirteen years in between, some of the most formative and adventure-filled of any person's life, were robbed from him by the sins of others.

Those initial days, first as the Midianites' captive and then as Potiphar's slave, must have been the worst of all. Joseph must have wondered how his change in fortune made sense in light of God's great promises to Abraham, Joseph's great-grandfather—promises to bless the world through his descendants. How did the pain and suffering of slavery fit into the dreams Joseph knew had been sent to him by that same God?

Some man of destiny he was, bowing and scraping before his Egyptian master! Joseph could barely comprehend the orders he was being given—how could he even imagine his brothers bowing down before him? How could such terrible things, unsought and undeserved, have barged into his life?

Recently I read a scholar's response to a man questioning God's existence. The man was seeking answers in view of his intense grief over the sudden death of a young son. The scholar carefully acknowledged that he himself had never personally dealt with such an agonizing loss, then suggested the grieving father wasn't dealing primarily with the intellectual problem of suffering—he was enduring its emotional aspects. The father really needed to speak to a pastor, not a philosopher.

In large measure, the scholar was right. Here was a man in a wheelchair, not an armchair, and there was nothing theoretical about what he was undergoing. But, at the same time, the division between the two aspects of suffering is too neat. What we feel greatly impacts what we think, just as certainly as what we think hugely influences how we feel. Distorted thoughts in our minds can deepen pain in the soul, while pain in the soul can breed doubts in our minds.

Few people illustrate the difference between the armchair and wheelchair views of suffering more vividly than John Feinberg. John is a gifted biblical scholar—a man with a strong Christian heritage, a robust God-centered theology, and a deep anchor in the Word of God. He enlisted his considerable intellectual skills in a study of the problem of evil and suffering, leading to a doctoral dissertation and a book drawn from his research: *The Many Faces of Evil*.[1] As he says, "If anyone had thought about this and was prepared to face affliction, surely it was I."[2]

Then, a few years later, Feinberg's wife was diagnosed with an illness that was, he says, beyond his worst nightmare. She suffered from

Huntington's chorea, a disease that would not only attack her brain with increasingly severe symptoms, but that may have been transmitted genetically to their children. Feinberg was overwhelmed with shock and confusion.

Suffering was no longer an armchair matter; it was up close and personal now. "I had," he writes, "all these intellectual answers, but none of them made any difference in what I felt. The emotional and psychological pain was unrelenting, and the physical results from the stress and mental pain were devastating."[3] The problem wasn't that intellectual answers had no value; it was that the pain and uncertainty of what they were enduring overwhelmed everything else.

Feinberg's depiction of his struggle is painfully honest, as he recounts things that did and didn't help. What was of special importance was a comment by his father: "John, God never promised to give you tomorrow's grace for today. He only promised today's grace for today, and that's all you need!" Reminded of that, he says, "I began to readjust my focus from the future to the present. I would begin each day asking God for the grace just to sustain me that day. As that prayer was answered day after day, I gained more assurance that God would be there when things got worse."[4]

The wheelchair view forces a new perspective on us. My daughter asked many questions, and I'm sure there were many more that she never voiced to anyone but her Lord. I asked questions too, as I helped Janice into her chair, then pushed her on one of our walks. We watched others coming and going, apparently living a normal life free from concern, while we struggled with obstacles we'd never faced, or even noticed, before. And there were questions about the future for which we had no answers.

Joseph must have felt the same way as he wrestled for sleep in the darkness of his slave quarters, struggling to keep hope alive. Some of his questions, obvious but inescapable, would have been ones we all share: "Why me? Why now? Why this? What next?" Others come from the depths of our souls, depths of our souls, and Joseph would have battled hopelessness and despair; outrage at the injustice and those who had caused it; fear of both the present and the future; a sense of abandonment and betrayal; immense sadness for loved ones lost to him, perhaps forever; and a multitude of questions about where a good and gracious God was in all of this.

Suffering is a universal experience. For much of our lives, we are only dimly aware of that fact, just as people who live in certain parts of southern California pass their lives only dimly aware that half of the state is mountain lion habitat. Then, one day, during an ordinary hike, an unsuspecting person finds on the trail a cougar, poised to attack. The animal cannot be ignored—he is unavoidable, inescapable, and very dangerous. Ready or not, the crisis is there.

So it is with suffering. We may recognize that people have classified suffering into categories such as moral evils (those due to the actions of people) and natural evils (impelled by more mysterious forces). However, when we find ourselves facing evil, such distinctions don't really help to deal with the cougar right before us on the trail. Neither would an explanation from an expert about why this particular lion is at this particular spot at this particular time. He is here—that is what matters most.

When I first typed that last sentence, a headline appeared on my computer: "132 children killed. *Why?*" Amazingly and tragically, as I edited this page many months later, word came that two armed individuals had entered a Christmas party at a government building less than six miles from my home, shooting and killing fourteen people and wounding almost two dozen more. The shadow of terrorism suddenly darkened my own world, especially when I learned that the couple who committed the atrocity lived just over a mile from my home in the quiet city of Redlands. If terrorists can take the form of an educated, well-employed couple with a six-month-old baby, and if they can strike in a place like where I live, ordinary life has been suddenly and permanently changed.

Evil and pain are not illusions, things we can overcome by wishful thinking or weaning ourselves away from all desires, as some philosophies or religions suggest. They do not reflect God's original intention for His good creation—they are the products of humanity's rebellion against a good and gracious God. Because of that rebellion, we live in world that groans (Romans 8:22), in which suffering is not necessarily "karma" for personal sins. Rather it is the pervasive reality of a fallen world.

There is a mysterious interweaving of the sinful deeds of human beings, the victimization of the innocent, and the brokenness of the world, all within the sovereign control of a gracious God "who works all things according to the counsel of His will" (Ephesians 1:11). Invisibly, He is working His purpose through all of these experiences. It was far too complex for Joseph to understand, yet we will see him begin to lay hold of this truth of God's mysterious sovereignty as he stumbles through blind curves in the maze of his painful journey.

Twenty-two years after his brothers sold him into slavery, he greeted them with a remarkable insight: "You sold me here, [but] God sent me before you to preserve life" (Genesis 45:5). In no way did God's purpose change the brothers' evil actions into something good. Nor did God's purpose erase the suffering of Joseph's days as a slave and a prisoner. But God used the very things that threatened to destroy Joseph as instruments to accomplish divine purposes through him. Those years of pain could have broken Joseph; instead God used them to build and prepare him.

Years ago, I was struck by an observation of pastor and author Warren Wiersbe that has often come to my mind since:

> The central challenge in our lives is not to explain suffering, but rather to be the kind of people who can face suffering and make it work for us and not against us. . . . Nobody will deny that what happens *to* us is important. But what happens *in* us is also important, because that will help to determine what happens *through* us.[5]

That kind of mature insight was probably a long way from Joseph's mind as he began his journey into slavery. He did possess the promises that God had made to Abraham, Isaac, and Jacob, as well as some knowledge of God's interventions in their lives. He also had his own remarkable dream experience. We, on the other hand, are privileged to face our journey with far greater resources than Joseph had. The story of God's work in and through Joseph's suffering is one example, but we have the entirety of Scripture, which sets forth a robust understanding of God's sovereignty, His unlimited knowledge, and His unchanging promise to be with and for His people, whatever may happen.

We also know of God's overruling of suffering in our lives for our good and His glory, His faithfulness declared and experienced, and His eternal home—the new heavens and the new earth—where we will enter into the fullness of His joy. In the light of all those things, we can proclaim with the apostle Paul, "I consider that the sufferings of this present time are not worth comparing with the glory that is to be revealed to us" (Romans 8:18).

Most of all, we have the cross of our Lord Jesus Christ—the climax of His God-appointed journey through suffering on our behalf, which He transformed into the path to resurrection life and victory over sin and suffering. In the light of the cross, suffering has a different significance. Seen through the eyes of faith, the worst suffering may not lose its sting, but it does lose something of its power. Why? Because we recognize that it is under God's control and somehow serves His all-good and all-wise, if usually inscrutable, purposes.

Here, as in everything, the cross makes all the difference. Theologian John Stott says it well:

> I could never myself believe in God, if it were not for the cross. The only God I believe in is the One Nietzsche ridiculed as "God on the cross." In the real world of pain, how could one worship a God who was immune to it? I have entered many Buddhist temples in different Asian countries and stood respectfully before the statue of the Buddha, his legs crossed, arms folded, eyes closed, the ghost of a smile playing round his mouth, a remote look on his face, detached from the agonies of the world. But each time, after a while, I have had to turn away. And in imagination I have turned instead to that lonely, twisted, tortured figure on the cross, nails through hands and feet, back lacerated, limbs wrenched, brow bleeding from thorn-pricks, mouth dry and intolerably thirsty, plunged in Godforsaken darkness. That is the God for me! He laid aside his immunity to pain. He entered our world of flesh and blood, tears and death. He suffered for us. Our sufferings become more manageable in the light of His. There is still a question mark against human suffering, but over it we boldly stamp another mark, the cross that symbolizes divine suffering.[6]

When we met with the surgeons to discuss Janice's second surgery, they did their best to explain exactly what they planned to do. It was a risky procedure, but there seemed to be no other options. Doing less would mean that death would come very quickly; only radical action could meaningfully extend the length of her life and the time she would have with her children—that time was now incredibly precious. The head surgeon was new to us, but we knew of his outstanding credentials and his excellent reputation. Still, it was an act of faith to entrust our daughter into his hands. This was only one in a number of surgeries he would do that week. But Janice was her children's only mother and our firstborn.

But suppose this surgeon had come to us and told us how deeply committed he was, within the limits of his abilities, to saving the life of our daughter.[7] Suppose further that he was a perfect match for her rare blood type, and that he would gladly donate his own. Suppose even further that, because of her situation as a single parent, he committed himself not only to perform the surgery but to pay all the costs of her hospital stay. That would have radically deepened my confidence that this was a surgeon into whose hands we could confidently entrust our daughter. That kind of love would make it clear that he was truly for us.

Drawing a similar comparison, Vince Vitale observes,

> The Christian claim is that this is precisely what God has done for each of us. When He saw us hurting and in need of healing, He provided His own blood. He chose to join us in our suffering and take on Himself whatever suffering was necessary for us to be healed. He displayed His love in such an extravagant way that we have strong reason to trust Him, even when we don't fully understand His ways.[8]

Janice's surgery did not produce the results that either the surgeons or we desired. But our daughter was in God's hands, not theirs, and nothing could separate her or us "from the love of God in Christ Jesus our Lord" (Romans 8:39).

The Lord's Unfailing Presence

We return to the story of Joseph. Having told us that he, as a slave, had become a member of Potiphar's household, Moses immediately declares, "The LORD was with Joseph" (Genesis 39:2). Three things stand out in that simple phrase.

First, this is the initial mention of God's personal name in the Joseph story. (The Hebrew name translated "The LORD" in many English

Bibles is Yahweh.) God is certainly present in the providential acts of Genesis, but He is never directly mentioned. Now He is not only mentioned but seen as the agent moving everything: "the LORD was with Joseph" (39:2); "the LORD was with him and . . . caused all that he did to succeed" (39:3); "the LORD blessed the Egyptian's house for Joseph's sake; the blessing of the LORD was on all that he had" (39:5).

Secondly, the name Yahweh also represents God's covenant name,[9] the name by which He would later reveal himself to Moses at the burning bush (Exodus 3) and at the start of the Exodus encounters with Pharaoh (Exodus 6:2–9). So this name, closely linked to God's declaration that He is "I AM" (Exodus 3:14), serves as both the personal and the covenant name of God. Remarkably, the only times it appears in the entire Joseph story are the eight references in this chapter (five times in verses 1–6 and three times in verses 21–23), plus one more in Genesis 49:18.

It is worth lingering here. When the Bible begins with the familiar declaration, "In the beginning God created the heavens and the earth" (Genesis 1:1), the Hebrew name is *Elohim*, emphasizing the power and majesty of God the Creator. It is, in a sense, the most general term for God, declaring that He is "the Mighty One." But what is He like? What is His nature and His attitude toward the people He made?

In grace, God reveals himself by entering into a covenant with the people He has chosen, and to them He makes known His personal, covenant name. Of all the peoples of the earth, Israel alone is given the privilege of knowing God by His "first name": Yahweh, the LORD.

But God's grace reaches even further. Believers in Christ are not only brought into a covenant relationship with God, they are adopted into His family. As the apostle Paul writes in Galatians 4, God sent forth His Son "so that we might receive adoption as sons. And because you are sons, God has sent the Spirit of his Son into our hearts, crying 'Abba! Father!'" (vv. 5–6). *Father* is the Christian name for God, richer, more intimate, and more assuring than simply "God" or even "Yahweh." When we suffer, whatever our circumstances may be, it makes all the difference in the world to know that "Father is with me."

Third, the declaration "Yahweh was with him" is repeated four times in this chapter. God's Word goes out of its way to tell us that, at the two hardest points in Joseph's life, despite all appearances to the contrary, the covenant-keeping God was not only aware of his situation but was present with him. Even a pagan slave owner could see it: "His master saw that the LORD was with him" (Genesis 39:3). Later, the Egyptian prison keeper would see the same thing (39:21–23).

We are not told exactly how Joseph experienced God's presence. That he was deeply aware of God's presence is evident in the fact that the Egyptians knew that Joseph was specifically loyal to Yahweh as opposed to some generic deity. At every critical point in Joseph's life, whether he is dealing with a temptress (39:9), imprisoned royal officials (40:8), Pharaoh himself (41:16, 25, 28, 32), his newborn children (41:51–52), or his brothers (45:5–9; 50:19–20), God's name is on his lips. Joseph was not a secret follower of his God, and, in turn, God's presence was a reality to him. Even as a slave or prisoner, Joseph was concerned to live in a way that honored God.

There is a principle here of great importance, expressed well by Jerry Bridges:

> Our first priority in times of adversity is to honor and glorify God by trusting Him. We tend to make our first priority the gaining of relief from our feelings of heartache or disappointment or frustration. This is a natural desire and God has promised to give us grace sufficient for our trials and peace for our anxieties (see 2 Corinthians 12:9; Philippians 4:6–7). . . . [But] God's honor is to take precedence over our feelings. We honor God by choosing to trust Him when we don't understand what He is doing or why He has allowed some adverse circumstance to occur.[10]

The promise of God's presence with His people is one of the great truths of Scripture. God is the omnipresent one—He fills all of space with His entire being. He is universal and inescapable. At the same time, He is present in a special way with His people. The Lord God had promised Joseph's grandfather, Isaac, "I will be with you" (Genesis 26:3), and declared that same thing to Joseph's father, Jacob (Genesis 31:3). Those events would have been part of the family's story, told often around the fires, and Joseph probably took them to heart as a young boy. His determination to honor God would become most evident when the fire of his own trials grew hottest.

During Janice's wheelchair days, Isaiah 41:10 took on special significance for both of us. I said and sang the words to her: "Fear not, for I am with you; be not dismayed, for I am your God; I will strengthen you, I will help you, I will uphold you with my righteous right hand." This is not a promise that we will be exempted from adversity; it is a promise that God will go through such things with us. No truth is more precious in times of trouble and suffering.

Nor is this confined to the Old Testament. The Lord's statement at the end of the book of Matthew reinforces it for us—"Behold, I am with you always, to the end of the age" (28:20)—a promise linked to the gift of the indwelling Spirit. We could wish He promised an explanation of our problems; He didn't. But He does promise His unfailing presence. In the majestic words of Isaiah 43:2:

> When you pass through the waters,
> I will be with you;
> and through the rivers,
> they shall not overwhelm you;
> when you walk through fire you shall not be burned,
> and the flame shall not consume you.

The presence of God, unexplainable but undeniable, not only enabled Joseph to survive, but to thrive. So we read, "The LORD was with Joseph, and he became a successful man" (Genesis 39:2). The Hebrew word rendered "successful" indicates that he advanced or prospered within the situation that he found himself.

Joseph's obvious gifts and abilities became evident to Potiphar, who gave him more and more responsibility. At each level, Joseph proved to possess both competence and character—he was skilled and reliable, absolutely trustworthy in the way he conducted his life. Yet Potiphar recognized that there was something more at work in Joseph's life: "His master saw that the LORD was with him and that the LORD caused all that he did to succeed in his hands. So Joseph found favor in his sight and attended him, and he made him overseer of his house, and put him in charge of all that he had" (39:3–4).

Joseph was quick to credit the Lord with his success, and Potiphar was fully aware of his spiritual convictions. This extraordinary rise to a position of great trust, which required the learning of a new language and culture, took place over a period of years. It is so remarkable that the writer repeats over and over that the blessing of God that was on Joseph, a blessing that overflowed to those around him. As one writer observes, "Regardless of what genius Joseph possessed, his successes were made possible by the Lord."[11]

As we read this account of the blessing of Joseph, even in his slavery, it is important that we view it through a wider lens. When God called Joseph's great-grandfather Abraham, He had said, in part, "I will bless you and make your name great, so that you will be a blessing. I will bless those who bless you" (Genesis 12:2–3). God was already beginning to fulfill His promise in and through Joseph, and God's blessing on Joseph, as Abraham's offspring, was beginning to overflow to foreigners. Despite all appearances, God was being faithful to His covenant promises.

At the same time, unknown to Joseph, the Lord was preparing him through his growing administrative responsibilities to become a source of blessing—to the nation where he was a slave, to other nations of the world, and specifically to his own family. In suffering, Joseph was finding and refining skills he might not otherwise have developed.

Dependence on God

Nothing in the journey through suffering is more valuable and precious than a confidence in the presence and faithfulness of God. One of the harsh blessings of the wheelchair is that it drives you to dependence. And very often that dependence on God reveals His faithfulness in fresh ways we might never expect.

Gerald Sittser is a theology professor who found his life changed in an instant. A drunk driver crossed the center line and hit Sittser's car head-on, killing three generations of the most precious women in his life—his mother, his wife, and his four-year-old daughter. The terrible loss plunged him into personal grief, but he was also confronted with the challenge of raising three other young children, who had also been traumatized by the tragedy. "Something incomprehensible and extraordinary had just happened," he wrote. "By some strange twist of fate or mysterious manifestation of divine providence, I had suddenly been thrust into circumstances I had not chosen and could never have imagined."[12] It was, he says, the test of his life, one he could neither evade nor escape. His journey was hard, as he faced huge responsibilities and equally huge questions. His book, *A Grace Disguised,* is a gift to all who read it, and the words with which he begins show hard-earned wisdom:

> Sooner or later all people suffer loss, in little doses or big ones, suddenly or over time, privately or in public settings. Loss is as much a part of normal life as birth, for as surely as we are born into this world, we suffer loss before we leave it. It is not, therefore, the *experience* of loss that becomes the defining moment of our lives, for that is as inevitable as death, which is the last loss awaiting us all. It is how we *respond* to loss that matters. That response will largely determine the quality, the direction, and the impact of our lives. . . . Response involves the *choices* we make, the *grace* we receive, and ultimately the *transformation* we experience in the loss. My aim is not to provide quick and painless solutions but to point the way to a lifelong journey of growth.[13]

Joseph's journey had already taken him from the favored son's special place to the pit of death to the slave quarters to the administrator's office in Potiphar's household. He had no idea it would take him to the prison, and then, astonishingly, to the prime minister's office. In the worst of his darkness—when he couldn't even see his own hand in front of his face—God's hand was on Joseph. God's presence was with Joseph, weaving His divine purpose through all that transpired.

And this is true for all of God's children. We do well, when life in the wheelchair is excruciating, to hear the words of Peter: "Let those who suffer according to God's will entrust their souls to a faithful Creator while doing good" (1 Peter 4:19).

FIVE

PERFORMING UNDER PRESSURE

Flight 1549 from New York's LaGuardia Airport, with 155 passengers and crew on board, was scheduled to take 87 minutes. Instead it lasted four minutes and forty-two seconds, ending not in Charlotte, North Carolina, as expected, but in the middle of the ice-filled Hudson River.

The first hundred seconds of the flight, with the copilot at the controls, were routine. Then the captain, Chesley "Sully" Sullenberger, shouted "birds!" The jet engines ingested a flock of Canada geese and began to grind to a halt. Within ten seconds, the engines went silent.

"My airplane," Sullenberger said as he took over the controls of what was now essentially an eighty-ton glider. Still at low altitude over one of the most densely populated cities in the world, the plane had no time to return to the airport. Nor were there any viable emergency landing areas.

Sullenberger recalls that he felt strangely confident, even though he'd never previously had to deal with an engine failure or land a plane anywhere but on a runway. Drawing upon forty-two years of military and commercial aviation experience, he immediately radioed "Mayday" to air traffic controllers. Then, having mentally processed all possible options, recognizing that he was too slow and low to get back to LaGuardia, Sullenberger calmly informed controllers, "We're gonna be in the Hudson."

Just over three minutes after striking the birds, the Airbus A320 settled onto the river. The crew carried out a brilliant evacuation, and a number of boats quickly came to retrieve all of the passengers and flight crew. It was a remarkably happy ending to a potentially tragic situation.

The entire episode became known as "the Miracle on the Hudson." Pictures of passengers, standing on the wings of the aircraft floating on the river, captivated people everywhere. "Captain Sully" catapulted to fame for his calm under enormous pressure. His own explanation was clear and memorable: "For forty-two years I've been making small regular deposits in this bank of experience, education, and training. And on January 15, the balance was sufficient so that I could make a very large withdrawal." On another occasion he observed, "I never knew in forty-two years that there would be 208 seconds on which my entire career would be judged."

When he left for work that day, Sullenberger had no way of knowing that he was about to experience a defining moment, a turning point for the rest of his life. Fortunately, his bank of experience stood him in good stead in his moment of testing.

There is an even more important bank where we all make deposits or withdrawals—the bank of character. Moments arrive, usually unheralded, unannounced, and unexpected, when we reveal whether we have enough "character capital" on which to draw. These are defining moments, occasions that challenge our values, test our commitments, and expose who we really are.

An old proverb declares, "Smooth seas don't make skillful sailors." You can't learn how to handle a ship by reading books, taking courses, or floating around a sheltered harbor. A sailor's most important skills can only be learned on the open seas, when the winds are howling and the waves are breaking over the bow. The obvious problem is that the same rough seas that produce seasoned sailors can also sink their boats.

So it is with all of us. We need life's stormy trials to teach and strengthen us, but on the other side of each trial is a temptation, calling us to take an easier or more enticing way. All of us know the pull and power of temptation, even though the things that entice me might not arouse much interest in you. Temptation presents itself in a multitude of forms, each designed specifically for us, taking into account our unique desires, life experiences, circumstances, and personality type. Then, like a heat-seeking missile, it targets our most vulnerable places. No wonder the playwright Oscar Wilde had one of his characters ironically declare, "I can resist everything except temptation."

The psalmist tells us that when Joseph was sold as a slave, "His feet were hurt with fetters; his neck was put in a collar of iron; until what he had said came to pass, the word of the LORD tested him" (Psalm 105:18–19). This is an inspired insight into the accumulating trials experienced by Joseph. They were, in part, a God-intended testing. The term is significant: *testing* refers to the refining of metals, whereby they are placed in a fire to be both purified of impurities and authenticated as to worth.

Joseph was indeed in a fire, but it was a refiner's fire. He was being refined, not destroyed; built, not broken. Although he could not know it at the time, he would emerge from the flames a stronger and better man than he had been before. Because he was in God's hands, the fire of suffering would produce endurance and character, as Romans 5:3–4 promises all believers.

To shift the analogy, the Lord was using rough seas to make Joseph a skillful sailor. In the hardest of times, the Lord's presence enabled Joseph to steer clear of a temptation to despair. Instead, Joseph "became a successful man" (Genesis 39:2). He rose through the ranks of Potiphar's household until his owner "made him overseer of all his house and put him in charge of all that he had" (39:4). These "worst of times" were the Lord's workshop, preparing Joseph for administrative responsibilities far greater than anything in Potiphar's household. Joseph was developing skills he might never otherwise have learned.[1]

Ironically, however, his very success, as he progressed to the top of the rung in Potiphar's house, exposed him to a different kind of temptation, one that would have life-altering implications for him.

The Test of the Flesh

Now Joseph was handsome in form and appearance. And after a time his master's wife cast her eyes on Joseph and said, "Lie with me." But he refused and said to his master's wife, "Behold, because of me my master has no concern about anything in the house, and he has put everything that he has in my charge. He is not greater in this house than I am, nor has he kept back anything from me except you, because you are his wife. How then can I do this great wickedness and sin against God?" And as she spoke to Joseph day after day, he would not listen to her, to lie beside her or to be with her.

But one day, when he went into the house to do his work and none of the men of the house was there in the house, she caught him by his garment, saying, "Lie with me." But he left his garment in her hand and fled and got out of the house.

Genesis 39:6–12

Joseph had been blessed by God with great abilities that had come to the fore, even when he was a slave. He had another quality, inherited from his mother, that was about to land him in a world of trouble. Rachel had been a beautiful woman (Genesis 29:17), and her son was an extremely attractive young man, "handsome in form and appearance" (39:6). The same word used to describe Rachel's beauty is now used of Joseph.

Had Joseph remained an anonymous slave, or even if he had been ordinary in looks, he might have escaped the notice of Potiphar's wife. But now that his responsibilities brought him into regular contact with her, she couldn't help but notice this gifted and desirable young man. Ironically, his faithfulness to Potiphar, combined with God's hand of blessing on him, had made Joseph an enticing target for an entirely new kind of temptation.

There is an important reminder here: God's blessings do not make us bullet-proof. Very often, they expose us to even stronger enticements. Climbing the ladder of godly success only stirs Satan's interest in bringing us down. The higher we are, the farther and harder we can fall.

We can only speculate about what was going on inside Potiphar's wife to trigger her lust-filled advances toward Joseph. She must have known she was playing a dangerous game as she pursued him. But she had become a slave to her lust for this young slave. Potiphar's wife turned all her wiles loose on Joseph in a shameless, direct way: "Lie with me" (39:7, 12). This was not a one-time thing; she propositioned

Joseph "day after day" (39:10). She had taken the measure of her target: a lonely, virile, single young man in his mid-twenties, anything but immune to the sexual longings she doubtless aroused within him. Aroused herself, she threw caution to the winds.

Wise people do their best to avoid temptations. But that was an option not available to Joseph the slave. He couldn't resign his job or transfer to another department—both the temptress and her enticement were inescapable. Nor could he merely dismiss his own sexual desires; in a twenty-five-year-old man, they can feel overpowering, and there is no reason to believe Joseph was any exception.

Joseph had no spiritual community to support him in his struggle, no moral examples to guide him in resistance, and no third party to whom he could turn for counsel or help. The temptation to rationalize self-indulgence with his master's wife must have been real; he was, after all, a slave under her authority! His male ego would have been flattered that such a woman wanted him so much, and who would ever know? The two of them could surely find a way to keep it secret. As the Proverbs say, "Stolen water is sweet, and bread eaten in secret is pleasant" (9:17).

The temptation confronting Joseph was blatantly sexual, a temptation that plays to some of the deepest drives and desires in human nature. Powerful as it is, however, it is clearly not the only form of temptation—and not always the most dangerous. Temptation itself is the product of a triad of enemies: the world, the flesh, and the devil. Interrelated though they are in their opposition to God's work in our lives, they operate in quite different ways. The world pressures us to conform, the devil to doubt, and the flesh to indulge. All our lives, this side of heaven, we will fight the battles these three enemies bring our way.

In the darkness of his enslavement, Joseph had already been encountering the primary temptation of Satan—the temptation to doubt God and His Word. He must have wrestled long and hard with the question of how his present circumstances could be reconciled with God's promise to bless the family of Abraham, and God's purpose for his own life, revealed in his dreams.

Cut off from his old life and situated in a new culture, Joseph had also faced the attack of the world. As his status in Potiphar's household grew there must have been an increasing temptation to "Egyptianize." Life in Egypt brought a constant pressure, a magnetic pull to conform, to adopt the values and even the gods of the surrounding culture, to fit into a lifestyle contrary to God's purposes and values for the family of Abraham.

And now, in the enticing form of Potiphar's wife, Joseph was facing the lure of the flesh, whose primary temptation is toward sensual indulgence and self-gratification in its various forms.

Because our temptations are multiform, wise Christians recognize their need to know their own weakness, to recognize the nature of sinful attacks, and decide ahead of time on a wise and godly response. We, as Christ-followers, have tools that Joseph did not possess. As Martin Luther declared, "Nothing is so effectual against the world, the flesh, and the devil, and all evil thoughts, as to be occupied with God's Word, in conversation and meditation." Even more, we have the indwelling Spirit of God.

Joseph must have known that either yielding to or denying this woman's advances would complicate his life immeasurably. Embracing her proposition might satisfy a momentary lust, both hers and his, but it was far more likely to arouse a desire for more. Gratifying her might also benefit Joseph by putting him in the good graces of someone who had enormous power over him. Saying no, on the other hand, could make her very angry. He could readily supply reasons for self-indulgence—we all have a great capacity to justify what we want to do. But, as a wise man once told me, "There is a big difference between reasons that sound good and good, sound reasons."

Joseph refused her advances clearly, directly, and consistently. His words are memorable: "Behold, because of me my master has no concern about anything in the house, and he has put everything that he has in my charge. He is not greater in this house than I am, nor has he kept back anything from me except you, because you are his wife. How then can I do this great wickedness and sin against God?" (39:8–9). It was an answer that showed him to be a man living by non-negotiable convictions about himself, morality, and God. Yet although his refusal was strong and clear, his temptress had no intention of surrendering so quickly. Even defeated temptations are amazingly resilient!

Joseph's refusal is important to us because it contains some fundamental principles of resisting temptation, in whatever form it arrives. First, *Joseph had a clear sense of who he was.* On the most basic level, that involved an understanding of his role as a slave entrusted with great responsibility by Potiphar, a trust that he would not violate. But beyond that, he had a deep sense of his God-given identity and destiny, as revealed in the dreams God had sent to him. He was God's man, not merely Potiphar's. Knowing who I am before God, by His grace, is a powerful incentive to live honorably even in the presence of the most enticing opportunities.

Second, *Joseph had a clear understanding of what sin was.* This was revealed clearly in his rhetorical question, "How then can I do this great wickedness and sin?" (39:9). Joseph named her proposition for what it was—an inducement to sin and wickedness. Temptation always pushes us to redefine what it calls us to do, rationalizing away its seriousness or downplaying the possible consequences. Our culture excels in redefining sin, but godly wisdom calls for us to name it for what it truly is: "great wickedness and sin." Only then will we find the strength to call on God for His help.

Third, *Joseph knew who God was*—the ever-present One in whose sight we constantly live and against whom all sin is ultimately directed. "The eyes of the LORD are in every place, keeping watch on the evil and the good" (Proverbs 15:3). Consenting to this woman's invitation would have been "great wickedness and sin against God," and Joseph was a deeply God-centered man. The Lord's presence and pleasure was more real to him than this very available woman—and he would not yield. Joseph wasn't committed simply to doing the right thing; he was committed to doing the right thing to honor his great God. For Joseph, this temptation was—as it is for all of us—a loyalty test, and he was determined to be loyal to his God.

But this was only one round of a protracted campaign of seduction by Potiphar's wife. For her, "No" simply meant "Not yet." "She spoke to Joseph day after day" (39:10), offering herself to him, hoping to wear away his resistance. Temptation is rarely a singular event, and its very presence can transform the unthinkable into the thinkable, the impossible into the possible. We all too easily underestimate the resilience of temptation, while overestimating our capacity to withstand its persistent attacks on our defenses. Joseph couldn't avoid the temptation, but he did resist it: "He would not listen to her, to lie beside her or to be with her" (39:10).

But Potiphar's wife still would not be denied. His rejections only inflamed her lust and she carefully laid a trap, arranging household affairs so that no one else would be in the house when Joseph arrived for work. We can imagine she had dressed in the most seductive manner possible—and when Joseph arrived, she launched herself at him. Grabbing at his robe, she brazenly commanded him, "Lie with me" (39:12).

Joseph bolted. Shrugging out of his cloak and leaving it in her hands, he fled the scene, determined to be true to himself, his master, and his God. He had passed the test of temptation, but there was no one to applaud him for his moral heroism. No other human knew anything of the battle he had fought and won. It was a very private victory, and it would not lead to a "happily ever after" ending. Sadly, in a fallen world, godly behavior not only fails to win applause, it is often scorned and even punished. So it would be with Joseph.

The Trial of Injustice

And as soon as she saw that he had left his garment in her hand and had fled out of the house, she called to the men of her household and said to them, "See, he has brought among us a Hebrew to laugh at us. He came in to me to lie with me, and I cried out with a loud voice. And as soon as he heard that I lifted up my voice and cried out, he left his garment beside me and fled and got out of the house." Then she laid up his garment by her until his master came home, and she told him the same story, saying, "The Hebrew servant, whom you have brought among us, came in to me to laugh at me. But as soon as I lifted up my voice and cried, he left his garment beside me and fled out of the house." As soon as his master heard the words that his wife spoke to him, "This is the way your servant treated me," his anger was kindled. And Joseph's master took him and put him into the prison, the place where the king's prisoners were confined, and he was there in prison.

Genesis 39:13–20

Few things are as hard as being punished for doing the right thing. But it is clear both from Scripture and our human experience that righteous behavior in this world may produce unfair consequences. The Lord Jesus is, of course, the supreme example of that. In a less significant way, so is Joseph.

I have had friends who lost promotions and even their jobs because they refused to engage in immoral and unethical behavior. I have known pastors attacked and slandered because they refused to condone sinful behavior or false teaching by some who were influential in their congregations. I have counseled wives who were abandoned by their husbands because they would not agree to immoral sexual behaviors. We regularly see the news media or the entertainment industry mocking people who have spoken against practices their Christian convictions would not allow them to affirm. Believers are persecuted and killed by hate-filled enemies in various parts of the world, simply because they claim the name of Christ-follower. And through no fault of his own, Joseph now found himself the object of a vengeful woman's anger.

In the late 1600s, poet William Congreve wrote a line that has evolved over time into "hell hath no fury like a woman scorned." Joseph had not intended to scorn Potiphar's wife. But maintaining his integrity meant refusing her, and now she was determined to exact revenge. Joseph had rejected her; now she would seek to have him killed.

Summoning the other male servants back into the house, she made them witnesses to her account of the events, determined get her version on the record first. Brandishing Joseph's robe, which was actually a token of her unbridled lust, she accused him of attempted rape. Shrewdly, she played to the racial resentments the other slaves probably harbored against their supervisor Joseph, labeling him "a Hebrew to laugh at us" (39:14).[2] Note too how she identified herself with the servants against Joseph ("at *us*"). At the same time she subtly laid blame on her own husband: "*he* has brought among us a Hebrew." She presented her account of events, taking the offensive while carefully twisting the facts: Joseph had initiated the interaction, disrobed and left his garment, and then fled in fear when she cried out for help. (Perhaps she had cried out in anger as Joseph left her).

Stage two of her plan was accusing Joseph directly to her husband. She set the scene carefully, remaining exactly where she had been when the attempted rape allegedly took place. When he returned, she was feigning deep trauma due to her "narrow escape" from Joseph's "brutality."

The story was carefully constructed to deceive her husband and indict Joseph. She followed the same plotline as she had with the slaves: an appeal to prejudice ("the Hebrew servant"), an implied accusation of her husband's complicity ("whom you have brought among us"), and a deceitful rewriting of events ("[Joseph] came in to laugh at me"). She was, she wailed, the innocent victim of a slave's lust and her husband's incompetence.

Potiphar's response appears to be exactly what she expected. No husband could be expected to carry out an objective inquiry and determine the precise truth in the face of such explosive accusations. She had pushed all the right buttons, and "his anger was kindled" (39:19). Yet, we wonder about other aspects of the story. Surely, capital punishment would be the normal consequence of an attempted rape of a nobleman's wife by a mere slave. There would be no trial, just swift and terminal justice since a master had absolute authority over his slaves. No one would question Joseph's execution.

But Potiphar only imprisons Joseph, a sentence far harsher than he deserved, but far less than expected for the crime of which he had been accused. Once again, Joseph's life was spared by the Lord's unseen hand, this time restraining Potiphar. Maybe he was motivated to act leniently, even in the face of such a damning scenario, because of his appreciation and admiration for Joseph. I suspect he had serious misgivings about his wife's truthfulness, perhaps because of what he knew of her character. However, a man in his position could not afford to take his foreign slave's side against his own wife.

So, once again, Joseph was suffering unjustly. Ironically, the book of Proverbs warns that adultery is like playing with a fire that will certainly burn: "Can one walk on hot coals and his feet not be scorched? So is he who [sleeps with] his neighbor's wife; none who touches her will go unpunished" (Proverbs 6:28–29). Joseph refused to touch his master's wife, but he was the one unjustly burned!

Joseph had been thrown down the ladder, from slave to prisoner. But things weren't quite what they seemed. God was at work, positioning Joseph to be in exactly the right place for the next part of his story.

The Unchanging Presence

> But the LORD was with Joseph and showed him steadfast love and gave him favor in the sight of the keeper of the prison. And the keeper of the prison put Joseph in charge of all the prisoners who were in the prison. Whatever was done there, he was the one who did it. The keeper of the prison paid no attention to anything that was in Joseph's charge, because the LORD was with him. And whatever he did, the LORD made it succeed.
>
> Genesis 39:21–23

Genesis 39 ends in the same way it began—with Joseph experiencing unjust suffering. Yet God is mysteriously present, bringing about unexpected success in the most unlikely place. Again Moses reminds us that Joseph is under the care of Yahweh, the covenant God. In this most unpleasant of places, "The LORD was with Joseph" (39:21).

How much Joseph felt of God's presence we cannot know. We must not imagine that Joseph was immune to these overwhelming experiences, the feelings that any of us would feel in such a situation. After all, jail is jail—all of us shudder at the thought of enduring time there. If that is true in our modern world, it would have been far worse in Joseph's time. Conditions would have been squalid and harsh. The wrongness of the situation must have set off storms that ravaged Joseph's emotions and threatened to overwhelm his mind with unending and unanswerable questions.

Joseph had endured mistreatment, misrepresentation, and injustice primarily because he had committed himself to honoring God in the way he dealt with temptation. He had performed heroically under pressure, doing the right thing and honoring his God! So how do we make sense of this imprisonment? Where exactly was God in all this?

Though he was likely unaware of it, at least three things are taking place during this phase of Joseph's life. First, *God's presence was being experienced*: "The LORD was with Joseph and showed him steadfast love and gave him favor in the sight of the keeper of the prison" (39:21). This reads like a rerun of verses 2 and 3, with the special note that Yahweh was showing Joseph His loyal love. The Lord chose not to remove Joseph's suffering, instead revealing His presence by supplying the grace and mercy Joseph needed in the darkness and ugliness of an ancient prison.

Second, *God's person was being prepared.* As in Potiphar's household, Joseph once again found himself in a position of responsibility, "in charge of all the prisoners who were in the prison. Whatever was done there, he was the one who did it" (39:22). In all that was happening, Joseph's character was being deepened and refined. The once self-confident, even arrogant, young man is being refined and purified—but the process is a painful one.

Third, *God's purpose was being furthered.* For a man in prison, with no future and no reason to hope, the dreams that once excited him now served only to mock him. He had reached his late twenties, and the dreams hadn't merely been derailed—they'd been destroyed. Yet the prison that threatened to engulf him would become his entryway into the presence of Pharaoh himself. As Old Testament scholar Gordon Wenham observes, "His present disgrace was a necessary preliminary to his future glory."[3] At no stage could Joseph have known the destination this long hard road would eventually reach. How strange God's pathways often are!

Within Genesis 39 are some truths that we must not miss. These things are true for all God's people, not just Joseph.

First, Joseph's experience is testimony to the fact that *when things are the darkest and hardest, God is most certainly present with us.* Once again the words of Isaiah 41:10 come to mind: "Fear not, for I am with you; be not dismayed, for I am your God; I will strengthen you, I will help you, I will uphold you with my righteous right hand."

Closely connected to that concept is this truth: *our Lord often uses the hardest of places to make us, not break us.* This was the confidence of Job, a man who suddenly and inexplicably lost everything he most valued in life. He didn't understand where God was or what He was doing, but he did know that the simplistic answers his friends were giving weren't true. Job was in "the furnace of affliction" (Isaiah 48:10), and everything that once seemed clear was now cloudy. Yet he cried out in Job 23:8–10:

"Behold, I go forward, but he is not there,
and backward, but I do not perceive him;
on the left hand when he is working, I do not behold him;
he turns to the right hand, but I do not see him.
But he knows the way that I take;
when he has tried me, I shall come out as gold."

Job was in a crucible, and yet he trusted that a good and gracious God was not breaking him but refining him. And God was with Joseph, building and refining him for a purpose Joseph could not yet see. So it is with us, although only eternity will reveal the end of God's mysterious ways. Our responsibility in such times is to keep making regular, small deposits in the account of character, so that when we have an urgent need of withdrawal, there is more than enough to cover what is required.

Joseph's loyalty test reminds us of ours—different in many details, but similar in essence. Temptations come in a multitude of forms, evolving with our circumstances and stage of life to maximize their effectiveness. "Temptation is, by definition, subtle and personality specific," Russell Moore writes, "with a strategy to enter as larvae and then emerge in the fullness of time as a destructive animal force."[4] We cannot and will not be able to withstand it on our own. *Knowing God and trusting that He is with us gives us the power and the motivation to say "No."*

SIX

FAITHFUL BUT FORGOTTEN

Seventeenth-century England was not an easy place to be a committed follower of Christ and His Word. On November 12, 1660, thirty-two-year-old Baptist preacher John Bunyan was thrown into jail in Bedford. The king, Charles II, had earlier been returned to the throne and the monarchy restored. He made it clear that he intended to stop virtually all religious gatherings apart from the state church, and to ban anyone from preaching who was not officially ordained. Parliament would make the king's desire the law of the land two years later. But Bunyan dared to go against the king's clear wish, and he became the first to be arrested and jailed. He certainly wasn't an ordained minister: he made his living making and selling pots and pans—a "tinker," as the craft was known.

Bunyan was an unlikely preacher. On one hand, he had very little education; on the other, he had a dubious past. In later life he would recall his youthful self: "From a child I had but few equals for cursing, swearing, lying, and blaspheming the holy name of God. . . . I was the very ringleader of all the youth that kept me company, in all manner of vice and ungodliness."

But when Bunyan was in his mid-twenties, the Lord Jesus and His gospel intersected the young man's life, radically changing his direction and gradually transforming his character. Though Bunyan was almost completely lacking in formal education, the Lord gave him a hunger for Scripture. Bunyan began to study and, eager to share what he had learned, preach to anyone who would listen. He was a naturally gifted speaker, and it wasn't long before crowds came to hear him proclaim God's Word with great power. We are told that, with a day's notice, twelve hundred people would come out to hear Bunyan at seven on a workday morning!

When the king's mandate that anyone who lacked the approval of royal and state officials became known, Bunyan refused to obey. As a result a zealous local judge decided to make Bunyan an example by sentencing him to jail for his horrendous "crime," even though Bunyan had broken no actual law. Bunyan was a recent widower with four children under age six—one of them blind. His new wife was pregnant, and he had no financial resources to leave his family. Those things had made his decision to defy the unjust law excruciatingly difficult.

He would later write from prison, "Parting with my wife and poor children hath often been to me in this place as the pulling of flesh from my bones . . . because I should often have brought to my mind the many hardships, miseries, and wants that my poor family was like to meet with . . . especially my poor blind child, who lay nearer my heart than all I had beside." But he refused to compromise. He would stay in that prison, without trial, for twelve long, hard years, the first to be arrested, and the last to be released after the king's mandate became law. He was finally released in 1672, only to be imprisoned again in 1676 for six more months. In all of this, Bunyan was apparently the helpless victim of evil men.

So many years of imprisonment seem like a waste. Yet, in a remarkable way, Bedford prison was an investment. As Bunyan would later write, "I never had in all my life so great an inlet into the Word of God as [in prison]. . . . Jesus Christ was never more real and apparent than now. Here I had seen Him and felt Him indeed." He became a prodigious writer, turning out more than sixty books, most from his jail cell. And it was in that jail, during his second confinement, that Bunyan conceived and largely wrote the book that made his name famous.

The Pilgrim's Progress was, for centuries, second only to the Bible as the world's best-selling book. It has been translated into more than two hundred languages, and greatly used by God to help generations understand the gospel in a new way. For Bunyan, prison proved to be more than a place of punishment—it was the launching pad for a written ministry that continues more than 350 years later!

When the Lord wants to prepare us, He rarely does so in ways we would expect. He put Moses into Pharaoh's palace for almost forty years, then sent him into the desert to herd sheep for another forty. Not until Moses was eighty did the Lord meet and call him at the burning bush, sending him back to Egypt to deliver the Israelites from their bondage. David, Israel's greatest king and the man after God's own heart, spent his youth as a shepherd. Then, in his early adult years, he was a fugitive from the jealous King Saul. Only after these experiences did God's appointed time come for David to take the throne.

Before either Moses or David, the Lord put His hand on Joseph. Through him, God purposed to deliver His chosen people from both physical starvation and their increasing spiritual and moral assimilation in Canaan. A significant part of Joseph's preparation involved undeserved confinement in prison, a most unlikely place to equip anyone to serve in high government positions. But Joseph was destined, in God's plan, to wield great authority at the right hand of the world's most powerful ruler—Egypt's Pharaoh.

Life in the Pit

We are not given many details about Joseph's time in prison, apart from what we learn in Genesis 40. A political prison in Egypt four thousand years ago was hardly a luxury resort, yet, in this worst of places, the Lord himself was with Joseph, and "whatever he did, the LORD made it succeed" (39:23). Encouraging as that sounds, it cannot remove the reality of the drudgery, difficulty, and perhaps even danger of Joseph's prison journey.

This favorite son of a wealthy man had first been stripped of his identity and dignity, sold as a foreign slave, deprived of his rights and his future. Now, because of the completely false accusation of a vengeful woman, he has lost his reputation. Joseph has been reduced to the lowest place on the social ladder.

His life may have been spared, but from all outward appearances, he was a forgotten, abandoned victim of injustice after injustice. Joseph would later describe his prison as "the pit" (40:15), using the same word that had described the cistern into which his brothers had thrown him in Dothan (37:24). In both cases, "the pit" had been the means of rescuing him from death—but each time he'd landed there only because evil people were treating him unjustly. All the while, he was doing the right thing.

Joseph's situation was unique, but suffering and mistreatment aren't. Even as I write this, unknowable multitudes of God's people around the world are encountering undeserved evils, untrue accusations, unjust treatment, unfair situations, and unchangeable circumstances. Recent events have made us aware of the depths of human depravity, as terrorists gleefully share videos of the executions of people whose only crime is to bear the name "Christ-follower."

You may number yourself among those who are being mistreated because you have refused to compromise your commitment to the Lord Jesus Christ. Such is life in a fallen world, where God's people often cry out with the martyrs of Revelation 6:10, "O Sovereign Lord, holy and true, how long?" Yet the Joseph story is eloquent testimony to the fact that God is always present with His people, even though that presence doesn't exempt any believer from suffering, difficulty, tragedy, injustice, and mistreatment. It didn't for Joseph, it didn't for the Lord Jesus, and it won't for us.

The Lord who promises, "I will be with him in trouble" (Psalm 91:15), was present in Joseph's squalid, hope-deprived, soul-crushing prison. That same Lord says, "I will rescue him and honor him" (Psalm 91:15). In God's good time, Joseph's degradation would lead to his elevation.

A Glimmer of Hope

Some time after this, the cupbearer of the king of Egypt and his baker committed an offense against their lord the king of Egypt. And Pharaoh was angry with his two officers, the chief cupbearer and the chief baker, and he put them in custody in the house of the captain of the guard, in the prison where Joseph was confined. The captain of the guard appointed Joseph to be with them, and he attended them. They continued for some time in custody.

And one night they both dreamed—the cupbearer and the baker of the king of Egypt, who were confined in the prison—each his own dream, and each dream with its own interpretation. When Joseph came to them in the morning, he saw that they were troubled. So he asked Pharaoh's officers who were with him in custody in his master's house, "Why are your faces downcast today?" They said to him, "We have had dreams, and there is no one to interpret them." And Joseph said to them, "Do not interpretations belong to God? Please tell them to me."

So the chief cupbearer told his dream to Joseph and said to him, "In my dream there was a vine before me, and on the vine there were three branches. As soon as it budded, its blossoms shot forth, and the clusters ripened into grapes. Pharaoh's cup was in my hand, and I took the grapes and pressed them into Pharaoh's cup and placed the cup in Pharaoh's hand." Then Joseph said to him, "This is its interpretation: the three branches are three days. In three days Pharaoh will lift up your head and restore you to your office, and you shall place Pharaoh's cup in his hand as formerly, when you were his cupbearer. Only remember me, when it is well with you, and please do me the kindness to mention me to Pharaoh, and so get me out of this house. For I was indeed stolen out of the land of the Hebrews, and here also I have done nothing that they should put me into the pit."

When the chief baker saw that the interpretation was favorable, he said to Joseph, "I also had a dream: there were three cake baskets on my head, and in the uppermost basket there were all sorts of baked food for Pharaoh, but the birds were eating it out of the basket on my head." And Joseph answered and said, "This is its interpretation: the three baskets are three days. In three days Pharaoh will lift up your head—from you!—and hang you on a tree. And the birds will eat the flesh from you."

Genesis 40:1–19

Waiting is hard work, and I'm not very good at it. I look for the shortest lines, fuss at slow drivers, grow annoyed as minutes tick by in waiting rooms, and grumble as I listen to those endless recorded apologies as I wait on hold on my phone.

The reality is that much of our waiting is simply a nuisance, rarely a significant problem. But waiting for reports on the progress of a disease or the success of a treatment is another matter. We did a lot of that during our daughter's illness. Other kinds of waiting can also be excruciatingly difficult: the phone call from a loved one bearing important news; word about acceptance by a chosen college; evidence that a long effort to overcome infertility has ended; a positive response to some desperate request we have made for help. Hardest of all may be waiting on God to do what only He can do on our behalf. Isaiah 40:31 is encouraging, though hard to put into practice: "They who wait for the LORD shall renew their strength; they shall mount up with wings like eagles; they shall run and not be weary; they shall walk and not faint."

Moses introduces us to the next major event in Joseph's life with the simple expression, "Some time after this" (Genesis 40:1). We are given no indication of how much time has passed. However, the end of chapter 39 indicates that Joseph had made himself indispensable to the keeper of the prison, just as he had with Potiphar. That hadn't occurred overnight. Over time, possibly months of daily drudgery, Joseph had lived responsibly and faithfully, doing right even though he had no way of knowing how his story could ever turn out for good—for him or anyone else.

"Faithful living" may sound simple, but it is incredibly difficult and demanding. It is also life-changing and life-saving. When we as a family found ourselves walking through the complex emotions, challenges, and decisions related to Janice's terminal illness, it was enormously helpful to recognize that our most immediate responsibility was rarely to solve long-terms questions. We were responsible to "do the next right thing." That much we were capable of, with the Lord's enabling strength, for the good of our daughter and her children, as well as ourselves.

That idea of doing "the next right thing" was etched on my wife's mind by her encounters with Elisabeth Elliot, whose first husband, Jim Elliot, was one of five missionaries killed in an attempt to reach the Waorani Indians in the jungles of Ecuador in 1956. Their story had an enormous impact on my life, as well as many others of my generation. My Elizabeth enjoyed the famed Elisabeth both through her writings and personal contacts.

Several years ago, Elizabeth and I had the immense privilege of flying deep into the Ecuadorian jungle with missionary friends who have faithfully served the Lord there for more than fifty years. We visited the actual place where those missionaries were killed, and also some of the Waorani believers who are the fruit of their sacrifice. Betty Elliot once wrote of the days immediately following Jim's death, as she returned to the remote jungle village where they had shared their home and ministry. She was dealing with the reality of her grief, as well as the care of a ten-month-old baby:

> When I went back to my jungle station after the death of my first husband, Jim Elliot, I was faced with many confusions and uncertainties. I had a good many new roles, besides that of being a single parent and a widow. I was alone on a jungle station that Jim and I had manned together. I had to learn to do all kinds of things, which I was not trained or prepared in any way to do. It was a great help to me simply to do the next thing. . . . So I went back to my station, took my ten-month-old baby, tried to take each duty quietly as the will of God for the moment.[1]

For Joseph, a routine, "do the next thing" kind of faithfulness put him in exactly the right place when God's special time arrived. For reasons unknown to us, but in full accordance with the sovereign purpose and providential working of God, Pharaoh became suspicious of two of his high-ranking officials—his cupbearer and his baker.

A cupbearer was entrusted not only with choosing a king's beverages, but also with making sure those drinks had not been tampered with in any way. He was therefore not just a butler, but a trusted royal confidant with significant influence. Bakers held a similar position of trust, since they directly oversaw the preparation and integrity of the ruler's food, and would have regular access into his presence.

The arrival of such prestigious political prisoners would have produced a significant disruption of jail routine. They required special treatment, demanding great wisdom and diplomatic skill on the jailer's part. Would the prisoners be found innocent or guilty? If handled too harshly or too leniently, there could be severe repercussions after their cases were settled. It is an evidence of the esteem in which Joseph was held by the prison keeper that he was given direct responsibility for the two men.

Joseph had no way of knowing that one of these men would hold the key to his future. He only knew that they came from exalted positions, people he would never have encountered otherwise. Now he was charged with their well-being. Joseph certainly knew that their situations were precarious, their lives hanging on the whims of Pharaoh. Doing the next right thing, Joseph chose to treat them humanely, thereby building their trust and confidence in him.

Prison life usually involves boring routines, and life in Pharaoh's prison would have been no different. However, God himself chose to interrupt the monotony of prison life by sending a pair of dreams; each of Pharaoh's imprisoned servants would have a similar dream on the same night. This marks the second of three life-shaping dream episodes in Joseph's life.

Dreams played an important role in ancient Egyptian culture, because of the belief that "sleep puts us in real and direct contact with the other world where not only the dead but also the gods dwell. Dreams therefore are a gift from the gods."[2] Given the cupbearer and baker's anxious uncertainty and tenuous hold on life itself, both men were convinced that these dreams were of extraordinary importance—portents of their future that should not be ignored. But they also knew that they were unable to penetrate the dreams' meanings by themselves.

In Egyptian culture, the interpretation of dreams was viewed as a science, a specialized skill carried out by highly trained experts. Confined to jail as they were, the royal prisoners lacked access to any such person. So their discomfort escalated. As one commentator observes, "A dream without an accompanying interpretation is like a diagnosis without a prognosis."[3]

As the two men's supervisor, Joseph had little reason to be concerned about their emotional state. His responsibilities concerned their physical needs. He could have reasoned that they had probably been imprisoned for good reasons, so why get personally involved? Joseph, however, had allowed his own experience with suffering to soften his heart, not to harden it. When he saw the men's troubled state, he couldn't simply ignore it.

Concerned about their well-being, Joseph felt moved to ask each man why he looked so despondent. The answer was immediate: Each had dreamed an unforgettably ominous dream. But with no one to interpret the dreams, they were paralyzed with fear.

Joseph's response is telling. He could have minimized their concerns, dismissing the significance of dreams. After all, his present circumstances contradicted his own dreams. Instead, he took them with great seriousness. Joseph was quick to deny any personal skill that enabled him to interpret dreams, but confidently affirmed his trust that God would reveal their meanings: "Do not interpretations belong to God? Please tell them to me" (40:8).

This is a profoundly important insight into Joseph's inner life at this point. Despite all the bad things that have happened to him, he is deeply God-centered, robustly confident of God's presence and His gracious empowerment that would enable him to interpret these dreams. Just as he had been aware of God's presence in the midst of Potiphar's wife's seduction, so now he was confident of God's empowering presence in the depths of Pharaoh's dungeon.

But Joseph's attitude went beyond *confidence* in God—he was determined that God alone must receive the *credit,* in advance, for the interpretation he was sure would come. That God-honoring attitude would be displayed even more clearly when, years later, Joseph would stand in the presence of Pharaoh himself (see 41:16, 25, 28, 32).

Whether he had genuine confidence in Joseph, or simply the sense that he had no other options, the cupbearer entrusted Joseph with his dream. It featured a vine with three branches, each of which produced an abundant cluster of grapes. The cupbearer had seen himself pressing those grapes into a wine that filled a cup in Pharaoh's hand. As soon as he finished recounting the dream, Joseph confidently and without ambiguity proclaimed its meaning: "In three days Pharaoh will lift up your head and restore you to your office, and you shall place Pharaoh's cup in his hand as formerly, when you were his cupbearer" (40:13).

Joseph saw a strategic opportunity to enlist the cupbearer as his advocate before Pharaoh, and he had no intention of missing it. The cupbearer, no doubt thrilled with Joseph's interpretation, had every reason to be well disposed toward him. So Joseph asked the man to reciprocate in "kindness," loyal love, by telling Pharaoh about his unjust confinement.

I cannot prove this, of course, but I can't help but wonder whether Joseph had, over the years, dreamed of an occasion like this. Perhaps he had even rehearsed what he would say, when he could finally speak to someone who could make a difference to his situation.

Joseph wanted the cupbearer to know that he was an innocent man, the victim of a series of terrible injustices: "For I was indeed stolen out of the land of the Hebrews, and here also I have done nothing that they should put me into the pit" (40:15). His had been a long, hard journey from the "pit" at Dothan to this "pit" in Pharaoh's Egypt.

These were not words of self-pity or manipulation. Joseph's interpretation of the cupbearer's dream hinged on the fact that the man was going to be released and restored to royal duty because he had been falsely imprisoned. The cupbearer, of all people, should be able to identify with an unjustly imprisoned Joseph. So Joseph made the injustice of his own situation clear: he was a man doubly victimized, first by human trafficking and then by this false imprisonment. Though he refused to become a victim of bitterness, he also refused to be passive, choosing instead to appeal for help from a man who would soon be able to put in a good word for him.

Encouraged by the good news his fellow prisoner received, the baker immediately recounted his dream to Joseph. Not surprisingly, it was about baked goods, three baskets full that he carried on his head. Bread was very important in Egypt—some researchers have observed that dozens of varieties of both cakes and breads are mentioned in ancient Egyptian literature. But this baker, in his dream at least, seemed strangely indifferent to the value of his product.

The baskets were intended for Pharaoh himself, and royal food must be protected from all mistreatment. But this man's dream depicted wild birds feasting on the bread; the baker, meanwhile, went on his way, doing nothing to chase the birds away.

Once again Joseph's interpretation was immediate and straightforward. This time, however, the meaning was unambiguously bad: in three days the baker's head would also be "lifted up," the same term he had used for the cupbearer. Only this time the "lifting up" would not be in exaltation and restoration—it would occur when the baker was found guilty, executed, and then, in the ultimate act of shaming, left unburied. The baker's corpse would be publicly exposed on a tree, where carrion birds would devour it. This cruel and painful death, compounded by shame, would undoubtedly lead to great problems for the baker's entire family.

We note both the certainty and the courage of Joseph. He did not hedge his bets by choosing evasive and vague language in his interpretations; he was very direct. Had he been wrong, he would have made a dangerous and determined enemy of both prisoners. But Joseph was a man of integrity, a truth-teller with the courage not to soften the harsh realities of God's warning. This is a quality deeply needed in a culture like ours, one that wants to soften the hard edges of God's truth and punish those who breech the conventions of political correctness.

Forgotten Again

> On the third day, which was Pharaoh's birthday, he made a feast for all his servants and lifted up the head of the chief cupbearer and the head of the chief baker among his servants. He restored the chief cup-bearer to his position, and he placed the cup in Pharaoh's hand. But he hanged the chief baker, as Joseph had interpreted to them. Yet the chief cupbearer did not remember Joseph, but forgot him.
>
> Genesis 40:20–23

The conclusion of Genesis 40 is anticlimactic, as Pharaoh's actions fully vindicated Joseph's interpretations. Pharaoh's birthday happened to fall three days after the dreams, a fact probably unknown to Joseph beforehand. In honor of this special day, Egypt's ruler held a feast for his retinue, using the opportunity to grant reprieves, declare amnesties, and complete unfinished royal business. Just as Joseph had predicted, the cupbearer was restored to his position of influence and affluence, while the baker was executed and publicly disgraced. Both proceedings confirmed Joseph's status as an accredited spokesman for his God.

While he probably grieved for the baker, Joseph's hopes must have soared on the news of the cupbearer's elevation. Surely the cupbearer would remember Joseph with gratitude, making his situation known to Pharaoh and bringing his saga of suffering to a happy end!

It was not to be. "The chief cupbearer did not remember Joseph, but forgot him" (40:23). And Joseph must have felt in some way forgotten by God. After all, he had only been able to interpret the dreams with God's help. Why wouldn't the same Lord who had given him those boyhood dreams do for Joseph what He had done for a pagan cupbearer?

"Hope deferred," Proverbs tells us, "makes the heart sick" (13:12). Joseph must have battled that kind of heartsickness, and the next two years must have dragged by at a snail's pace. One of the hard realities of life is that God's timetable isn't the same as ours, and one of life's hardest disciplines is waiting on God. From our perspective, knowing Joseph's entire story, we realize that while the Lord was shutting the prison door, He was preparing to open the palace door. Had Joseph been released just after the cupbearer was, he probably would have been returned to Potiphar's service, sold to another master as a slave, or perhaps allowed to leave the land as an unwanted foreigner. While those would have likely been preferable to languishing in prison, they were not what God had purposed to do to and through him. The time was not yet ripe.

God's plan, however, came at great cost to Joseph. As Iain Duguid observes, "In order for that plan to progress, Joseph had to continue to experience injustice at the hands of men. He had to go on suffering undeserved pain in order ultimately to free others from death."[4] Knowing nothing of that greater plan, this strong, immensely gifted man must have thought the prime years of his life were vanishing before his eyes. He must have fought a relentless daily battle against despair and hopelessness, as his old dreams served only to mock him. He must have fought hard to hold fast to what he knew of the goodness, grace, and sovereign power of his God, amid circumstances that seemed to suggest the exact opposite.

The earlier events of Genesis 40 had opened a window of hope in his life: if the dreams of pagans could come true exactly as God had indicated, why wouldn't the same thing happen with his own dreams?

But hope is a fragile thing, and the lengthening months of imprisonment became a loyalty test every bit as difficult as any he had endured to this point in his life. We know his remarkable change of fortune was coming. Joseph did not.

———————————————■———————————————

Looking back over this stage of Joseph's journey, we should observe some lessons. In Joseph's careful attention to his prison duties, we are reminded that *routine integrity and faithfulness aren't routine.* Sometimes we believe that we honor God in the extraordinary and special events of life, not in its normal routines. However, most of life is lived in the ordinary. Joseph's routine faithfulness caused the prison keeper to give him responsibilities that put him in contact with the very person who would provide a connection with Pharaoh. The way in which Joseph chose daily to do the "next right thing"—even in the midst of undeserved suffering—was the means God used to launch him into a position he couldn't have imagined.

Another truth that runs throughout Joseph's life stands out clearly: *It is our view of God that determines our attitude to the circumstances in which we find ourselves.* It is impossible to exaggerate the importance of this.

Years ago, when I was a college student, words of A. W. Tozer etched themselves on my consciousness: "What enters into our minds when we think about God is the most important thing about us."[5] He goes on to say, "Wrong ideas about God are not only the fountain from which the polluted waters of idolatry flow; they are themselves idolatrous. . . . Perverted notions about God soon rot the religion in which they appear."[6] Tozer's point isn't simply about theological accuracy, important as that is. My view of God shapes my response to everything in my life, especially the hardest things. There is an unresolvable mystery about the ways of God. We will never fully comprehend His ways because He is God and we're not. But He has revealed the truth about himself in His Word, and supremely in His Son.

When we were in the midst of our daughter's terminal illness, all of us took refuge in our God's personal presence, even while the storms of our questions and concerns battered our hearts. As we walked with our precious grandchildren through the agonizing news of their mother's illness, her growing weakness, and her dying moments in our home, we had no answers to "Why?"—but together we knew "Who" was the enduring foundation of her life and theirs. As we now take a major role in raising these children in our home, realizing that the sand in the hourglass of our lives is diminishing, our confidence must be in the truth that God will be with them when we cannot be. We believe that nothing can separate them or us from the love of God that is in Christ Jesus our Lord (Romans 8:39).

We as Christians today actually know much more about God than Joseph did, because we have both the gift of the incarnate Son and the completed Scriptures. Still, Joseph was a man of robust faith in God, a faith that had been tempered and tried in the pit of affliction. As the psalmist said of him, "Until what he had said came to pass, the word of the LORD tested him" (Psalm 105:19). Joseph was able to "keep on keeping on" in the worst of times, not because he was made of superior stuff, but because his God was with him. That was true even when God's presence and enabling power were hidden by the dark clouds of circumstances.

Closely related to our knowledge of God is our confidence in God, and this brings up a third lesson from Joseph's life: *We can trust God's promises and purposes even when we don't understand His timing.* Waiting is one of the most difficult assignments God gives us. There is a story about a famous preacher of the nineteenth century, Phillips Brooks, best known today as the author of "O Little Town of Bethlehem." A friend found Brooks pacing back and forth in evident frustration. "What's the problem, Phillips?" he asked. "I'm in a hurry and God isn't," he responded.

All of us, brought up in a microwave culture, can identify. We want the solution to our situation "yesterday," especially in the midst of life's hard things. So we need to hear the words of James 1:2–4 (NIV): "Consider it pure joy, my brothers and sisters, whenever you face trials of many kinds, because you know that the testing of your faith produces perseverance. Let perseverance finish its work so that you may be mature and complete, not lacking anything." Because waiting is hard, so is endurance. But the truth remains: "The LORD is good to those who wait for him, to the soul who seeks him. It is good that one should wait quietly for the salvation of the LORD" (Lamentations 3:25–26).

Those two years of silence from the palace must have been difficult for Joseph. But the Lord was completing an important work in his life, as well as preparing him for what lay ahead. Joseph hadn't been forgotten; he was being forged, hardened by the fire.

So, too, with us in our hard times of waiting. That is why Peter urges us, "Let those who suffer according to God's will entrust their souls to a faithful Creator while doing good" (1 Peter 4:19). That exhortation is coupled with a great promise: "After you have suffered a little while, the God of all grace, who has called you to his eternal glory in Christ, will himself restore, confirm, strengthen, and establish you" (1 Peter 5:10). Armed with those promises, we find that even waiting in a pit becomes possible through God's strengthening grace.

Malcolm Muggeridge was a well-known British journalist and media figure in the mid-twentieth century. In his youth he was an ardent socialist and outspoken agnostic; later in life, he not only became more conservative politically, he became an outspoken Christian. He would write of the fame, success, and pleasure he achieved, but declare, "I say to you and beg you to believe me. Multiply these tiny triumphs by millions, add them together, and they are nothing—less than nothing, a positive impediment—measured against one draft of that living water Christ offers to the spiritually thirsty, irrespective of who or what they are."[7]

Toward the end of his life, Muggeridge looked back with words that are of particular relevance to the concept of waiting on the Lord, even in the hardest of times and places:

> I can say with complete truthfulness that everything I have learned in my seventy-five years in this world, everything that has truly enhanced and enlightened my existence, has been through affliction and not through happiness, whether pursued or attained. In other words, if it ever were to be possible to eliminate affliction from our earthly existence by means of some drug or other medical mumbo jumbo, as Aldous

Huxley envisaged in *Brave New World*, the result would not be to make life delectable, but to make it too banal and trivial to be endurable. This, of course, is what the Cross signifies. And it is the Cross, more than anything else, that has called me inexorably to Christ.[8]

Joseph endured suffering not because of sins he had committed, but because God purposed that suffering for good—to position Joseph to become the life-giver who delivered others from certain death. In that, Joseph foreshadows our Lord Jesus Christ, who endured unjust suffering, supremely that of the cross, so He might deliver us from sin and death.

As Christ-followers, we may learn from Joseph—but it is to the Lord Jesus that we primarily look: "Consider him who endured from sinners such hostility against himself, so that you may not grow weary or fainthearted" (Hebrews 12:3).

SEVEN

FROM PIT TO PALACE

She was, by any measure, a very ordinary looking woman. She seemed totally out of place auditioning for the television show *Britain's Got Talent*. A few moments earlier, she had told offstage interviewers that she was an unemployed single woman who had never been kissed. The judges treated her with thinly veiled amusement, while the audience chuckled in anticipation of a comical performance. But then Susan Boyle began to sing.

Snickers turned to looks of wonderment and then smiles; cynical chatter turned to amazement. The audience spontaneously rose to applaud the performance, while judges stumbled for words to express their delight. Susan Boyle's song was a well-known standard, "I Dreamed a Dream," and when the video of her audition caught the world's attention, she was launched into a way of life that certainly surpassed any dream she had ever dared to dream. In an instant, her life changed from one of obscurity and hardship to one of fame—and possibly fortune.

There is something compelling about a genuine "rags to riches" story, of someone achieving his or her "big break." An unknown author writes a book that receives multiple rejection slips; when a publisher does take a chance on the story, it strikes a chord that creates an international bestseller. A persistent entrepreneur invents a product that creates an entirely new market. An athlete "comes out of nowhere" to become a star. Such things do happen, although much less often than we may be led to believe, and reality tells us that the "rags to riches" idea tends to downplay years of hard work and tenacious persistence in the face of rejection and failure.

Then there are the "overnight successes." They "go viral," blasting off like rockets, quickly achieving their "fifteen minutes of fame." Just as quickly, they vanish from public view or they crash to the ground with a resounding thud, done in by the shallowness of their achievement or their inability to resist the temptations their success had brought them. The music world is full of "one-hit wonders," the athletic world of performers remembered for a brilliant but unrepeated season, the business world of highly-acclaimed start-ups that vanish almost as dramatically as they first appeared.

Few "overnight successes" have been as dramatic, sudden, and far-reaching as that experienced by Joseph. The old adage, "What a difference a day makes," was never more applicable. A truly innocent man was set free from a terrible injustice, not because he was found innocent, but because he had become indispensable to a pagan king. And he was not only released, he was catapulted to one of the highest political offices in the entire world. Second only to the king of Egypt himself, Joseph found himself lavished with all the power, prestige, and privilege of such a position.

The changes were astonishing in their suddenness and extent. Joseph awakened in prison one morning, as he had for months, then went to bed in a palace that night! In the morning, his youthful dreams seemed to mock him; by nightfall, they were coming to fulfillment. From having no foreseeable future, he suddenly had unlimited prospects. The ascent was dizzying, and its attendant dangers were real. Only the strongest can resist the temptations that sudden success brings: as the Scottish writer Thomas Carlyle observed, "Adversity is sometimes hard on a man; but for one man who can stand prosperity, there are a hundred that will stand adversity."

Although Joseph's change of status was breathtakingly quick, his success was far from sudden. Slavery and imprisonment had been his training grounds for thirteen years, and he had experienced a version of success even in those disagreeable places. Long years of routine faithfulness and diligence in the hardest of circumstances had taught Joseph lessons and forged characteristics that prepared him for the next stage of God's intended journey. Joseph's experience had been hard, but it wasn't a wasted time because of what God was doing within him.

Joseph's victories over the temptations that plagued him in adversity had built qualities that would help him to deal wisely with prosperity. It is evident in the way he handled both his moment of opportunity before Pharaoh and the blessings that followed that Joseph had allowed God to work in the deepest parts of his life. His story allows us a glimpse into the often mysterious ways God works in the lives of all His people.

Opportunity Knocks

After two whole years, Pharaoh dreamed that he was standing by the Nile, and behold, there came up out of the Nile seven cows attractive and plump, and they fed in the reed grass. And behold, seven other cows, ugly and thin, came up out of the Nile after them, and stood by the other cows on the bank of the Nile. And the ugly, thin cows ate up the seven attractive, plump cows. And Pharaoh awoke. And he fell asleep and dreamed a second time. And behold, seven ears of grain, plump and good, were growing on one stalk. And behold, after them sprouted seven ears, thin and blighted by the east wind. And the thin ears swallowed up the seven plump, full ears. And Pharaoh awoke, and behold, it was a dream. So in the morning his spirit was troubled, and he sent and called for all the magicians of Egypt and all its wise men. Pharaoh told them his dreams, but there was none who could interpret them to Pharaoh.

Then the chief cupbearer said to Pharaoh, "I remember my offenses today. When Pharaoh was angry with his servants and put me and the chief baker in custody in the house of the captain of the guard, we dreamed on the same night, he and I, each having a dream with its own interpretation. A young Hebrew was there with us, a servant of the captain of the guard. When we told him, he interpreted our dreams to us, giving an interpretation to each man according to his dream. And as he interpreted to us, so it came about. I was restored to my office, and the baker was hanged."

Then Pharaoh sent and called Joseph, and they quickly brought him out of the pit. And when he had shaved himself and changed his clothes, he came in before Pharaoh.

Genesis 41:1–14

Two years is a long time to wait. Just before my final year of university, I suffered a detached retina, which threatened the loss of vision in my right eye. At that time, medical treatments for my condition were far less advanced than they are today. I had a procedure done that required me to lie blindfolded, flat on my back in a hospital bed for three weeks, in the hope that scar tissue would enable my retina to reattach. That was followed by strong restrictions on the use of my eye, with television and reading greatly limited. All the while I wore sunglasses, taped to force me to look straight ahead through a narrow slit.

Nevertheless, I was determined to graduate, so I began my senior year on schedule. But the operation wasn't successful; four weeks later, the retina detached again. Providentially, the hospital had acquired new technology in the intervening weeks, and I underwent a different procedure that enabled me to return to normal activity much more quickly. By God's grace, that solution has endured for almost fifty years!

I had missed five weeks of classes, though, and had to make up a great deal of ground. That meant going to each of my professors to explain my situation and request special consideration. I'll never forget one professor's response: genuinely concerned for my well-being, he strongly advised me to withdraw from school for the year, to heal completely and not put myself under unnecessary pressure. He might as well have been speaking a foreign language. The very idea seemed incomprehensible—I was twenty-one, itching to get to the next stage of my education. A year seemed impossibly long! So the professor graciously relented, modifying my requirements and enabling me to finish on time.

I tell that story to make the point that even a year seems enormously long to people in their twenties. Joseph must have felt that much of his life had already irretrievably slipped past him. The silence from the palace after the cupbearer's release was agonizing. Joseph had been forgotten. . . . But he hadn't been. He was actually in God's waiting room, not Pharaoh's. God was working, following His own schedule. He was preparing a time for Joseph, and Joseph for that time.

It is remarkable how many of God's people in Scripture had extended periods of "delay" in their lives—people like Abraham, Moses, David, Jeremiah, Daniel, John the Baptist, Peter, Paul, and John. Most of those biblical figures even knew the bitter experience of imprisonment—or a near equivalent! Their resulting wisdom, from the school of hard experience, is expressed well by David in Psalm 27:14: "Wait for the LORD; be strong, and let your heart take courage; wait for the LORD!" But staring into a seemingly bleak future, the call to wait is hard to accept.

Joseph was still waiting. His best and only hope, the cupbearer, had failed him. Perhaps Joseph wondered whether that prison was where he would spend the rest of his life. What about those God-given dreams? Ironically, had Joseph been released when the cupbearer was, Pharaoh would have had no need of him, and Joseph would probably have vanished into complete obscurity. It was not yet God's time.

Despite this crushing disappointment, however, Joseph made a saving choice. He would continue to carry out his assigned duties, as well as he could. There is a powerful lesson here, helpfully articulated by pastor and US Senate chaplain Richard Halverson:

> The [person] who keeps waiting for the *big* chance never recognizes it when it comes. Downgrading the ordinary, day-to-day affairs conditions him for failure in extraordinary times. If a [person] is not great when it doesn't matter, he will not be when it does! "It is required of a steward that [he] be found faithful," admonished the Apostle Paul (1 Corinthians 4:2).[1]

Suddenly, after long years, God's time arrived. The Lord intervened into the innermost part of Pharaoh's unconsciousness, inspiring a pair of dreams that caused great distress. One commentator observes, "This is not so much a story about Joseph as about God's faithfulness to his promises through providential acts."[2]

As we have noted, Egyptians viewed dreams with great importance; royal dreams especially so. The pharaoh was seen as the earthly representative of the gods, and dreams were a primary way in which the gods revealed messages to him. This night, Pharaoh's dreams were clear enough to arouse alarm, but not so clear that he could understand why they felt so ominous.

The first dream put Pharaoh in a familiar setting: by the banks of the mighty Nile River. The Nile was the bloodstream of Egypt, the source of its strength and prosperity. Egypt was far less dependent on local rains than neighboring areas, because the Nile's headwaters arose deep in Africa, in regions where rain was plentiful. Each year the river would flood, bringing with it both abundant water and rich alluvial soil. As a result, famines were rare in Egypt. But when they did occur, they were especially devastating, because Egyptian irrigation practices were completely dependent on the regularity of the river's flooding. Without that abundant water, crops could not survive the summer's withering heat.

Cows were also a common feature of Egyptian life. Valued primarily for their milk, they would often be seen wading in the river to avoid the oppressive heat and swarming flies. This initial part of Pharaoh's dream would not have been surprising: plump cows wading in the Nile, emerging to feed on the green growth by the river's edge, was life as normal. It was, however, startling to see those seven fat cows pursued by seven scrawny ones, who feasted on the fat cows rather than the reeds. Cannibal cows were bizarre and ominous, troubling enough to shock Pharaoh out of his sleep—probably in a cold sweat.

Distressed though he was, he was tired enough to fall back to sleep. But he would experience a second, equally disturbing dream. Again it began with a good sign—seven good plump heads of grain on a single stalk of wheat, an evidence of the abundant fertility that made Egypt the breadbasket of the region. Then this dream also turned bizarre: seven thin heads of wheat, shriveled by a hot wind, appeared to attack and devour the plump heads of wheat. Now plants were becoming cannibals!

This time, when Pharaoh awoke, it was impossible to get back to sleep. These, he knew, were not ordinary dreams but supernatural messages. Cows don't eat cows; heads of wheat don't devour other heads of wheat. The message was obviously bad, but what could it be? Overcome with anxiety, Pharaoh summoned his experts to hear and interpret the dreams. They completely failed. Despite all their training and their experience, the meaning eluded them.

All this time, the cupbearer had been a silent spectator to his master's growing frustration at his experts' failures. Finally, Pharaoh's increasing anger and distress caused the cupbearer to experience a mental flash-back to a season of his life he had tried his best to bury. His ordeal in prison was not one he cared to dwell on, or to have Pharaoh recall. But now the memory came flooding back, especially of the Hebrew prisoner who had proven so helpful by accurately interpreting the dreams of each of the men. (He may also have remembered Joseph's plea to mention him to Pharaoh.)

Whatever the case, the cupbearer knew he could not keep this information to himself. He recounted his story to Pharaoh, who was desperate enough to try anything to get an interpretation of his trou-bling dreams. Suddenly the forgotten slave and prisoner was the subject of conversation in the palace of Egypt!

God's time had come.

Called Before the King

Then Pharaoh sent and called Joseph, and they quickly brought him out of the pit. And when he had shaved himself and changed his clothes, he came in before Pharaoh. And Pharaoh said to Joseph, "I have had a dream, and there is no one who can interpret it. I have heard it said of you that when you hear a dream you can interpret it." Joseph an-swered Pharaoh, "It is not in me; God will give Pharaoh a favorable answer." Then Pharaoh said to Joseph, "Behold, in my dream I was standing on the banks of the Nile. Seven cows, plump and attractive, came up out of the Nile and fed in the reed grass. Seven other cows came up after them, poor and very ugly and thin, such as I had never seen in all the land of Egypt. And the thin, ugly cows ate up the first seven plump cows, but when they had eaten them no one would have known that they had eaten them, for they were still as ugly as at the beginning. Then I awoke. I also saw in my dream seven ears growing on one stalk, full and good. Seven ears, withered, thin, and blighted by the east wind, sprouted after them, and the thin ears swallowed up the seven good ears. And I told it to the magicians, but there was no one who could explain it to me."

Then Joseph said to Pharaoh, "The dreams of Pharaoh are one; God has revealed to Pharaoh what he is about to do. The seven good cows are seven years, and the seven good ears are seven years; the dreams are one. The seven lean and ugly cows that came up after them are seven years, and the seven empty ears blighted by the east wind are also seven years of famine. It is as I told Pharaoh; God has shown to Pharaoh what he is about to do. There will come seven years of great plenty throughout all the land of Egypt, but after them there will arise seven years of famine, and all the plenty will be forgotten in the land of Egypt. The famine will consume the land, and the plenty will be unknown in the land by reason of the famine that will follow, for it will be very severe. And the doubling of Pharaoh's dream means that the thing is fixed by God, and God will shortly bring it about. Now therefore let Pharaoh select a discerning and wise man, and set him over the land of Egypt. Let Pharaoh proceed to appoint overseers over the land and take one-fifth of the produce of the land of Egypt during the seven plentiful years. And let them gather all the food of these good years that are coming and store up grain under the authority of Pharaoh for food in the cities, and let them keep it. That food shall be a reserve for the land against the seven years of famine that are to occur in the land of Egypt, so that the land may not perish through the famine."

Genesis 41:14–36

For months stretching into years, Joseph's life had been shaped by the daily drudgery of prison routines. As he awoke, he would have expected the day to be just like every day—the same old same old. Why expect anything different?

Then, suddenly, the tedium was broken by the noise of footsteps and shouts of his name. Breathlessly, the keeper of the prison announced that Joseph was wanted immediately by none other than Pharaoh himself. Joseph had been taken out of a pit once before, only to be sold as a slave into Egypt. This time would be entirely different: he would stand in the presence of the most important person in his world!

Joseph couldn't go as he was. Since Egyptians were clean-shaven, he was required to remove his Semite beard to be presentable. He was then given garments appropriate for such an auspicious occasion. The uniform of the prisoner was gone, replaced by clothes that hinted at the new life he was about to enter.

We don't know if Joseph had advance information about what Pharaoh expected of him. But the mere fact that the great king was looking to a foreign prisoner for help indicated the almost desperate nature of Pharaoh's concern. So Joseph's heart must have pounded as he followed his escort into the king's presence. This was the golden moment, the kind of opportunity he had longed for. His future hung in the balance and, knowing that his handling of the next few minutes was critically important, he probably turned to his Lord in prayer.

Kings don't need to explain themselves, so without any fanfare, Pharaoh set the agenda: "I have had a dream, and there is no one who can interpret it. I have heard it said of you that when you hear a dream you can interpret it" (41:15). Joseph's response is remarkable, and it reveals an enormous amount about him: "It is not in me; God will give Pharaoh a favorable answer" (41:16). Joseph had no polished words of flattery for the king, and he completely resisted the opportunity to ingratiate or advertise himself. His answer, pointing away from himself, revealed both his humility and his confidence in God. Joseph had no intrinsic ability or credentials to claim, but he did know his Lord.[3]

Joseph's consistency and integrity are self-evident. On a much less important occasion, he had said virtually the same thing to the cupbearer and baker: "Do not interpretations belong to God?" (40:8). Now, in the presence of Pharaoh, he returns over and over to this same theme: "God has revealed to Pharaoh what he is about to do" (41:25); "God has shown to Pharaoh what he is about to do" (41:28); "The thing is fixed by God and God will shortly bring it about" (41:32). In Egyptian eyes, Pharaoh was both the human representative of the gods and also the embodiment of Egyptian religion, based on a multitude of gods. Joseph was humble enough to declare his utter dependence upon God and courageous enough to risk declaring his faith in a God unknown to the Egyptians. Despite all his suffering and unjust treatment, Joseph was unshakably loyal to the God he knew to be the only true and living God.

Joseph's poise and confidence prompted Pharaoh's trust, and he recounted the dreams. Joseph's immediate response is remarkable: he didn't ask for time to consider what he'd just heard, or even to pray for divine help. Instead he immediately set out the interpretation.

Pharaoh's dreams, Joseph boldly declared, were about the imminent future: "God has revealed to Pharaoh what he is about to do" (41:25).

In fact, the two dreams were separate versions of a single dream, a fact Joseph repeated three times (41:25, 26, 32). The seven plump, good cows and the seven good ears of grain both represented seven years of abundant harvests, a time of great plenty. In contrast, the seven scrawny cows and the blighted heads of grain foretold seven harsh years of famine—famine so severe it would erase all trace of the good years and threaten mass starvation. The dreams were doubled because, as Joseph said, "the thing is fixed by God and God will shortly bring it about" (41:32).

For all his immense earthly power, Pharaoh's dreams told of events completely beyond his control. The weather wasn't in his hands. It was, however, in God's—the same sovereign God whose providence stood behind the events of Joseph's life and who had invaded Pharaoh's sleep with dreams was now arranging weather patterns to bring about His plan of great harvests followed by even greater famine.

Kings don't like to hear bad news, especially about events beyond their control. But Joseph refused to hold back, giving some very bad news with unflinching honesty. However, he wasn't content just to be the bearer of bad news—without being asked, he quickly gave the king unsolicited advice on how to handle the problem he now faced. Joseph had had no time to think about the implications of the dreams, nor had he been asked to propose a plan of action. Yet he did so, in obvious confidence that God himself had provided instant wisdom.

The realities of God's plan were certain and could not be changed. An unprecedented famine was coming, a fact that called not for resignation and passivity but wise planning and strategic action. The coming famine was not a judgment from God that must be yielded to, but a challenge that could and must be managed. So Joseph set forth his proposal: Pharaoh should appoint a food czar, "a discerning and wise man" (41:33). This man would build a network of overseers who would impose a 20 percent tax on the produce of the good years, gathering that portion of the bumper crops into storage facilities throughout the seven years of plenty. That reserve would be stockpiled for use during the harsh years of famine to come, and people's lives would be preserved. It was a daring, brilliant plan.

Promoted!

This proposal pleased Pharaoh and all his servants. And Pharaoh said to his servants, "Can we find a man like this, in whom is the Spirit of God?" Then Pharaoh said to Joseph, "Since God has shown you all this, there is none so discerning and wise as you are. You shall be over my house, and all my people shall order themselves as you command. Only as regards the throne will I be greater than you."

And Pharaoh said to Joseph, "See, I have set you over all the land of Egypt." Then Pharaoh took his signet ring from his hand and put it on Joseph's hand, and clothed him in garments of fine linen and put a gold chain about his neck. And he made him ride in his second chariot. And they called out before him, "Bow the knee!" Thus he set him over all the land of Egypt. Moreover, Pharaoh said to Joseph, "I am Pharaoh, and without your consent no one shall lift up hand or foot in all the land of Egypt." And Pharaoh called Joseph's name Zaphenath-paneah. And he gave him in marriage Asenath, the daughter of Potiphera priest of On. So Joseph went out over the land of Egypt.

Joseph was thirty years old when he entered the service of Pharaoh king of Egypt. And Joseph went out from the presence of Pharaoh and went through all the land of Egypt. During the seven plentiful years the earth produced abundantly, and he gathered up all the food of these seven years, which occurred in the land of Egypt, and put the food in the cities. He put in every city the food from the fields around it. And Joseph stored up grain in great abundance, like the sand of the sea, until he ceased to measure it, for it could not be measured.

Before the year of famine came, two sons were born to Joseph. Asenath, the daughter of Potiphera priest of On, bore them to him. Joseph called the name of the firstborn Manasseh. "For," he said, "God has made me forget all my hardship and all my father's house." The name of the second he called Ephraim, "For God has made me fruitful in the land of my affliction."

The seven years of plenty that occurred in the land of Egypt came to an end, and the seven years of famine began to come, as Joseph had said. There was famine in all lands, but in all the land of Egypt there was bread. When all the land of Egypt was famished, the people cried to Pharaoh for bread. Pharaoh said to all the Egyptians, "Go to Joseph. What he says to you, do."

So when the famine had spread over all the land, Joseph opened all the storehouses and sold to the Egyptians, for the famine was severe in the land of Egypt. Moreover, all the earth came to Egypt to Joseph to buy grain, because the famine was severe over all the earth.

Genesis 41:37–57

"The king's heart," the Proverbs tell us, "is a stream of water in the hand of the LORD; He turns it wherever He will" (21:1). Instantly, the Lord opened Pharaoh's heart to recognize the truth of Joseph's words and the brilliance of his proposal.

The plan did have its challenges. After all, ancient Egyptians wouldn't like a huge tax increase any more than modern people do. And this tax increase would be based on the unproven dream interpretation of an obscure Hebrew slave and prisoner! But the Lord had mysteriously inclined Pharaoh's heart and mind to Joseph. Turning to the assembled royal court, he asked in approving astonishment: "Can we find a man like this, in whom is the Spirit of God?" (41:38).

Despite the capitalized "Spirit" in our English translation, the pagan Pharaoh was not referring to the Holy Spirit, since he knew nothing about him. He meant simply that "the spirit of the gods" was present in Joseph. However, we know, in the light of further Scripture, that Pharaoh was speaking better than he knew—Joseph was indeed indwelt and guided by God's Spirit. Pharaoh recognized that Joseph's God had not only given him the proper interpretation of his dreams, but also the wisest solution to the coming problem. Such remarkable abilities could only be God-given.

Pharaoh's declaration went even further. Joseph had not offered his plan with any self-interest in mind. His proposal that Pharaoh appoint "a discerning and wise man" (41:33) over the famine project was strategically the right course of action. But the king, recognizing the wisdom of the plan, also realized that the man he needed was standing right before him.

While the court officials may have agreed that Joseph's plan was wise, it is very likely that Pharaoh's next words shocked them—and probably Joseph as well. Some of those present would have had ambitions for just such a position. And who was a less likely candidate than a foreign slave who had been in prison only moments before? But you don't argue with Pharaoh, unless you want to forfeit your life!

When the king announced his decision, it was not impulsive, but God-implanted. Acknowledging Joseph's God and His revelation to and through Joseph, Pharaoh changed Joseph's life in a moment: "You shall be over my house and all my people shall order themselves as you command. Only as regards the throne will I be greater than you. . . . See, I have set you over all the land of Egypt" (41:40–41).

In the blink of an eye, Joseph went from the depths of suffering, obscurity, and bondage to the highest levels of status and authority—an elevation seemingly out of all proportion to his contribution of interpreting the dreams. Furthermore, Pharaoh had completely approved and adopted Joseph's plan. It was not Pharaoh who opened the door of the palace to Joseph, but God himself.

The royal court must have been dumbstruck. A previously unknown foreign slave and prisoner had suddenly been promoted over all of them! And Pharaoh wasn't even finished. Summoning the appropriate servants, he invested Joseph with the official symbol of high office, a signet ring granting him royal authority. This was accompanied by status symbols like fine clothing, a gold chain, and the equivalent of a presidential limousine—Pharaoh's own second chariot, now devoted to Joseph's use.

Joseph was to be treated with royal dignity, with all the kings' subjects commanded to "bow the knee" (41:43) before him in acknowledgment and respect. Unwittingly, Pharaoh was commanding the fulfillment of those dreams God had given to Joseph so long ago and far away! We can only wonder whether that thought flashed through Joseph's mind as he listened to Pharaoh's orders.

But with such immense privileges came significant pressures, including the weight of his new responsibilities. A more subtle pressure was Pharaoh's desire to turn Joseph into a full-fledged Egyptian, integrating him into the mainstream of national life. He had already given him duties throughout Egypt, which required him to have both an Egyptian name and a suitable Egyptian wife. Joseph probably had little say in either.

The new name is a tongue-twister: Zaphenath-paneah. It probably means "God speaks and lives," in honor of Joseph's interpretation of

Pharaoh's dreams, and was intended to reinforce his new identity. But it also unwittingly testified to the reality of a living, speaking God, a powerful contrast to the dead, dumb idols of Egypt. Wouldn't it be great if people were inspired to attach that kind of name to us!

Marriage into one of Egyptian's aristocratic families followed. It was a sign of great royal favor to be made son-in-law of Potiphera, priest of On, the center of worship of the solar deities Ra and Atum. We know nothing about Joseph's wife Asenath other than her family of origin and that she gave birth to at least two of Joseph's sons.

Such accumulation of Egyptian power and status must have presented powerful temptations for Joseph to completely assimilate to an Egyptian lifestyle and worldview. From a human perspective, there were good and sufficient reasons to leave his identity as a Hebrew far behind. Life in Egypt was suddenly proving to be much better than anything he had known in Canaan.

Years later, when Joseph's brothers encountered him in Egypt, they did not have the slightest hint that the man standing before them was anything other than Egyptian, even though they had repeated meetings with him. But Joseph's outward appearance belied his inner reality. At the core of his being he remained completely Hebrew, part of God's chosen people. That self-identity was evident when Joseph gave his firstborn a Hebrew name, not an Egyptian one. *Manasseh* is a name formed from a Hebrew word meaning "to forget," and Joseph chose it carefully: "God has made me forget my hardship and all my father's house" (41:51).

There is irony in this name. Calling the boy "Forgotten" would actually serve to remind Joseph, every time he said the name, of what he claimed to have forgotten. Joseph's point was not so much to declare that he had driven the past from his memory as that he had put it behind him. He had no intention of continually looking back, rehearsing the wrongs done to him. He chose by God's grace to live looking forward.

So his son's name represented a kind of forgiveness, a declaration that Joseph saw those terrible injustices through the lens of God's constant goodness, faithfulness, and providential care. Scars of the past abuse would remain forever; the rawness of his wounds he had placed in God's hands.

Suppose that, rather than "forgetting," Joseph had chosen to hold a grudge, keeping his mistreatment in the forefront of his mind. What then?

Researchers at Erasmus University in the Netherlands carried out a creative experiment to discover the effects of nursing our grievances. As part of the study, they asked 160 undergraduates to write about a time they had experienced conflict. Some of the group were told to reflect on a time when they didn't forgive the offender; others were told to think about a time when they did forgive; a third group was asked to write about an unimportant social interaction with a friend or coworker, with no reference to conflict. All of the participants were then given a small physical challenge: to jump five times, as high as they could. The results were intriguing: those who had thought of someone they had forgiven jumped about 30 centimeters on average, while the "non-forgivers" jumped only 22 centimeters. The researcher who led the study observed, "A state of unforgiveness is like carrying a heavy burden. . . . Forgiveness can 'lighten' the burden."[4]

Something about this experiment rings true emotionally. We feel ourselves dragging the weight of unresolved issues and people who remain unforgiven. There can be little doubt that Joseph lived more freely, because he had given the burden of his past to his Lord. That freedom is why God's Word exhorts us, whatever our situation: "Humble yourselves, therefore, under the mighty hand of God so that at the proper time he may exalt you, casting all your anxieties on him, because he cares for you" (1 Peter 5:6–7).

The name of Joseph's second son also revealed his God-centered focus. This boy was also given a Hebrew name—*Ephraim*—which means "doubly fruitful." This is Joseph's declaration of gratitude: "God has made me fruitful in the land of my affliction" (41:52). As good as life in Egypt was, it was still "the land of affliction" because Joseph's true home was elsewhere. Yet within and despite his afflictions, the Lord had given Joseph a double measure of blessing, both two sons and an abundance of other good things. Fruitfulness was God's good gift to him; Joseph was deeply aware that his current situation came from God's hand, not his personal merits. The true source of his blessing, he knew, was not Pharaoh.

Living at the pinnacle of power, Joseph may have looked fully Egyptian. Yet he remained a devoted follower of his Lord in this foreign land. And his children, seeing the integrity of his life, were to follow him. We know that his two oldest sons identified themselves with their father's family, not their mother's because, when the Exodus came centuries later, the descendants of Ephraim and Manasseh were numbered among the twelve tribes as "the children of Israel." They may have been born in Egypt of an Egyptian mother, but they were Israelites to the core of their being.

By the end of Genesis 41, Joseph's external circumstances bore no resemblance to those in which he began the chapter. His predictions about the years that lay ahead proved to be precisely true. The rollout of his survival plan had worked exactly as he had forecast. "There was famine in all lands, but in all the land of Egypt there was bread" (41:54). As a result, Joseph's prestige and authority grew exponentially. He possessed Pharaoh's complete confidence, as evidenced by Pharaoh's instruction to those who came to him: "Go to Joseph. What he says to you, do" (41:55). Indeed, Joseph's impact was international: "All the earth came to Egypt to Joseph to buy grain" (41:57). Through Joseph, a descendant of Abraham, blessing was coming to the nations, just as God had promised (Genesis 12:2–3).

All of these external changes, however impressive, were not as important as the internal changes God was working in Joseph's character. This reveals a fundamental truth of God's work in our lives: *While external changes in our circumstances may be a great blessing, the greater blessing is the God-produced change in our character.* Thirteen years is a very long time, but they had not been wasted for Joseph—it was a time of investment. The slave house and prison had been much more than waiting rooms. God had been building things of lasting value into Joseph.

On a superficial level, he had become fluent in the Egyptian language and skilled in administration. On a deeper level, God had been building his character. Through the fire of adversity, the Lord was forging a man of faith and faithfulness, equipped to deal with the responsibilities and challenges that lay ahead. Difficult circumstances not only reveal our character—as we walk with the Lord, they also change us, as the Lord uses them to refine us.

The way God works is found in Moses's striking challenge to the people of Israel, as they were about to enter the Promised Land. He recounted the often overwhelmingly difficult experiences they had encountered during their wilderness journeys, saying they were so "he might humble you and test you, to do you good in the end" (Deuteronomy 8:16). Humility teaches our dependence on God, and Joseph certainly learned that he was utterly dependent on God to deliver him from his circumstances. The great truth is that God delights to aid those who rely on Him: "'God opposes the proud but gives grace to the humble.' Humble yourselves, therefore, under the mighty hand of God so that at the proper time He may exalt you" (1 Peter 5:5–6).

A second principle unfolds throughout this chapter: *While God's timing and ways may be mysterious, God's faithfulness to His promises is certain.* Joseph's thirteen years of waiting for the dreams to be fulfilled had been excruciatingly long. During that time, everything valuable seemed to have been stripped from him. But God had not forgotten Joseph's dreams and, in God's time, His purpose had been revealed and realized.

The dungeon seemed to be a dead end. Instead, it proved to be God's means to bring Joseph into contact with the cupbearer, and then, when all hope appeared to be gone, before the great Pharaoh himself. The words of Richard Halverson are worth heeding: "To say 'Now!' to God is as presumptuous as saying 'No!' Submission to God's will involves submission to God's timing."[5]

There is a third principle: *We need the Lord as much in success as in distress.* Few have written as perceptively on issues of Christian leadership as the missionary statesman Oswald Sanders. He warns, "Not everyone can carry a full cup. Sudden elevation frequently leads to pride and a fall. The most exacting test of all to survive is prosperity."[6] Clearly, Joseph needed the Lord's presence in the darkest of times. But now, in the "best" of times, he needed God's presence every bit as much to keep him on his divinely appointed course.

The danger of adversity is that it grinds us down, producing despair and cynicism. The danger of prosperity is that it puffs us up, making us proud, arrogant, and self-sufficient. It can steal our hearts, and Joseph was in danger of being enticed by the riches of Egypt to turn away from the living God.

When Moses told the Israelites that God had used their wilderness sufferings "to do you good in the end," he also warned them about the prosperity they were about to experience in the Promised Land. "Take care," he said, "lest you forget the LORD your God. . . . Beware lest you say in your heart, 'My power and the might of my hand have gotten me this wealth'" (Deuteronomy 8:11, 17). Prosperity has its own very real dangers.

Centuries ago, the Puritan Thomas Watson observed a fact as true now as it was then: "People are usually better in adversity than prosperity. A prosperous condition is not always so safe. True, it is more pleasing to the flesh—but it is not always best. Many look at the shining and glittering of prosperity, but not at the burdens of prosperity."[7]

As I have mentioned, Joseph's story is not, in the final analysis, about Joseph—it is about God himself. *This part of the story of Joseph gives us a powerful picture of the gospel.*

Joseph was prepared and equipped to be Israel's deliverer through a humiliation that refined his character. Our greater Savior was qualified to become our Deliverer, not so that His character might be refined, but so that He might become like us in our weakness and suffering. The writer of Hebrews tells us that the Lord Jesus "had to be made like His brothers in every respect, so that He might become a merciful and faithful high priest in the service of God, to make propitiation for the sins of the people" (Hebrews 2:17).

We also see that through the intervention of a mediator—the cupbearer—Joseph the innocent was released from bondage and elevated to the highest place, receiving the greatest blessing Pharaoh could bestow. In contrast, because of the intervention of our Mediator—the Lord Jesus—we, the guilty, are released from the penalty and punishment of our sins and elevated to the privileges of sons and daughters of the living God, who has "blessed us in Christ with every spiritual blessing in the heavenly places (Ephesians 1:3).

EIGHT

WHEN THE PAST BECOMES PRESENT

When the future thirty-fourth president of the United States was a ten-year-old boy, his parents refused to allow him to accompany his two older brothers while they went trick-or-treating on Halloween. Any boy would be disappointed, but Dwight Eisenhower was infuriated. None of his pleading, shouting, or begging changed his parents' minds, so when his brothers left, he stomped into the back yard and vented his anger on an apple tree, pounding on its trunk until his hands bled. His father finally pulled the boy away from the tree, gave him a significant spanking, and banished him to his room. There Eisenhower continued to sob and scream into his pillow.

After some time, Dwight's mother entered his room and began to care for his badly bruised and bleeding hands. She then quietly began to talk to him about his hot temper. Pointing to Dwight's battered hands, she gave him some advice he would remember for the rest of his life. Hating, she said, was self-defeating. The person with whom he was angry probably didn't care, and, even if he did, wasn't going to change just because Dwight got angry. The only one he had injured during his tantrum was himself—the tree wasn't wearing bandages or bearing bruises, but Dwight certainly was.

Many years later, he recalled this conversation as one of the most valuable of his life. Anger, he realized, only wasted his time and clouded his judgment. That insight led him to begin a practice he followed throughout his illustrious career, a habit he reflected on during his retirement years:

> To this day I make it a practice to avoid hating anyone. If someone's been guilty of despicable actions, especially toward me, I try to forget him. I used to follow a practice—somewhat contrived I admit—to write the man's name on a piece of scrap paper, drop it into the lowest drawer of my desk and say to myself: "That finishes the incident, and so far as I'm concerned, that fellow." That drawer became over the years a sort of private wastebasket for crumbled-up spite and discarded personalities. Besides, it seemed to be effective and helped me avoid useless black feelings.[1]

Historians would have loved to rummage through that bottom drawer! But while Eisenhower's desk would have produced some fascinating historical insights, it doesn't provide a very healthy example.

It is undeniably tempting to write people out of our lives—to cut them out of our social circle or even to unfriend them on social media—living our lives as if they no longer existed. I suspect this never really works, for us or for a president of the United States. Troublesome people have a way of refusing to just disappear. Most of the people who deeply wrong us have an annoying habit of scrambling out of our "drawer of discarded personalities."

The reality is that most such people are permanent parts of our lives—parents, siblings, children, relatives, in-laws, friends of friends, former spouses who share the parenting of children, business associates, and so on. They won't just go away. Rather than remaining in relational limbo, they keep turning up in our lives. How do you avoid that relative who will certainly be present at family functions, or that gossiping coworker who continually undercuts you at the office? If we can't discard them, something deep within us yearns to retaliate, to lash out and give them a taste of their own medicine. As my rugby coach used to say, "Don't get mad, get even."

Broken relationships are sad, hard, and unavoidable facts of life in a broken world. The most painful are those involving the very people we ought to love and value most. Often, the initial offense is relatively trivial, but misunderstandings have a way of escalating. Other actions are so wrong, so painful, and so hurtful that they cannot and must not be ignored or tolerated. Most of us know that we are called to love even our enemies, which means that we shouldn't stoop to retaliation or revenge. But does that mean that we just grin and bear what was done? What if the offender endangers other people who need to be warned? Do we have a responsibility to them that prevents us from simply suppressing the past? What if the offender doesn't or won't admit any wrongdoing? Do we forgive anyway? And if there is some expression of regret, should that be sufficient for us?

These clearly are not theoretical questions. At some point in each of our lives, we will wrestle with some major issue of this sort. And we will almost inevitably hear someone try to reassure us with the mantra, "Well, time heals all wounds." It doesn't, of course. That tired cliché is plainly untrue. Even on a physical level, we know that untreated, unclean wounds don't vanish; they fester. Unacknowledged cancers don't heal themselves; they kill.

When she was a teenager, my oldest daughter complained of a severe pain in her foot. My examination of the wound site discovered no sign of any problem, especially when the purple surrounding the "wound" turned out to be a dye that washed off quickly. It looked okay to me, so I told her the problem was probably something that would soon go away.

I was wrong. Janice's pain only increased, until it became unbearable. Finally, a trip to the emergency room revealed that she had stepped on a needle, which was now embedded deeply into her foot. Following my advice—to keep walking—had only driven the needle in deeper. Extracting it proved far more difficult and painful than it would have been had I not misled her into thinking things were all right.

We have all experienced relational splinters that are buried from sight. Even though we have ignored them and tried to wish them away, they haven't gone away. Our relational wounds are like physical ones: only when an infected wound is lanced and cleaned does healing really begin. But our relational healing must go deep: a superficial reconciliation resembles a Band-Aid that covers, but can't cure, a wound. True healing occurs only on the basis of deep repentance, authentic character change, and costly forgiveness.

Happily, even when circumstances don't allow for such healing, Christ-followers can enter into the truth of a gracious God who "heals the brokenhearted and binds up their wounds" (Psalm 147:3).

It is hard to overstate the trauma Joseph had experienced, and that is what makes his story so compelling. He clearly was numbered among the brokenhearted. Time and again, he had been sinned against in awful ways. He was forced to battle the powerful temptation to become bitter or to wallow in despair. He had learned to lean hard on his ever-present Lord, even when nothing else in his world made sense. Joseph's positive responses to very hard situations witness to the fact that the Lord was healing His brokenhearted servant.

Then, suddenly, without any opportunity to prepare, Joseph found himself catapulted to unimaginable power, prestige, and prominence. This was a new and equally intense test: breathtaking prosperity. For seven years the former slave and prisoner enjoyed life at the highest levels of Egyptian society, as he maneuvered the nation through the bounty he'd predicted.

Joseph had embraced the gift of a new family God had given him, and managed to keep his balance through these dizzying experiences. The Hebrew names of his sons witness to his spiritual grounding: "Manasseh" declared that God had enabled Joseph to put the past behind him, "Ephraim" that God had made Joseph fruitful, even in the spiritual desert of Egypt. Egypt was now the land of thriving; Canaan only a bad memory.

Then came the pressure-filled years of dealing with the famine. He knew it was coming, so he was undoubtedly prepared for the challenge. But I wonder how well prepared he was for the challenge that faced him one ordinary workday: there, in line of foreigners seeking permission to buy food, were his treacherous brothers. God's hidden hand was at work once again.

The brothers were totally unaware of what they were about to encounter in the obviously high ranking and powerful "Egyptian" official to whom they must make their appeal—their own brother, whose life they had valued at twenty shekels of silver seventeen years earlier. They couldn't know that they were not only completely at Joseph's mercy, but also potentially in great danger. Joseph could do with them whatever he pleased. Were he in the mood for revenge, they could be about to die.

For his part, Joseph suddenly faced a personal test every bit as demanding as the test of injustice and suffering the brothers had made him endure. This was a defining moment for the entire family: Would Joseph take revenge? No one would question his actions if he did. Should he give the brothers the hard justice they so richly deserved? Should he confine them to his "drawer of discarded personalities," leaving them to their fate? Should he ignore their atrocities and embrace them, satisfying his longing for reunion with his family, whatever the cost? Or should he allow the Lord to use him for a larger purpose?

At that moment, God was fitting together the broken pieces of Joseph's life to accomplish a divine plan. Joseph was probably unaware of exactly what God was doing. But he did know that his family had been called by God, through Abraham, to have a special role in God's program for the world. He also knew that his brothers had shown that they were totally unprepared for such a role. Could he become an agent of healing toward the very men who had done him such harm?

Over the years, Joseph had probably brooded over his family's downward course in Canaan, the inexorable loss of their Abrahamic identity and their assimilation to a pagan lifestyle. His immediate choice was clear: he could strike back in revenge against his brothers, or reach forward, pursuing restoration and reconciliation. Joseph's response to that defining moment would determine the future of his entire family. And he had only moments to choose his course of action.

Moved by a Hidden Hand

When Jacob learned that there was grain for sale in Egypt, he said to his sons, "Why do you look at one another?" And he said, "Behold, I have heard that there is grain for sale in Egypt. Go down and buy grain for us there, that we may live and not die."

So ten of Joseph's brothers went down to buy grain in Egypt. But Jacob did not send Benjamin, Joseph's brother, with his brothers, for he feared that harm might happen to him. Thus the sons of Israel came to buy among the others who came, for the famine was in the land of Canaan.

Genesis 42:1–5

God had a purpose that He was working out in history to bring salvation and blessing to the world through the family of Abraham—a purpose that would culminate in the incarnation of the Lord Jesus. So the story of Joseph isn't just about an interesting but deeply flawed family, a kind of ancient soap opera. Rather, it is the story of God himself bringing His salvation. By the time we reach the fourth generation of Abraham's family, the central agent of God's program is Joseph.

Behind all that transpires, we must see the hand of the sovereign God. To a contemporary observer, the seven years of remarkable agricultural prosperity in Egypt and the following years of severe famine would be seen as the result of unexplainable, possibly unprecedented meteorological phenomena. To the eyes of faith, it is all the result of God's special plan for His people Israel.

Joseph, by his God-given wisdom to interpret Pharaoh's dreams, had been used by God to bring blessing not only to Egypt but the world. God had made Joseph fruitful in his personal life, and was working through him to bring into effect the Lord's promise to Abraham: "In you all the families of the earth shall be blessed" (Genesis 12:3). At the heart of God's covenant was the promise, "I will make of you a great nation" (12:2). So the focus of the story now shifts back to Canaan, to Joseph's badly broken, dysfunctional family.

The children of Israel were, at this time, neither a nation nor a source of blessing to anyone, including themselves. God's purpose wasn't just to save them from famine, but to forge them into a people who would become the instrument of His blessing to the world. In their current condition, that was clearly impossible. It would become possible only if they were first delivered from their downward course of assimilation.

That would require a self-sacrificing commitment to unity, a cohesion only possible were they to experience deep repentance and transformation. God would use Joseph to accomplish this.

Famine had reached its tentacles into Canaan as God's hidden hand was forcing Jacob's family to look toward Egypt for help. Genesis 45:6 tells us that the famine was in its second year when Joseph finally saw his brothers again. Since he was elevated to power at the age of thirty, and the seven years of plenty had passed, that means it had been twenty-two long years since Joseph had been part of the family's life. Sold at the age of seventeen, Joseph was now thirty-nine years of age; his father now about 130. But time certainly hasn't healed all wounds! Joseph had been physically absent, but it was an absence that haunted the family—especially the still-grieving Jacob. In the intervening years the family had grown into a community of almost seventy family members, served by a multitude of servants. The deepening famine had now become a looming threat to all of their survival.

Jacob had been slowed by age, but he seems to have been more alert to the realities of the situation than his sons, who appear frozen into passivity and inaction. Calamity was at hand; their only hope was immediate and decisive action. Word had reached Jacob that food was available in Egypt, so the old man told his sons that was where salvation lay: "Go down and buy grain for us there, that we may live and not die" (42:2). He had no idea how much better "living" would soon be!

Even at his advanced age, Jacob was still the undisputed leader of the family, and the brothers, now men in their forties and fifties, neither protested nor complained. Instead, they immediately set out for Egypt. But their youngest brother, still in his twenties, was a significant exception: Benjamin stayed behind.

Jacob had aged, but he hadn't changed: he "did not send Benjamin, Joseph's brother, with his brothers, for he feared that harm might happen to him" (42:4). It isn't clear what dangers he feared, but he wasn't taking any chances. Benjamin was the new "special son," the one now holding the place once held by Joseph.

The old, ugly pattern of favoritism remained. It is understandable that Jacob's ties to Benjamin were very strong. In light of the disappearance of Joseph, Jacob's youngest son was the only surviving link to his beloved Rachel. He could risk the others, but not Benjamin. Is it possible that he even harbored suspicions of the ten oldest brothers, given the strange case of Joseph? Throughout the next chapters of Genesis, we will never hear Benjamin speak—but he is the central issue behind the events that unfold.

The Past Becomes Present

> Now Joseph was governor over the land. He was the one who sold to all the people of the land. And Joseph's brothers came and bowed themselves before him with their faces to the ground. Joseph saw his brothers and recognized them, but he treated them like strangers and spoke roughly to them. "Where do you come from?" he said. They said, "From the land of Canaan, to buy food." And Joseph recognized his brothers, but they did not recognize him. And Joseph remembered the dreams that he had dreamed of them. And he said to them, "You are spies; you have come to see the nakedness of the land." They said to him, "No, my lord, your servants have come to buy food. We are all sons of one man. We are honest men. Your servants have never been spies."
>
> He said to them, "No, it is the nakedness of the land that you have come to see." And they said, "We, your servants, are twelve brothers, the sons of one man in the land of Canaan, and behold, the youngest is this day with our father, and one is no more." But Joseph said to them, "It is as I said to you. You are spies. By this you shall be tested: by the life of Pharaoh, you shall not go from this place unless your youngest brother comes here. Send one of you, and let him bring your brother, while you remain confined, that your words may be tested, whether there is truth in you. Or else, by the life of Pharaoh, surely you are spies." And he put them all together in custody for three days.
>
> Genesis 42:6–17

When the brothers arrived in Egypt, they "just happened" to find themselves required, as foreigners, to get special permission from the man in charge of foreign grain sales. On this day, that person "just happened" to be Joseph himself. It is extremely unlikely, given all his other responsibilities, that this was always Joseph's duty. Be that as it may, on this day he "just happened" to be working at the time and place of his brothers' arrival.

When the brothers finally reached the head of the line, in accordance with Eastern customs and desperate to gain favor, they immediately bowed before Joseph in deference. It was a common courtesy but, unknown to them, they were fulfilling the very dream for which they had been willing to kill "the dreamer"!

It is hardly surprising that the brothers failed to recognize Joseph. That it could be him would have been the farthest thing from their minds. Twenty-two years had passed, and Joseph was, to them, as good as dead. Furthermore, the clean-shaven man before them was clearly an Egyptian, speaking fluent Egyptian, bearing an Egyptian name, wearing Egyptian clothes, holding an Egyptian government position, and surrounded by Egyptian officials. He was obviously a very powerful official, to be approached with great care.

But Joseph recognized his brothers. Their clothing and beards made it clear that they were foreigners. Their language revealed their Hebrew identity, and their features and mannerisms would have tapped into some of Joseph's deepest memories. Given the realities of the famine, he might even have expected that they would be among the throngs who came seeking food.

We can only guess all that went through Joseph's mind at the moment of recognition. But we are told of one thought: "Joseph remembered the dreams that he had dreamed of them" (42:9). This was his moment of vindication! The emotions must have been nearly overwhelming. But what would he do with these men? They were absolutely at his mercy. He could do virtually anything he pleased.

He could avoid them, sending them away without explanation and without engagement as "discarded personalities." That, however, would cut him off from any information about his father or his brother Benjamin, and from any possibility of future relationship with his family. *He could punish them*, meting out the justice they so richly deserved, smacking his lips on the sweetness of revenge. *He could embrace them*, instantly forgiving them, sweeping away the past as though it had never happened. But such a reunion would be superficial, covering the past without cleansing it and leaving his family unchanged. Something deeper and more enduring was needed if there was truly to be a new future: *he could wisely love them*, reaching for an entirely new relationship grounded in genuine repentance, true forgiveness, and authentic reconciliation.

Joseph's initial response makes us wonder what option he chose, especially when we read that "he treated them like strangers and spoke roughly to them" (42:7). He was speaking through an interpreter, but both his tone and his words made his attitude toward the men clear. He was deeply suspicious.

The harshness seems to suggest that a desire for revenge has captured Joseph's heart. Yet what follows makes it clear that something else was going on. Joseph has instantly opted for a complicated plan intended to test and refine his brothers, a plan that, in the end, would forge an entirely new kind of family relationship. Joseph's plan would involve great pain for his brothers, but his motivation wasn't revenge—rather, it was love and reconciliation. With a wisdom given by God, Joseph chose a course of action that used the pain of the past to reach for a new future.

The process began with a blunt and serious accusation that the brothers were spies. Joseph repeats the accusation four times in this encounter. It was a shock attack, and not entirely unreasonable given the circumstances. During this period of their history, Egyptians were very conscious of the need for border security, even during normal times. They had developed a rather sophisticated system of frontier defenses, which would be elevated in a time of regional famine, when Egypt had the only viable food resources.

The part of the Egyptian frontier of greatest concern was the northeast, the very direction from which Joseph's brothers came.[2] So when they heard this very serious accusation, they passionately jumped to their own defense. The man had it wrong—they weren't spies, they were family, ten brothers, the sons of one man. Spies wanted to be invisible. They certainly wouldn't come in such an obvious group.

Joseph's biting accusation had been, of course, a pretext to get information about his own family—and the brothers gave it to him. Perhaps Joseph bit his lip when they claimed that they were "honest men" (42:11). But their answer to his next charge told him what he really wanted to know: "the youngest [brother] is this day with our father" (42:13). Both Jacob and Benjamin were still alive! But I wonder what emotions surged through him as they mentioned a missing brother: "and one is no more" (42:13).

To all appearances, Joseph refused to accept their plea of innocence. He repeated his accusation that they were guilty of being spies. But he also proposed a means by which they could prove their innocence, and he chose a word that revealed his intentions: "By this you shall be tested" (42:15). As we saw earlier, Psalm 105:19 describes Joseph's time in slavery and prison as the word of the Lord testing him, a test that made Joseph a person of faith and faithfulness. Now, the tested one becomes the one giving the test.

Joseph was concerned about much more than famine relief. His intention is to put his brothers through a fire—not to destroy them but to refine them. His test would expose their innate qualities, and also put them through a severe process intended to purge their worst tendencies. The brothers had thrown Joseph into the pit of testing years before. Now the roles would be reversed.

First, Joseph declared that he planned to confine most of the brothers in an Egyptian prison, while allowing one to return to Canaan with a specific purpose: to bring back the youngest brother the men claimed to have. Joseph had accused them of being spies; they had claimed to be "honest men." Only the actual presence of this brother in Egypt would prove their honesty. Otherwise, they would be treated and punished as spies, a threat that almost certainly carried with it the likelihood of the death penalty. Joseph obviously had a very personal reason for this demand: he wanted to see Benjamin and, perhaps, bring him under his protection.

Then Joseph was through talking. He had the ten men imprisoned for three days to make clear the seriousness of their legal position. More importantly he was testing them in a way that would reveal their attitude toward both their father and his special son. Were these the same men who had planned the murder of a younger brother, being restrained only by the opportunity to sell him as a slave for twenty shekels? The issue at this point wasn't whether Joseph was willing to forgive his brothers. The real question was whether the brothers had the capacity to properly respond to such forgiveness.

Awakening Consciences

> On the third day Joseph said to them, "Do this and you will live, for I fear God: if you are honest men, let one of your brothers remain confined where you are in custody, and let the rest go and carry grain for the famine of your households, and bring your youngest brother to me. So your words will be verified, and you shall not die." And they did so. Then they said to one another, "In truth we are guilty concerning our brother, in that we saw the distress of his soul, when he begged us and we did not listen. That is why this distress has come upon us." And Reuben answered them, "Did I not tell you not to sin against the boy? But you did not listen. So now there comes a reckoning for his blood." They did not know that Joseph understood them, for there was an interpreter between them. Then he turned away from them and wept. And he returned to them and spoke to them. And he took Simeon from them and bound him before their eyes. And Joseph gave orders to fill their bags with grain, and to replace every man's money in his sack, and to give them provisions for the journey. This was done for them.
>
> Genesis 42:18–25

Those must have been the longest three days of the brothers' lives, a small taste of the suffering they had inflicted years earlier on Joseph. Summoned again into Joseph's presence, they learned that he had reconsidered the terms of their confinement. Perhaps he had realized that keeping nine of the brothers in Egypt, while allowing only one to return for Benjamin, would endanger all those left behind in the Promised Land. After all, one person would be unable to carry enough food to meet the family's needs. As well, the absence of nine more brothers would push Jacob to the edge, make it all but certain that he would refuse to allow Benjamin to be put at such risk.

So Joseph revised his conditions. Only one of the brothers would remain in custody, while the others would be permitted to return to Canaan. The one brother would be a hostage, released only if and when the rest returned, bringing with them their youngest brother. Only on that basis would they be allowed to purchase more food in Egypt. Compliance would prove that they were not spies, releasing them from the death penalty that hung over them and allowing continued access to essential food.

The brothers were in no position to bargain, so they accepted the Egyptian's terms. Yet, even as they did, they seemed to experience a kind of group flashback: they were transported two decades into the past to the atrocity they had tried to bury inside. Their total inability to make this powerful man listen to their protestations of innocence reminded them of that time when they themselves sat, eating their food and callously discussing the murder or sale of Joseph. All the while, his cries of distress from inside a dry cistern only yards away rang in their ears.

Then, the brothers had been completely indifferent; Joseph had been terrified and powerless. Now the roles were reversed. Suddenly, they had an inkling of what Joseph had gone through, and how hard their hearts had been. Assuming that they could not be understood by the Egyptians, they confessed to one another in their native Hebrew: "In truth we are guilty concerning our brother, in that we saw the distress of his soul, when he begged us and we did not listen. That is why this distress has come upon us" (42:21).

I suspect this was one of the very few times that the brothers dared to speak even with one another about their terrible secret. Now they saw it in an entirely different light. Even more, they felt it. What convicted them wasn't just the determination they needed to rid themselves of their brother. It was their utter hard-heartedness as they witnessed Joseph's intense distress. Their own undeserved suffering had opened their hearts to identify with the suffering they so unjustly inflicted on their young brother all those years ago.

They were seeing the situation, perhaps for the first time, from God's perspective. So it is no surprise that they concluded that their present experience was, in some mysterious way, justice—repayment from a righteous God. Time had covered that shameful moment in the mists of the past, but it hadn't erased it. The missing Joseph was suddenly alive and active in their consciences.

Reuben, with self-righteousness and more than a little self-deception, was quick to point his finger in blame: "Did I not tell you not to sin against the boy? But you did not listen. So now there comes a reckoning for his blood" (42:22). His words were obviously self-serving, but he did get one thing right: the brothers' act hadn't been a mistake. It was a great sin, a violation that brought blood guilt before a holy God. Their current distress was God's time of reckoning.

———————————————

This was a hugely important moment. A dark secret, undisclosed for more than twenty years, was being openly discussed and lamented by those who were guilty. But we need to step back and ask an important question: Was this discussion an indicator of genuine repentance or merely of deep regret? The two may be linked, but they are not the same. Were the brothers regretful about the circumstances in which they now found themselves, consequences of a long-past sin, or were they actually repenting of the sinful deeds themselves?

This is a question I have been forced to ask, when as a pastor I have listened to people sharing stories of being caught in sin. There are nearly always declarations about the shame they are feeling, as well as fear of the likely consequences. However, I always find myself asking whether there is more concern about the consequences of their actions than over the innate sinfulness of what they have done. One response signals regret; the other points toward repentance. Regret makes us feel bad; repentance drives us to change and to make whatever amends are possible.

At this stage in Joseph's story, it is not clear how much true repentance is evident in the men's declaration of guilt about their treatment of their brother. Nevertheless, this represents an important first step in the right direction. The older brothers' own suffering had sensitized their hearts so that they began to see both Joseph and themselves in a different light.

The moment was too much for Joseph. Unknown to the brothers, he had heard and understood everything they'd been saying. Joseph got a glimpse through the window of their hearts, only to see a painful reminder of that awful moment two decades before. Since this was not the time to reveal himself to them, he quickly and quietly withdrew from the room. For the first of six times in his encounters with his brothers, he wept.[3] As Gordon Wenham observes, "For all his apparent harshness toward his brothers, this action proves that he still loves them and that if they continue to show a change of heart, reconciliation will be possible ultimately."[4]

When he returned to the room, Joseph's tears were gone. The harsh visage returned. He chose Simeon to be a hostage, binding him in the brothers' sight. We are not told why Joseph chose Simeon; as the oldest, Reuben was the recognized leader of the brothers, responsible for their well-being, and probably a more likely choice. Yet Joseph had just heard Reuben remind the others that he had tried to dissuade them from their evil plan, so perhaps Simeon, as next oldest, became Joseph's choice. He was bound as a prisoner and led to confinement.

The nine other brothers were then sent back to Canaan. But they didn't leave empty-handed. Joseph not only gave them the grain they had come for, he chose to pay for his family's food. Joseph had his servants secretly place in the grain sacks the money the brothers had used to purchase the food. He also provided necessities for the journey itself. Both were acts of kindness, but given the brothers' recent experience of imprisonment, the discovery of the money would be a further jolt to their systems. It would weigh heavily on their consciences.

What Do We Do About Benjamin?

Then they loaded their donkeys with their grain and departed. And as one of them opened his sack to give his donkey fodder at the lodging place, he saw his money in the mouth of his sack. He said to his brothers, "My money has been put back; here it is in the mouth of my sack!" At this their hearts failed them, and they turned trembling to one another, saying, "What is this that God has done to us?"

When they came to Jacob their father in the land of Canaan, they told him all that had happened to them, saying, "The man, the lord of the land, spoke roughly to us and took us to be spies of the land. But we said to him, 'We are honest men; we have never been spies. We are twelve brothers, sons of our father. One is no more, and the youngest is this day with our father in the land of Canaan.' Then the man, the lord of the land, said to us, 'By this I shall know that you are honest men: leave one of your brothers with me, and take grain for the famine of your households, and go your way. Bring your youngest brother to me. Then I shall know that you are not spies but honest men, and I will deliver your brother to you, and you shall trade in the land.'"

As they emptied their sacks, behold, every man's bundle of money was in his sack. And when they and their father saw their bundles of money, they were afraid. And Jacob their father said to them, "You have bereaved me of my children: Joseph is no more, and Simeon is no more, and now you would take Benjamin. All this has come against me." Then Reuben said to his father, "Kill my two sons if I do not bring him back to you. Put him in my hands, and I will bring him back to you." But he said, "My son shall not go down with you, for his brother is dead, and he is the only one left. If harm should happen to him on the journey that you are to make, you would bring down my gray hairs with sorrow to Sheol."

Genesis 42:26–38

If the trip to Egypt had been unexpectedly dramatic, the trip home had its own surprises. Apparently the men had two kinds of sacks—the equivalent of checked baggage (sacks of grain) and carry-on luggage (sacks containing provisions for the journey). At one stop, an unnamed brother chose to open his larger sack to feed his donkey. To his surprise and consternation, he discovered the money Joseph had secretly placed inside. Under the circumstances, the brothers could only conclude that this was bad news.

The stern Egyptian governor's strange actions and their guilty consciences caused them to imagine the worst and "their hearts failed them" (42:28). They feared that the man would somehow use this against them, accusing them of being not only spies but also thieves. Worse yet, they sensed in this strange happening the judicial hand of an offended God, once again moving against them. The despairing question, "What is this that God has done to us?" (42:28), was almost certainly said in consciousness of the great wrong they had done to their brother decades earlier. God, not Joseph, was closing in on them.

Surprisingly, none of the other brothers dared at that time to open their sacks to see if money had been returned to them as well. They probably just decided it was better not to know. But now they faced another problem: they had to answer to their father. If looking back to Egypt made them fearful, looking ahead to meeting Jacob with one of their number missing—again—made them even more nervous. How could they face their father with the fact of Simeon's absence and the demand for Benjamin's presence in Egypt?

When they finally reached home, they poured out their story to Jacob. The account of their encounter with the mysterious "lord of the land" of Egypt (42:30) was carefully designed to put matters in the best possible light. The basic facts of their meeting were all present: the man's harsh accusation, their pleas of innocence and family connectedness, and the man's insistence on Benjamin's presence as a condition for Simeon's release and their ability to trade for more food. But the brothers carefully omitted or glossed over some rather significant details. They hadn't just been accused of being spies; they had been imprisoned for three days. They didn't "leave" Simeon (42:33); he had been taken hostage, with a death penalty hanging over him. They worked hard to emphasize the positive, quoting the ruler as saying, "I will deliver your brother to you, and you shall trade in the land" (42:34).

We see a major difference now, compared with the time they had brutally confronted their father with Joseph's "demise." Then, the brothers had callously produced Joseph's blood-covered and shredded special coat to maneuver their father toward false conclusions about Joseph's death. This time, they treated their father with sensitivity and thoughtfulness. Is this another indication of the change their own encounter with suffering had produced in their hearts?

Jacob may have been older, but his mind was still clear. I suspect he was less than impressed with their story, especially when each of the brothers discovered his food money buried in his sack. That curious fact, along with the absence of Simeon, likely deepened the old man's suspicions. Ironically, when the brothers had lied to him about Joseph, Jacob had believed them; now he found it very hard to believe them.

Once again, Jacob had lost a son, and the finger of blame pointed squarely to the others: "You have bereaved me of my children; Joseph is no more, and Simeon is no more, and now you would take Benjamin. All this has come against me" (42:36). This was grief talking, not reason. But it is impossible not to sympathize with an old man who was seeing all he had valued in life slipping from his grasp. Still, his refusal even to consider parting with Benjamin posed an enormous problem for Simeon's well-being. Jacob was talking as if his son in Egypt was already dead: "Simeon is no more" (42:36).

As the firstborn son, Reuben was the titular leader of his brothers. He had proven incompetent in stopping the brothers from selling Joseph, and now he put his lack of discernment on display again. The issue was now Benjamin, and Reuben needed to convince Jacob that there was no option but to send his special son if Simeon was to be freed. And only then would the family be able to buy the food they needed to avoid starvation.

So Reuben blurted out a sincere, if utterly foolish, offer to his father: "Kill my two sons if I do not bring [Benjamin] back to you. Put him in my hands and I will bring him back to you" (42:37). As if the possibility of losing Benjamin and then killing two grandchildren was a proposal any sane person would agree to!

Jacob's response was immediate and final. He would not, under any circumstances, allow Benjamin to go to Egypt. Reuben's proposal seems only to have hardened his resistance: Who would entrust a special son to the care of a man willing to let his own sons be killed? The loss of Benjamin would kill Jacob, and under no conditions would he take that chance. After all, Benjamin was special, "the only one left," as the old man called him (42:38). His others sons couldn't possibly miss the point: none of them really mattered compared to Rachel's only remaining son. They were expendable, Benjamin wasn't. In Jacob's eyes, the possibility of losing Benjamin was far more significant than the prospect of restoring Simeon.

The question of Benjamin's destiny has become central to the story. Would the brothers overrule their father to do what was necessary to preserve their families and rescue a brother in distress? Would the father give up his favored son for the greater good? Would the brothers' recognition that they had sinned against Joseph, their father, and most of all God himself, grow into a deepening change of heart, or would it wither and die? So the storyteller pauses, leaving us this question: What about Benjamin?

When Joseph recognized his brothers and chose to build a bridge toward reconciliation rather than take revenge, he opened an entirely new chapter in the family's history. These initial encounters between the brothers make it very clear that time hasn't healed all wounds. As we have observed, it isn't time alone, but what you do with time that determines whether wounds heal or fester. For twenty-two long years, the wounds caused by the brothers' sin had been festering. The memories of their atrocity against Joseph had become remarkably fresh, despite the passing of the years, and Joseph's intention was to lance those wounds.

Joseph's own wounds were clean, since he had entrusted what happened into the hands of God. He affirmed, every time he called his son "Manasseh," that "God has made me forget all my hardship and my father's house" (Genesis 41:51). The tears he hid from his brothers made it clear that this meeting in Egypt has reopened the wounds in some way. But he was free to reject revenge and work toward reconciliation, since he had entrusted himself to God.

The brothers, on the other hand, had spent years covering their disgusting acts against their brother, hiding them from their father, and presumably barely speaking of them to one another. But hope was birthed in the midst of their suffering. Their consciences were stirred and their hearts opened when they experienced a small taste of what they had caused their brother to endure. For the first time in the account, they began to speak of God and their guilt before Him.

Proverbs 28:13 captures an abiding truth: "Whoever conceals his transgressions will not prosper, but he who confesses and forsakes them will obtain mercy." The brothers, in their God-orchestrated adversity, had begun to reveal their transgressions. Only time would tell whether they would forsake those transgressions for new patterns of behavior.

These principles are as true for us, in our brokenness and failures, as they were for Joseph's brothers. Genuine guilt is a profound gift of God, because it reveals our deep need for repentance. That, in turn, opens the possibility of our receiving forgiveness.

Joseph probably couldn't have articulated the principles that guided him as he put his brothers to the test. He clearly recognized that a superficial reunion with his brothers would be foolish, since *superficial reconciliations produce superficial healing and superficial relationships.* Authentic reconciliation requires deep repentance and personal transformation. A time would come when he could stand before his brothers and declare his forgiveness of them. But that would only be after a process in which they were tested and changed.

Behind all that happened in this part of the Joseph story is the mysterious hidden hand of God, a hand that moves clouds and winds first to produce bumper crops and then to cause an international food crisis. His is a hand that directs the plans of a national public works program, and a hand that works through the choices and challenges of a single family. In all things, God was working to achieve a bigger purpose than saving Jacob's family—He was carrying out His eternal plan to bring salvation to the world through the coming of His Son, the Lord Jesus Christ. And He would carry that out in ways we would never have expected.

The wonder of the gospel is that God, against whom we have all sinned at countless times and in countless ways, did not write our names on a paper that He then assigned to His "drawer of discarded personalities." Instead, He sent His only beloved Son to do for us what we could not do for ourselves. This Son—Jesus—was not an unwilling victim like Joseph was. Rather, our Lord willingly accepted humiliation, suffering, and unjust imprisonment. Our worst sin, the crucifixion of the Lord Jesus (after all, it was our sin, not just that the Jewish leaders and Roman soldiers, which nailed him there), became the means God used to provide a substitute, the Sin-bearer. Through His death we are reconciled to God, when we have faith in this One who loved us and gave himself for us. That is a story far greater than Joseph's!

NINE

SEEDS OF CHANGE

It was, on many levels, an inspiring story. A fiercely competitive young American began to reach high levels of success in cycling, a sport long dominated by Europeans. Then, apparently on the cusp of great stardom, Lance Armstrong received a heartbreaking medical diagnosis: at the age of twenty-five he had advanced testicular cancer. It had spread through his body, and although doctors were not quite so candid at the time, they felt his chances of recovery were almost nil. If survival was doubtful, any thought of continuing his cycling career was unimaginable.

But survive he did. Armstrong not only beat his cancer, he drove himself to return to competitive cycling—and he did so in spectacular fashion. From 1999 to 2005, he won the sport's most prestigious race, the Tour de France, an astonishing, record-shattering seven successive times. Acclaimed as an authentic American hero, Armstrong made millions of dollars from endorsement deals, inspired multitudes with his story of victory over cancer, and rallied people to contribute to cancer research. His yellow "Livestrong" bracelets became commonplace.

It was a story that seemed almost too good to be true. Sadly, it was.

Cycling, like too many other sports at that time, was infested with the use of performance enhancing drugs. There were persistent rumors that Armstrong was a user, even though he had passed numerous tests. At first, the accusations seemed like the attacks of jealous competitors. But rumors increasingly swirled around him, with accusations from former teammates, other fellow cyclists, race officials, and reporters.

Typical of his general approach to life, Armstrong fought back aggressively. He vehemently attacked any accusers who dared to suggest that he was guilty of personal involvement in doping. Armstrong accused them of professional jealousy, of fraud and deceit, or of carrying out witch hunts. He instigated lawsuits and privately issued personal threats, all the while publicly demeaning his accusers' character or integrity. Armstrong's denials were emphatic, his retaliations swift and harsh.

But as evidence mounted against him, Armstrong's denials seemed less and less credible. Before long, virtually no one doubted that Armstrong had blatantly and persistently cheated, while bullying his teammates into doing so as well. As a result, he was first suspended and then banned from participation in sanctioned professional racing. Still, he vigorously protested his innocence.

Finally, in a carefully arranged setting, he admitted to Oprah Winfrey on national television that he had, in fact, "crossed the line." But he quickly followed that statement with his justification: everyone else was doing it, and if he hadn't, he would have been at a competitive disadvantage. He was only seeking to level the playing field.

Armstrong's fall from grace was quick and hard. Overnight, the icon became a pariah. Sponsors dropped him, his charity cut ties with him, former sponsors sued him, and multitudes of fans felt betrayed. Early in 2015, in an interview with a BBC reporter, Armstrong acknowledged that "the fallout has been heavy, maybe heavier than I thought."[1] He admitted, in the course of the interview, that "My actions and my reactions, and the way I treated some scenarios, were way out of line, so I deserved some punishment."

Armstrong followed that with a carefully framed acknowledgement that he had cheated, expressing both remorse and a desire for forgiveness. He had changed, he said. Yet when asked whether he would use the substances again, he responded, "If I was racing in 2015, no. I wouldn't do it again, because I don't think you have to. If you take me back to 1995, when it was completely and totally pervasive, I'd probably do it again." Clearly, that is a long way from repentance!

There is a certain honesty in the admission. Yet Armstrong's statement exposed the depths of his heart. His words admitted wrongdoing but also revealed that Lance Armstrong, at his core, was still the same man, one who would do whatever it took to reach his goal. He was still worshipping the same idol of athletic fame and success, and, given the same circumstances, he would do it all over again. In his own words, "I would change the man who did those things, maybe not the decision, but the way he acted."

But that is precisely the point: you can't truly "change the man" without changing his core values. You can't become a new man while you are still defending and rationalizing the decisions the old man made. Character and conduct are inextricably intertwined as issues of the heart. That is why God's Word counsels, "Keep your heart with all vigilance, for from it flow the springs of life" (Proverbs 4:23).

You may wonder what all of this has to do with the story of Joseph. I don't know Lance Armstrong personally, and you probably don't either. Whatever he did, it wasn't directed at me—and I'm in no position to forgive him. But his story illustrates a fundamental issue at the heart of that portion of the Joseph story we have now reached.

Joseph must engage the very brothers who had grievously sinned against him, even though they didn't recognize who he really was. In that defining moment, Joseph chose not to retaliate, though he easily could have done so, without any repercussions for him. On the other hand, Joseph also chose not to immediately embrace the brothers and overlook their sin against him. Instead, he followed a course of action intended to redeem the past by bringing about authentic repentance. Only in that way could there be the possibility of true reconciliation.

Joseph wanted more than to simply restore the past. Why would anyone want to reproduce the sinful dysfunction that had plagued the family during his teen years? His goal was to build a bridge to a new future, one that was possible only if his brothers responded constructively to the suffering they were presently experiencing. God-sent famine and Joseph-induced anxiety combined to form a crucible in which the brothers could be tested and, hopefully, refined. They needed to become a different kind of men—not just men who would make different choices.

But more was in play than Joseph's efforts. God himself was working through these events, pursuing a much larger goal than Joseph was. The Lord's intent wasn't merely to restore the relationships among an elderly man and his twelve sons. He was seeking to build them into a people He could both bless and make a blessing to the nations.

Signs of Hope

Now the famine was severe in the land. And when they had eaten the grain that they had brought from Egypt, their father said to them, "Go again, buy us a little food." But Judah said to him, "The man solemnly warned us, saying, 'You shall not see my face unless your brother is with you.' If you will send our brother with us, we will go down and buy you food. But if you will not send him, we will not go down, for the man said to us, 'You shall not see my face, unless your brother is with you.'" Israel said, "Why did you treat me so badly as to tell the man that you had another brother?" They replied, "The man questioned us carefully about ourselves and our kindred, saying, 'Is your father still alive? Do you have another brother?' What we told him was in answer to these questions. Could we in any way know that he would say, 'Bring your brother down'?" And Judah said to Israel his father, "Send the boy with me, and we will arise and go, that we may live and not die, both we and you and also our little ones. I will be a pledge of his safety. From my hand you shall require him. If I do not bring him back to you and set him before you, then let me bear the blame forever. If we had not delayed, we would now have returned twice."

Then their father Israel said to them, "If it must be so, then do this: take some of the choice fruits of the land in your bags, and carry a present down to the man, a little balm and a little honey, gum, myrrh, pistachio nuts, and almonds. Take double the money with you. Carry back with you the money that was returned in the mouth of your sacks. Perhaps it was an oversight. Take also your brother, and arise, go again to the man. May God Almighty grant you mercy before the man, and may he send back your other brother and Benjamin. And as for me, if I am bereaved of my children, I am bereaved."

So the men took this present, and they took double the money with them, and Benjamin. They arose and went down to Egypt and stood before Joseph.

Genesis 43:1–15

When the brothers returned from Egypt, Jacob had drawn a clear line in the sand with them, saying in essence, "There is no way that Benjamin is leaving me to go down to Egypt. I simply won't risk him." Hard times, however, have a way of moving hard lines, and a growling stomach did that for Jacob. The rains didn't come, the famine didn't end, and the food supplies dwindled ominously. Finally, Jacob could avoid the subject of a return to Egypt no longer—the family's survival was at stake.

The Lord was using the famine to expose the elephant in this family's room: the privileged position of Benjamin, the current form of Jacob's undying preference for his beloved Rachel. He must have known that he couldn't avoid the issue, but he did his best, couching his directions as a suggestion, not a command: "Go again, buy us a little food" (43:2). Perhaps Jacob hoped that, having waited so long to make the suggestion, the brothers would respond to the urgency of the situation and immediately set off for Egypt, leaving Benjamin behind.

What followed was hugely significant: Judah responded, not Reuben, the firstborn. Reuben had probably lost credibility in the family because of past sins against his father (see Genesis 35:22) and his pathetic suggestion to use his own sons as collateral—suggesting that Jacob should kill them—if he didn't bring Benjamin back from Egypt (42:37). Whatever the reason, Judah now stepped forward as leader and spokesman for the brothers. It was a role he would assume from this point forward—here with his father, later when the men stood before Joseph in Egypt (note the expression "Judah and his brothers" in Genesis 44:14), and when the family prepared for its move to Egypt (46:28).

Judah seems a most unlikely candidate to lead his brothers in an honorable direction. Earlier in our story, Judah saw a golden opportunity to get rid of the hated brother in a way that would avoid direct murder and also provide some cash in the process: "Come, let us sell

149

him to the Ishmaelites, and let not our hand be upon him, for he is our brother, our own flesh" (37:27).

The next time Judah appears in Scripture, he is seen in an even worse light. In Genesis 38, Moses interrupts the account of Joseph's journey to Egypt with one of the most sordid stories in the Bible. Judah is shown to be deeply compromised by Canaanite values, choosing to marry a Canaanite woman by whom he had two children. Judah's oldest, Er, also married a Canaanite, a woman named Tamar. Er was a terribly corrupt man; his sins are not recounted but he was so "wicked in the sight of the LORD" that "the LORD put him to death" (38:7).

Er's demise brought the ancient Near East custom called "levirate marriage" into play. It may seem bizarre to us, but when a brother died childless, this custom demanded that the next oldest brother take the widow as his wife. Any males born of that relationship would be considered the sons and heirs of the first brother.

The next brother, Onan, had no intention of complying with the custom—probably because it would dilute his own share of the family inheritance. Outwardly, he followed the custom by taking Tamar as his wife. But he used her as a sexual plaything, enjoying her body but withdrawing from her prematurely so she couldn't become pregnant. God was not pleased with Onan: "What he did was wicked in the sight of the LORD, and he put him to death also" (38:10).

I do not need to belabor the sad aftermath of these events, recounted in Genesis 38. Judah, as head of the family of which Tamar was part, was now responsible to care for her. But, having lost two sons, he apparently viewed her as both bad luck and a nuisance. Against all prevailing cultural norms, Judah sent Tamar back to her father, saying he would give her in marriage to his youngest son at some future date—a promise he had no intention of keeping. This left Tamar marginalized and defenseless, bearing the triple shame of being widowed, childless, and without prospects for another husband.

Her growing disgrace and shame led her to launch a desperate and dangerous plan. At some point in the course of events, Judah's own wife had died. Tamar, knowing his character, disguised herself as a prostitute to entice Judah while he was on his way to a pagan harvest festival. She succeeded, and Judah eagerly sought her services. Apparently, Judah lacked cash for the liaison, so he promised a future payment. But Tamar knew that Judah was not a man whose word could be trusted—and she shrewdly required certain of his possessions as a pledge.

The first part of Tamar's plan succeeded: she became pregnant. When Judah learned that she was expecting a baby, his hypocritical response to the news was to demand her death as an adulteress. But when Tamar was brought out for punishment, she produced the pledge Judah had given her—a staff, a cord, and his own personal signet—clearly revealing the identity of her client.

Judah immediately recognized his guilt, releasing Tamar from punishment with the declaration, "She is more righteous than I" (Genesis 38:26). This is the first good action recorded of Judah. Confronted by evidence of his guilt, he openly admitted his sin—perhaps the first sign of moral change in Judah. Out of that sordid series of events came two more sons, twins named Perez and Zerah.

It is an ugly story. One wonders, at first glance, why the Holy Spirit would choose to record this episode in Scripture. It becomes even more amazing when we learn that the tribe of Judah was the line chosen by God to carry the ruler's staff among the children of Israel (Genesis 49:10). That meant that Judah's son Perez, born of his sleazy dalliance with Tamar, would become the ancestor not only of the great King David, but of our Lord Jesus Christ himself (see Matthew 1:1–18, especially v. 3).

Remarkably, out of Judah's awful sins—first against Joseph and then against Tamar—God brought blessing and salvation into his life, and through him to the world. Joseph's bondage in Egypt would result in him saving the family from starvation in Canaan. But it was Tamar's son who began the ancestral line through which God brought into the world our Lord Jesus Christ. As the Redeemer, He would pay the price of every sin—Judah's and ours—through His death on the cross.

None of that was apparent, of course, when Judah stepped forward to challenge his father. While he deferred to the old man's leadership, Judah faced the situation directly: it would be both foolish and futile to return to Egypt without Benjamin. "The man" had made it abundantly clear that, without Benjamin, Simeon's life would be forfeit, the other brothers' lives would be in jeopardy, and the family would be left without food. "The man" had been explicit: "You shall not see my face, unless your brother is with you" (43:5).

Jacob attempted to evade the issue by blaming his sons for telling the Egyptian about "another brother" (43:6), but they all followed Judah's lead by asserting that events had been out of their control. How could they have known that "the man" would demand Benjamin's presence when they innocently answered questions about their family?

Jacob's fear was understandable—he stood to lose what he valued most in the world. It was at this point that Judah displayed something deeper in his character than anything seen before. Whereas Reuben had been willing to put his sons' lives on the line, Judah offered to put his own life and future there: "Send the boy with me. . . . I will be a pledge of his safety. . . . Let me bear the blame forever" (43:8–9). Jacob's concern for Benjamin was putting the whole family at risk, and so "Judah risks his own family fortune and life to save the rest of the family."[2]

Ironically, when Judah spoke of being a "pledge," he used the same word recorded in chapter 38 to describe the items he left with Tamar, disguised as a prostitute (vv. 17–18, 25). That pledge had been a symbol of Judah's self-indulgent and immoral lifestyle, and became the means of his exposure by Tamar. Now, Judah himself was the pledge, as he hazarded himself for the well-being not only of Benjamin, but also of Jacob and the entire family. For the first time, one of the brothers was acting sacrificially for the good of the others. This may have been only a small step forward, but it was an important one. Only such an attitude would be able to save this broken family.

Jacob knew he had no real options. Bowing to the inevitable, he reluctantly released Benjamin to Judah's protection. Then, as a shrewd pragmatist, he gave the brothers some sage direction. Jacob told his sons to take gifts to "the man," fine products of Canaan—"a little balm and a little honey, gum, myrrh, pistachio nuts and almonds" (43:11). Such gifts were a normal courtesy when a petitioner approached someone of higher rank seeking favor. And in a time of famine, these particular items would be doubly precious. Perhaps they would smooth the way with this mysterious Egyptian who had so much power over the brothers.

As a further precaution, Jacob instructed the brothers to take not only the money they needed to purchase food, but also the silver that had mysteriously appeared in their sacks on the first journey back from Egypt: "Perhaps it was an oversight" (43:12). Their return of the money would make it clear that they were neither spies nor thieves, but the "honest men" they claimed to be.

Jacob's parting words were a prayer and a lament, a strange combination of self-pity and dependence on God. It is easy to criticize his self-absorption, but the one thing of greatest value to Jacob—actually, the one person, Benjamin—was embarking on a trip from which he might never return. For the first time, Jacob spoke of God—God Almighty, in Hebrew "El Shaddai."

I wonder if, as Jacob used this divine name, he recalled it being spoken over him. His father, Isaac, had used this name as Jacob was about to flee from his brother, Esau: "God Almighty bless you and make you fruitful and multiply you, that you may become a company of peoples. May he give the blessing of Abraham to you" (28:3–4). Or did Jacob recall the time when, fearful for his family's life, he had returned to Bethel where the Lord appeared, blessing Jacob and saying, "I am God Almighty: be fruitful and multiply. A nation and a company of nations shall come from you" (35:11). El Shaddai was a name of God closely linked to His covenant promises to His people. How appropriate that Jacob filled his heart and mind, as well as those of his sons, with the character and promises of God when their very existence as a family was in danger.

In this scene, Jacob may not impress us as a mighty man of faith. But what he does in his weakness is what we should do in ours: fill our minds and hearts with the promises of a faithful God. In my own family, as we walked through the valley of the shadow of death, we have been sustained over and over by the faithfulness of our triune God. During our times of great weakness and need, El Shaddai—the God of mercy and power—met our needs, just as He met Jacob's.

The prayer of Jacob is the prayer of a weak man, fearing the worst. But he knew enough to turn to a great and gracious God with those overwhelming fears: "If I am bereaved of my children, I am bereaved" (43:14). Would Jacob ever see any of his sons again—especially Benjamin?

An Unexpected Meal

So the men took this present, and they took double the money with them, and Benjamin. They arose and went down to Egypt and stood before Joseph.

When Joseph saw Benjamin with them, he said to the steward of his house, "Bring the men into the house, and slaughter an animal and make ready, for the men are to dine with me at noon." The man did as Joseph told him and brought the men to Joseph's house. And the men were afraid because they were brought to Joseph's house, and they said, "It is because of the money, which was replaced in our sacks the first time, that we are brought in, so that he may assault us and fall upon us to make us servants and seize our donkeys." So they went up to the steward of Joseph's house and spoke with him at the door of the house, and said, "Oh, my lord, we came down the first time to buy food. And when we came to the lodging place we opened our sacks, and there was each man's money in the mouth of his sack, our money in full weight. So we have brought it again with us, and we have brought other money down with us to buy food. We do not know who put our money in our sacks." He replied, "Peace to you, do not be afraid. Your God and the God of your father has put treasure in your sacks for you. I received your money." Then he brought Simeon out to them. And when the man had brought the men into Joseph's house and given them water, and they had washed their feet, and when he had given their donkeys fodder, they prepared the present for Joseph's coming at noon, for they heard that they should eat bread there.

When Joseph came home, they brought into the house to him the present that they had with them and bowed down to him to the ground. And he inquired about their welfare and said, "Is your father well, the old man of whom you spoke? Is he still alive?" They said, "Your servant our father is well; he is still alive." And they bowed their heads and prostrated themselves. And he lifted up his eyes and saw his brother Benjamin, his mother's son, and said, "Is this your youngest brother, of whom you spoke to me? God be gracious to you, my son!" Then Joseph hurried out, for his compassion grew warm for his brother, and he sought a place to weep. And he entered his chamber and wept there. Then he washed his face and came out. And controlling himself he said, "Serve the food." They served him by himself, and them by themselves, and the Egyptians who ate with him by themselves, because the Egyptians could not eat with the Hebrews, for that is an abomination to the Egyptians. And they sat before him, the firstborn according to his birthright and the youngest according to his youth. And the men looked at one another in amazement. Portions were taken to them from Joseph's table, but Benjamin's portion was five times as much as any of theirs. And they drank and were merry with him.

Genesis 43:15–34

In their wildest imaginations, the brothers could not have foreseen the reception that awaited them in Egypt. They had left under accusations of espionage, as well as strong threats of punishment and refusal of service if they failed to return with their youngest brother. Their trepidation must have reached new heights the closer they came to "the man." Though Benjamin was now with the brothers, the Egyptian's behavior on their earlier visit had been entirely unpredictable. Would it be the same this time?

But this morning, rather than facing a hostile inquisition, Jacob's sons heard "the man" instruct his steward to take them to his home. The steward should slaughter an animal in preparation for a special meal that the official would share with them. Suddenly, the brothers were not being treated as suspected spies, but honored dignitaries! What was going on?

This was no spur-of-the-moment decision. Joseph had had months to consider how he would test and refine his brothers. This meal was only part of a carefully constructed plan. Eating together would give him the benefit of closer contact, as well as an opportunity to assess their attitude toward Benjamin, the favored son. It would also provide credibility for Joseph's next accusation—that the brothers had stolen his special goblet—the critical piece of his intricately designed strategy. Nothing was happening by accident.

Joseph's kindness initially aroused fear and suspicion, not gratitude, in the brothers. Everything seemed too good to be true. Why were they being singled out for such special treatment? What had happened to those spying charges? The whole situation smelled of a trick.

Still hanging over them was the problem of their mysteriously refunded money. Surely, they whispered to one another, they were being set up. Paranoia began to run wild. This was all happening, they concluded, so that the Egyptian "may assault us and fall upon us to make us servants and seize our donkeys" (43:18). On one hand, such a concern was laughable. What did one of the richest men in Egypt want with their donkeys? But there was a more ominous note in their words. Their fear corresponded precisely to what they had done so long ago to Joseph: they had assaulted him and fallen upon him to make him a slave.

Guilty consciences were plaguing the brothers. However, when they approached Joseph's steward, telling of the surprising discovery of the money and their intent to return it, he proved to be completely uninterested. Dismissing their concerns, he insisted that they had paid their bill: "Your God and the God of your father has put treasure in the sacks for you. I received your money" (43:23). Ironically, it was a pagan steward who assured the men that their God was active on their behalf! Confirming that their account had been settled and that there were no remaining issues, the steward brought Simeon to them. Then he provided them with exactly what they needed to prepare for a luncheon in "the man's" house: water so they could wash and make themselves presentable for such an auspicious occasion.

Later in the day, when Joseph returned home, the brothers instinctively prostrated themselves before the unpredictable man who had so much power over them. They had done so on their first encounter (42:6), and now they did so once again, not realizing that they were fulfilling the dream that had long ago aroused their deep hatred toward their young brother.

Formal courtesies of such an occasion followed—the presentation of the brothers' gift to their host, and his polite inquiries after "the old man" (43:27), their father, Jacob. The question was routine, but of course, it was far more than a mere formality for Joseph. His father was aging, and famines are especially difficult for the very old. His question came from the heart: "Is your father well? Is he still alive?" (43:27).

Assured that Jacob was alive, Joseph turned to his other great concern: his mother's son and his full brother, Benjamin. Still playing a role, Joseph asked, "Is this your youngest brother, of whom you spoke to me?" (43:29) Joseph, of course, knew the answer: he had instantly recognized his brother. What may have surprised the brothers was the blessing that fell from his lips as he focused his gaze on Benjamin: "God be gracious to you, my son!" (43:29).

The brothers were likely puzzled by the emotion that suddenly overtook the austere Egyptian official. No matter how many times Joseph had played out this scenario in his imagination, no matter how carefully he had prepared for this moment, nothing had prepared him for the surge of emotions that rushed from the depths of his being as he addressed his full brother. Caught off guard, Joseph was forced to rush out of the room, probably inventing an excuse for such a sudden departure. He could weep in private and compose himself for what was to follow. After all, "Weeping will give away his subterfuge. People in power do not normally weep publicly, although they may make others weep."[3]

All of us who have been caught by an unexpectedly powerful surge of emotions can identify with Joseph at this moment. Those tears were years in the making. At their first meeting, tears were triggered when the brothers spoke regretfully of their terrible indifference to Joseph's suffering (42:24); here they are incited by the presence of his longed-for younger brother, Benjamin. In part, they were tears of relief that Benjamin had come through his brothers' hatred and jealousy better than Joseph had. They were also tears of release, venting the pent-up yearnings for his family that he had been carefully suppressing. They were probably also tears prompted by restraint—Joseph wanted to say much, but he couldn't yet. This was not the time for his brothers to see his true feelings; that time would come. For the present, Joseph needed to resist any premature and superficial reconciliation.

The meal itself had its own surprises. We don't know who else was on the guest list, but Egyptian protocol was carefully followed: the diners were carefully separated by status and ethnicity. The aristocratic Joseph was served at a table by himself, while lower ranking "fellow Egyptians" enjoyed their own company. The reason proves to be important: "the Egyptians could not eat with the Hebrews, for that is an abomination for the Egyptians" (43:32).

Abomination is a strong word. It is used in the Old Testament to describe something that, on religious grounds, is morally or ritually repulsive. In this case the normal Egyptian aversion to foreigners was probably reinforced by the fact that these men were shepherds, "for every shepherd is an abomination to the Egyptians" (Genesis 46:34).

This simple fact of prejudice gives us an insight into the divine strategy behind Israel's sojourn in Egypt. "Whereas the Canaanites were willing to integrate and absorb the sons of Israel, the Egyptians hold them in contempt."[4] Jacob's family was slowly being assimilated in Canaan, but now God would use the Egyptians' sinful sense of superiority and disdain for others to work to His people's advantage. They would be forced to live apart, enabling them to develop and preserve their distinct identity as God's people.

The most remarkable thing took place at the table designated for the brothers. They were astonished to discover that they had been seated in their exact birth order, from Reuben to Benjamin. To say the least, that must have seemed like an amazing coincidence—how could it happen by chance? Adding to their surprise, Benjamin's end of the table was loaded with food, five times the amount anyone else received.

This bizarre state of affairs was clearly at the direction of Joseph, since the food was taken directly from his table to theirs. The brothers must have wondered why their youngest brother, Rachel's son, was being singled out for preferential treatment, even here in Egypt. That was, of course, no accident—Joseph was probing to discover whether jealousy and sibling rivalry were still festering in his family.

The meal apparently took a large part of the afternoon. There was good food, abundant wine, and pleasant conversation, so that "they drank and were merry with him" (43:34). The former accusations of espionage seemed to have vanished. For some inexplicable reason, they were being treated as friends. As the brothers ate and drank more and more, I can imagine their anxieties melted away. They began to look forward to their journey the next morning, when they would head home loaded with food and supplies, accompanied by both Benjamin and Simeon. Sleep that night must have come easily to the eleven.

But probably not to Joseph. All had gone according to his plan, but that plan would reach its climax that very next day. This day had been far harder on Joseph than anyone realized; the next day would determine everything. While he longed for reunion and reconciliation with his family, his question remained: Had they really changed? When the heat was on, would they revert to type and act only to protect themselves? How did they really feel about the unexpected favoring of Benjamin? Would they sacrifice him to save themselves? Was there any hope that the family could really be a family? Only time would tell. It was probably a night Joseph spent tossing and turning on his bed, with his mind racing and his heart pounding.

When Lance Armstrong's interview was made public, reactions were predictable. The great majority were skeptical and dismissive: "Once a liar, always a liar." Others, usually those at a distance from any personal involvement, were willing to say, "Let bygones be bygones. We need to just move on. Forgive and forget." A few found it a significant opportunity to consider the distinction between regret and repentance.

It was easy to hear some regret in Armstrong's words; it was far harder to hear genuine repentance when he proclaimed that, given the same circumstances, he would probably do the same thing. No one can fully know another person's inner self, but if we take him at his word, Armstrong isn't very convincing when he claims that he is now an entirely different man.

Repentance isn't about feeling bad, but about owning my sins—without rationalizing or minimizing them—and then turning to move in a new direction. We can only hope Lance Armstrong will go farther than he has. More importantly, we can pray that he will recognize that his greatest need is not to be restored to public favor, but to be reconciled to a holy God through His Son, the Lord Jesus Christ.

At many points in our lives, we find ourselves standing on one side or the other of the repentance gap—either as sinner or sinned against. But whatever side we are on, our greatest need is vertical, not horizontal. If we are the offender, we must seek the Lord's forgiveness. If we were sinned against, we must roll our hurt, bitterness, and anger on God, asking Him to prevent us from hardening our hearts or turning to some form of revenge.

That vertical response, however, also requires horizontal action. As offenders, we need to acknowledge the truth, the whole truth, and nothing but the truth, not simply in regret but in repentance. And repentance means turning in a new direction, where we can then "bear fruits in keeping with repentance" (Luke 3:8). The sinned against are called to Jesus's cross to seek the power to forgive and, as God guides and enables, that will lead to their adversaries' genuine repentance, and hopefully, deep reconciliation between them.

Joseph reminds us that there are no shortcuts to this process, and that it is costly on both sides of the repentance gap. The journey of reconciliation brings tears to Joseph as well as his brothers. But the apostle Paul reminds us that there is such a thing as godly sorrow, which "brings repentance that leads to salvation and leaves no regret." Worldly sorrow, on the other hand, "brings death" (2 Corinthians 7:10 NIV).

At this point in the story, Joseph's brothers are full of remorse and regret. Will that flourish into life-changing repentance and reconciliation? The journey home would reveal the answer.

TEN

TURNING POINT

The first years of the Second World War had gone very badly for Great Britain and her allies. The German war machine had swept westward, occupying most of France and Western Europe, and only an amazing rescue effort on the beaches of Dunkirk had saved the British Army from virtual annihilation.

Adolf Hitler then turned his attention east, and Nazi forces began to push deep into Russia. At the same time, the Afrika Korps, led by one of Germany's greatest commanders, Field Marshall Erwin Rommel, was surging across North Africa in an attempt to seize the Suez Canal. If successful, the Allies would be cut off from the most efficient supply route for desperately needed Middle Eastern oil—and Germany would be poised to seize those same oil fields, an outcome catastrophic to the Allied cause.

Though the United States had joined the war at the end of 1941, after the Japanese attack on Pearl Harbor, her entrance did not quickly translate into significant military achievements. England was still enduring the blitz, German U-Boats were causing havoc in the Atlantic, and Japan was rampaging through the Pacific. The Allies were determined, but a thick fog of despair had settled over them. Was there time for America to engage? Could Hitler be stopped?

In this context an obscure little town in the barren deserts of western Egypt became a hinge of history. Rommel's rapid advance across North Africa had been spectacular, but it had stretched his supply lines precariously thin. The newly appointed general of the British Eighth Army, Bernard Montgomery, recognized Rommel's vulnerability. So, in October 1942, he determined not only to make a defensive stand at the village of El Alamein, but also to launch an unexpected and daring counterattack. For a brief moment, Montgomery held a significant numerical superiority in men, military equipment, and air support. He needed to seize the opportunity.

The resulting campaign was a brutal one, with the two sides seesawing back and forth. Finally, on November 2, with supplies almost exhausted, Rommel ordered his armies to retreat, and he began a fighting withdrawal to the west. Resolution would take months of bitter combat, but finally German troops and their Italian allies were forced to withdraw entirely from North Africa. With that, the entire momentum of the war shifted significantly.

When news of the German retreat first reached British Prime Minister Winston Churchill, he was ecstatic. This was the first real victory he would be able to share with the British people since the war had begun three long years earlier. But he was wise enough to know that many battles and much suffering still lay ahead. As Churchill said in a speech eight days after he received the news of Rommel's retreat, "Now this is not the end. It is not even the beginning of the end. But it is, perhaps, the end of the beginning."

Joseph could have said the same thing at this point in his story. Unrecognized by anyone else, he had been fighting a battle for his family. Despite a painful legacy of abuse spawned by the hatred of his brothers, Joseph had risen to the pinnacle of power in Egypt. Then, after an interval of twenty-two years, those brothers had reappeared, standing before him in desperate need of food to stave off the famine threatening their families with starvation. God had used the prediction of that very famine to elevate Joseph to his position of enormous power and prestige. Now, in the midst of the crisis, he was being forced to come to grips with people and issues buried deep in his past.

Despite all that his family had done, Joseph could not bring himself to ignore or reject them. Instead, he had made a healing choice to seek reconciliation, not revenge; restoration, not retaliation. Graciously, the Lord implanted in Joseph the wisdom to recognize that, if the brothers were still the same as they had been, an instant reunion would only be shallow and temporary. They needed to experience a deep repentance of the heart, birthed in the crucible of suffering, compelling them to truly acknowledge what they had done to their hated brother. Only then would it be clear that they were capable of an entirely new kind of future for their family.

We have witnessed Joseph's plan unfolding. Now we come to the moment of truth, when both the brothers and Joseph stand revealed in their true colors. The narrator slows down the pace of his storytelling, devoting almost two full chapters of Genesis to a single day. That fateful day would not be the end of Joseph's battle, but it could prove to be "the end of the beginning."

While this story is uniquely Joseph's, it raises issues common to broken families and shattered relationships. It is a story played out in a thousand different forms in people's lives every day: when I unexpectedly encounter the relative who abused me, the spouse who deserted me, the employer who wrongly dismissed me, the "friend" who slandered or betrayed me—and on and on it goes. This person, standing right in front of me, sinned against me deeply. What do I do now? Where do I go from here?

Benjamin and the Silver Cup

Then he commanded the steward of his house, "Fill the men's sacks with food, as much as they can carry, and put each man's money in the mouth of his sack, and put my cup, the silver cup, in the mouth of the sack of the youngest, with his money for the grain." And he did as Joseph told him.

As soon as the morning was light, the men were sent away with their donkeys. They had gone only a short distance from the city. Now Joseph said to his steward, "Up, follow after the men, and when you overtake them, say to them, 'Why have you repaid evil for good? Is it not from this that my lord drinks, and by this that he practices divination? You have done evil in doing this.'"

When he overtook them, he spoke to them these words. They said to him, "Why does my lord speak such words as these? Far be it from your servants to do such a thing! Behold, the money that we found in the mouths of our sacks we brought back to you from the land of Canaan. How then could we steal silver or gold from your lord's house? Whichever of your servants is found with it shall die, and we also will be my lord's servants." He said, "Let it be as you say: he who is found with it shall be my servant, and the rest of you shall be innocent." Then each man quickly lowered his sack to the ground, and each man opened his sack. And he searched, beginning with the eldest and ending with the youngest. And the cup was found in Benjamin's sack. Then they tore their clothes, and every man loaded his donkey, and they returned to the city.

Genesis 44:1–13

The brothers must have been euphoric as they packed up to leave Egypt that morning. Things couldn't possibly have gone better! Benjamin was still with them, Simeon had been restored to them, and their donkeys were loaded with sacks of food for their families. All of the charges and suspicions against them had mysteriously vanished. Still, "the man's" change of attitude must have been puzzling. How had it swung so completely, from hostility and suspicion to overflowing hospitality and kindness? On the other hand, who wants to look at the dark side, when everything is turning out so well?

"Can you imagine how dad will feel when we tell him what happened?" they may have said to one another as they rode their donkeys toward the border. But hidden in their sacks, by the direct instruction of "the man," was a ticking time bomb, set to explode in their faces. The hardest part of their journey lay before, not behind, them.

Hospitality in the ancient world had a significance that it does not have in ours. Today, the idea involves opening our homes to friends and relatives, but in biblical times, hospitality was shown to strangers and travelers. It was not merely a courtesy, but a matter of personal honor and sacred obligation. An aristocrat like Joseph would hardly be expected to invite foreign commoners into his palatial home. Nevertheless, once he had done so, he was obliged to extend himself to generously provide protection, food, and whatever else his guests might have required. Conversely, recipients were expected to respond with gratitude and courtesy. To breach hospitality was a severe offense; to steal from a host was an unthinkable violation, both socially and morally.

I can identify. My family has vivid memories of a "friend of a friend" who came to our home for a birthday party for one of our grandchildren. When she left, so did an expensive camera she had admired. Years later, we still feel violated when we think about this woman's behavior. It is hard to fathom the kind of person who comes as a guest and is treated kindly, but then leaves with a valued possession.

Victor Hugo's famous novel *Les Misérables* tells the story of Jean Valjean, a man unjustly jailed for nineteen years for stealing bread to feed his sister's children. Paroled, but required to carry a yellow card branding him as a criminal, he turned up one night at a bishop's door, seeking a place to stay. The bishop kindly welcomed Valjean, fed him, and provided clothing and a bed. But in the middle of the night, Valjean arose to steal much of the bishop's silverware and flee into the night.

Captured by police, Valjean was dragged back to the house, so the bishop could identify both the stolen goods and the offender. But the bishop told police that he had, in fact, given the silverware to Valjean as a gift. He even rebuked Valjean for not taking a silver candelabra as well! Faced with the bishop's response, the police could only release their prisoner. When the officers left, the bishop urged the astonished Valjean to use the silver to become an honest man. It was an encounter of grace that, as Hugo tells the story, transformed the guilty Valjean into a repentant, honorable, giving man.

Joseph's use of his silver was exactly the opposite of the bishop's, but it was also an act of grace. We can call it a "severe mercy." Joseph had his special silver cup planted in Benjamin's sack so the brothers could be accused of a crime. What followed would be a huge miscarriage of justice: an innocent man, in this case Benjamin, would be made to appear guilty of a serious theft from a revered person, a gross violation of both law and hospitality.

Joseph's test was simple but significant: Under pressure, would the brothers revert to type and act in protective self-interest, leaving Benjamin to his fate? He was, after all, the favored son, whose apparently reckless and foolish act was now endangering the entire family, including their father, far away at home. Or would the older brothers rally to protect Benjamin even at great risk to their own well-being?

Not long after the men departed on their euphoric journey home, Joseph sprung the trap. He sent his servant, probably accompanied by soldiers, after them. We all know the sinking feeling that comes when we see flashing red lights behind us, even if we're not speeding. Undoubtedly, the brothers' hearts sank when they realized that they were being pursued. As they recognized Joseph's steward, they knew that it could not be good news.

Joseph had given the steward explicit instructions, which he followed to the letter. When the brothers heard his stunning accusation, a bad situation became very much worse. The charge was not only surprising, it was dangerous: the theft of a high official's personal property went much further than breaching his hospitality and kindness. Stealing "the man's" own personal cup, the one from his own dining table, his favorite goblet used not only for drinking but also practicing divination[1] was an unthinkable outrage. Their guilt, as arranged in Joseph's plan, was a matter of record: "You have done evil in doing this" (44:5).

Dumbfounded, the brothers could only protest their innocence: I can imagine their sputtering defense: "Why would you say something like that? We're not that kind of people! That doesn't make any sense—don't you remember that we brought back the money from last time? Thieves don't do that. We'd never steal anything from your master's house." As they had told Joseph at their first meeting, "We are honest men" (Genesis 42:11).

Confident of their innocence, they invoked the death penalty on the supposed thief, and a penalty of enslavement on the rest: "Whichever of your servants is found with it shall die, and we will also be my lord's servants" (44:9). The steward modified their proposal, saying that only the guilty party would suffer; he would not be killed, but would become a slave. The rest would be free to go, as innocent men. So the brothers took their sacks off their donkeys, believing (or perhaps hoping) that the steward's search would vindicate each and every one of them.

That was not to be. Showing the same mysterious knowledge of the brothers' birth order as he had when he arranged the dinner seating in Joseph's house, the steward began with Reuben's sack. It must have been disconcerting when the search once again revealed that the purchase money was at the top of the sack. But there was no goblet, either, a pattern that continued through the first ten brothers. Then, suddenly, there it was—the worst of all possible outcomes. Benjamin, the special son, was unquestionably guilty, caught red-handed.

The discovery must have stunned the brothers, as they treated it like a death in the family, tearing their clothes in a time-honored cultural symbol of grief and mourning. Still, the steward had been clear that only the guilty brother would be held; the others were free to go. Why not take that option? Sure, it would be difficult to face their father with the news that Benjamin had not been allowed to return. But, as far as they could tell, that was Benjamin's own fault. He alone had been caught red-handed with the goblet. The choice was clear: the older brothers could save themselves or try to save their guilty youngest brother—their father's favorite.

There were sufficient reasons to rationalize abandoning Benjamin to his fate. He had made his own bed; let him lie in it. Didn't the others have a responsibility to provide for their own families with the food they were carrying? Why should they starve because Benjamin had been caught doing a foolish and sinful thing? Why should their families suffer the loss of husbands and fathers, especially in such a difficult time? Why should so many suffer for one person's mistake? Abandoning Benjamin to save themselves would be the path of common sense.

That was almost certainly the choice they would have made years earlier. But not this time: "Every man loaded his donkey, and they returned to the city" (44:13). The decision was momentous: to return meant going toward trouble, not away from it. Returning meant putting aside their own safety and self-interest—they were uniting to do whatever they could for the well-being of a brother. And not just any brother: it was Daddy's boy, Benjamin, the favored one, Rachel's son, the full brother of the hated dreamer!

The biblical text gives us no indication that their journey back was filled with denunciation or criticism of their "stupid younger brother." They just went—and we recognize that these are not same men who had coldheartedly plotted a vulnerable brother's murder before deciding to sell him into slavery for a petty profit. These men, united in defense of a brother, head back into unknown but real danger. They would stand or fall together. In that simple act of banding together, they had, unwittingly, passed a critical test.

"Take Me, Not Him"

When Judah and his brothers came to Joseph's house, he was still there. They fell before him to the ground. Joseph said to them, "What deed is this that you have done? Do you not know that a man like me can indeed practice divination?" And Judah said, "What shall we say to my lord? What shall we speak? Or how can we clear ourselves? God has found out the guilt of your servants; behold, we are my lord's servants, both we and he also in whose hand the cup has been found." But he said, "Far be it from me that I should do so! Only the man in whose hand the cup was found shall be my servant. But as for you, go up in peace to your father."

Then Judah went up to him and said, "Oh, my lord, please let your servant speak a word in my lord's ears, and let not your anger burn against your servant, for you are like Pharaoh himself. My lord asked his servants, saying, 'Have you a father, or a brother?' And we said to my lord, 'We have a father, an old man, and a young brother, the child of his old age. His brother is dead, and he alone is left of his mother's children, and his father loves him.' Then you said to your servants, 'Bring him down to me, that I may set my eyes on him.' We said to my lord, 'The boy cannot leave his father, for if he should leave his father, his father would die.' Then you said to your servants, 'Unless your youngest brother comes down with you, you shall not see my face again.'

"When we went back to your servant my father, we told him the words of my lord. And when our father said, 'Go again, buy us a little food,' we said, 'We cannot go down. If our youngest brother goes with us, then we will go down. For we cannot see the man's face unless our youngest brother is with us.' Then your servant my father said to us, 'You know that my wife bore me two sons. One left me, and I said, "Surely he has been torn to pieces," and I have never seen him since. If you take this one also from me, and harm happens to him, you will bring down my gray hairs in evil to Sheol.'

"Now therefore, as soon as I come to your servant my father, and the boy is not with us, then, as his life is bound up in the boy's life, as soon as he sees that the boy is not with us, he will die, and your servants will bring down the gray hairs of your servant our father with sorrow to Sheol. For your servant became a pledge of safety for the boy to my father, saying, 'If I do not bring him back to you, then I shall bear the blame before my father all my life.' Now therefore, please let your servant remain instead of the boy as a servant to my lord, and let the boy go back with his brothers. For how can I go back to my father if the boy is not with me? I fear to see the evil that would find my father."

Genesis 44:14–34

When Moses, the writer of Genesis, tells us that "Judah and his brothers came to Joseph's house" (44:14), he is signaling a significant change in the family's relationships. Judah has become the recognized leader of the brothers. From this point on, he acts as the brothers' spokesman, and he leads them toward the change they so desperately need. When they arrived at Joseph's house, "he was still there" (44:14). All of his other business had been set aside, as he anxiously awaited the results of his carefully conceived plan. This was the make-or-break moment, the climax to which his strategy had been pointing. What happened in the next few hours would be decisive for his own destiny, as well as that of his entire family.

On the brothers' arrival, Joseph immediately seized the initiative. As the men fearfully prostrated themselves before him—that dream again!—Joseph, with feigned anger, accused them of shameful and criminal behavior. Their very posture trumpeted their recognition that they were completely at this man's mercy. Benjamin had been caught red-handed, and the brothers had no mitigating evidence or feasible explanation of that incontrovertible fact. The stolen goblet had been in Benjamin's possession. Judah made no attempt at a defense: "God has found out the guilt of your servants" (44:16).

Against the background of the brothers' crime against Joseph, we cannot help wondering whether Judah was speaking merely of the stolen cup. The return of all of the brothers' money, along with the mysterious presence of Joseph's cup, must have raised questions in his mind about what was really going on—especially if, as I imagine, Benjamin was insistently protesting his innocence. Lurking underneath the immediate situation was an unshakeable, persistent, fresh feeling of guilt about their treatment of Joseph so long ago. It was this guilt that had bubbled to the surface during their first confrontation with the Egyptian official they didn't recognize as Joseph himself: "In truth we are guilty concerning our brother. . . . That is why this distress has come upon us" (42:21).

Now, as Judah stood before their judge once again, he knew it was futile to protest innocence. Even if the brothers were not guilty of this particular crime, a much greater crime haunted them. God's justice has finally found them out.[2] If stealing a cup deserved judgment, what should be the penalty for stealing their brother's life by selling him into slavery and oblivion? Seen in that light, the men fully deserved their punishment, whatever it might be. And they would take their punishment alongside Benjamin, the one "in whose hand the cup has been found" (44:16). Judah was willing to pay the price of his brother's guilt, and of his own.

Two things stand out in Judah's statement. The first is the lingering effect of guilt. Guilt has a bad reputation in our modern world. We are told it is a crippling emotion that destroys energy and devastates our sense of self-worth—guilt feelings are to be avoided like the plague. Now, there is certainly such a thing as false guilt, and it does no good to wallow in it; that kind of guilt is a gift that keeps on giving, and it gives all the wrong things. Regret and remorse are cheap forms of guilt—they make me feel bad, but leave me unchanged for the better.

Change for the better is the second thing that stands out in Judah's statement. While the brothers have tried over the years to bury their guilt, its continuing reemergence is a sign of hope that God is working in their lives. Like pain, guilt can be a profound gift of God—like a red light on a dashboard, it is a signal that something is wrong and needs to be corrected. The brothers' willingness to stand with their apparently guilty brother is a very good sign. They refused to abandon him, choosing to bind their destiny with his.

But Joseph would have none of it. He echoed what his steward had said earlier: "Only the man in whose hand the cup was found shall be my servant. But as for you, go up in peace to your father" (44:17). With that, the trap had been fully sprung.

Joseph had maneuvered his brothers into a situation strikingly like the one in which they found themselves twenty-two years earlier. The ten brothers were free to serve their own interests and to go home, even though they would be abandoning their younger brother, their father's favorite. Returning home without him would probably break their aged father's heart, but Benjamin was the guilty one, not them. Why should they suffer for the actions of Jacob's favored son? Why should their families be deprived of their presence because of Benjamin? Joseph's heart was probably beating fast as he waited to hear how his brothers would respond. What would they do this time? Was there any chance at a new family future?

Responsibility to respond fell squarely on the shoulders of Judah, the brothers' spokesman, and his answer revealed that he was now a man with a different heart. The cynical and ruthless brother who, two decades earlier, had cavalierly suggested selling Joseph to the Midianites was no more. His speech is not only the longest one recorded in the book of Genesis, it is one of the most important. He begins by retracing the events that brought the brothers to this point.

Judah first acknowledged "the man's" righteous indignation at the offense committed against him, and begged him for patience—"let not your anger burn against your servant" (44:18). He also expressed his recognition and respect for the Egyptian official's authority—"you are like Pharaoh himself" (44:18). He then, in verses 19–23, recounted the brothers' interaction with him, noting Joseph's demand that they return with their youngest brother or lose any further opportunity to buy food—"you shall not see my face again" (44:23). In Judah's retelling, the brothers emphasized how precious Benjamin was to their father, a fact not recorded in chapter 42: "He alone is left of his mother's children, and his father loves him. . . . The boy cannot leave his father, for if he should leave his father, his father would die" (44:20, 22).

Note two key things about this introduction. First, there is a focus on and a sensitivity to Jacob, a compassion completely absent from the events of chapter 37. Judah uses the word *father* fifteen times in his speech to Joseph, making it clear that Jacob's well-being is a primary concern. Second, he displays a very different attitude to Jacob's favoritism. Jacob had not changed: Rachel's son mattered more to him than all the other brothers. But they had come to accept their father's favoritism; it was no longer a constant source of bitterness, jealousy, and anger. Rather, they now saw it as a reason to show mercy and compassion to a heartbroken old man.

Judah emphasized how devastating the loss of Benjamin would be for their father (verses 24–29), recounting the resistance Jacob had shown against any possibility of the brothers returning to Egypt with Benjamin. Joseph must have struggled to contain himself as Judah recalled their father's words, "My wife bore me two sons. One left me, and I said, 'Surely he has been torn to pieces,' and I have never seen him since" (44:27–28). It was precisely because he had lost his special son that Jacob had objected so strenuously to putting Benjamin at risk: "If you take this one also from me, and harm happens to him, you will bring down my gray hairs in evil to Sheol" (44:29).

With that poignant picture in "the man's" mind, Judah made his direct plea in verses 30–34. But he was not asking for the merciful release of Benjamin, accused of a crime. Rather, he was asking for mercy of a very special kind. Judah had pledged to his father that he would care for Benjamin, taking full responsibility for the young man. So Judah would now atone for his brother's wrongdoing by taking on himself the penalty due to Benjamin: "Please let your servant remain instead of the boy as a servant to my lord, and let the boy go back with his brothers" (44:33). The one who once counseled selling a brother was now asking to be the substitute for another brother, paying the penalty the other man deserved. He would give his own life so that the "guilty" brother could go free—not primarily for his brother's sake, but for his father's: "For how can I go back to my father if the boy is not with me? I fear to see the evil that would find my father" (44:34).

There is no reason to believe that Judah was anything but sincere. His heart was full of concern for his father, whose very life was "bound up in the boy's life" (44:30). The old man's existence was inextricably tied into Benjamin's well-being; this youngest son had become the old man's only reason for living. Should Benjamin not return with his brothers, the result would be calamitous for Jacob: "He will die" (v. 31).

Judah was a different man. Once, he had joined his brothers in dipping Joseph's special coat in goat's blood and presenting it to Jacob, knowing it would break their father's heart. Now, he was a man willing to pay the highest price imaginable to spare his father pain. An innocent man was willing to surrender his own life and future by becoming a slave in Egypt.

This sacrificial proposal showed that Judah and the brothers had met and passed Joseph's hard test with flying colors. There could now be no doubt that these men were different than the ones who had victimized Joseph so many years ago. They were now capable of sacrificial love, of uniting to protect a vulnerable brother. They were willing to pay whatever price was required to show love to a father who had failed them in significant ways. And it was Judah who had taken the lead.[3] In a major way, both for Judah and Joseph, this marked a major step toward the destiny God intended for them.

Before we look at the great moment of reconciliation in Genesis 45, we should ponder the ways in which Judah models essential elements of repentance, the kind that make genuine reconciliation possible.

First, Judah has *an attitude of humility*. He stands before Joseph as a man with no claims of merit or achievement, making no attempt to impress his judge. Rather, he used the word *servant* twelve times to describe himself and his brothers; nine times he addressed Joseph as "my lord." Humility causes us to understand that we are dependent on mercy, not merit, to meet our need. Judah acknowledged that he could only rely on Joseph's kindness, not his own worth or status. He did not attempt to resolve this problem by bargaining his way through it.

Second, closely linked to his humility, Judah *admitted guilt, accepting full responsibility for what had happened.* He made no excuse for the presence of the cup in the sack, and offered no alternate explanations of how it might have gotten there. He himself was innocent, and perhaps he believed Benjamin was as well—we have no way of knowing for sure—but the evidence for the prosecution was insurmountable. More importantly, even if the ten oldest brothers weren't guilty of the theft of the goblet, they were certainly guilty concerning Joseph. As Judah acknowledged when he first stood before Joseph, "God has found out the guilt of your servants" (44:16). Repentance begins with owning our sin and wrongdoing, without evasion. It is tempting to weasel out with *if* declarations: "*If* I've offended you. . . . *If* you think I've done something wrong. . . ." As C. S. Lewis observed, "Forgiveness needs to be accepted as well as offered if it is to be complete; and a man who admits no guilt can accept no forgiveness."[4]

Finally, partnered with accepting responsibility, Judah *made no attempt to blame, excuse, or justify himself.* How tempting it must have been to blame Benjamin's youth or character. How easy it would have been to bemoan their father's favoritism, suggesting that it had distorted Benjamin into a spoiled, irresponsible, immature young man. All too often our "repentance" takes the form, "I have sinned and I have several excellent excuses."

Jacob had sinned against Judah and all of his brothers. His favoritism toward the sons of Rachel had scarred the souls of the ten older men. But their father's sin against them did not justify their sinful response to Joseph, understandable though it may have seemed. They had hated Joseph primarily because they deeply resented their father.

The partiality toward Joseph had been repeated in Jacob's obvious preferential love for Benjamin. Judah was not blind to that favoritism; he mentioned it several times in his speech before "the man," saying, "his father loves him" (44:20); "his life is bound up in the boy's life" (44:30); "as soon as he sees that the boy is not with us, he will die" (44:31). *Judah was now able to be sinned against without responding sinfully.* He had chosen to accept his father's shortcomings, and to love him deeply anyway.

All of this leads to the culminating point: *Repentance isn't simply a change of mind or emotions—it is a change of direction.* Judah proposed a radical exchange: he would pay the price of Benjamin's sin. Innocent of any complicity in Benjamin's apparent theft, Judah would become a substitute, taking the punishment deserved by the guilty. He would pay Benjamin's penalty so Benjamin could go free. Judah had moved from a cold indifference that could sell his own brother to human traffickers to a sacrificial compassion—he was willing to become a slave so that another brother could go free.

Genuine repentance may involve heartfelt sorrow over the wrong we have done. But it involves more than an emotional or verbal response to our sin. Repentance has been described as a "return to reality" about ourselves; that is true as far as it goes, but repentance also requires a fundamental change of our direction and behavior. The New Testament makes it clear that *repentance is an honest facing of who we are in God's sight that produces a heart-deep turning from our sin that, in turn, leads to new patterns of behavior, in utter dependence upon God and His grace.* In other words, it is a Spirit-produced heart change that progressively brings about Spirit-empowered behavior and character change.

Judah has emerged as the leader of his brothers. More importantly, he is willing to become a substitute, to pay a heavy penalty to set free his apparently guilty brother. Later in Genesis, we will learn that God has a special destiny for Judah and his descendants. From the way this story has unfolded, we would expect Joseph to be father of the royal family of Israel. But, typical of the Lord's mysterious ways, that privilege goes to Judah. Speaking under the direction of the Holy Spirit, his father, Jacob, prophesied,

> "Judah, your brothers shall praise you; your hand shall be on the neck of your enemies; your father's sons shall bow down before you. Judah is a lion's cub; from the prey, my son, you have gone up. He stooped down; he crouched as a lion and as a lioness; who dares rouse him? The scepter shall not depart from Judah, nor the ruler's staff from between his feet, until tribute comes to him; and to him shall be the obedience of the peoples."
>
> Genesis 49:8–10

We are never told precisely why the line of Judah is chosen as the royal tribe, the one that will bear the ruler's staff among all of Jacob's descendants. It is hard to resist the thought that this occasion—when Judah steps forward to serve as the leader among his brothers—is a significant part of the reason. He is not merely a leader but a servant leader, willing to sacrifice himself for the well-being of the rest of his family.

Judah is an ancestor of the great King David, whose descendants would bear the throne in Israel. But most of all, Judah was the ancestor and anticipator of the Lord Jesus, "the Lion of the tribe of Judah"

(Revelation 5:5). Judah, a sinful man, interceded with the judge to offer himself as substitute for the apparently guilty, making possible the reconciliation of his broken family. Jesus is the greater Judah, the sinless one who stood as Mediator between a holy God and sinful people (1 Timothy 2:5). He gave himself as the God-appointed Substitute, taking our sins on himself (2 Corinthians 5:21) so He might bring us to God (1 Peter 3:18).

The story of Judah gives us a small window into the wonderful reality of Jesus. We stand in need of a Substitute who can reconcile us to God. The marvel of the gospel is that God, in Christ, "was reconciling the world to himself, not counting their trespasses against them" (2 Corinthians 5:19). When we repentantly bow before Him, in faith laying hold of His provision for us, we enter as new people into His eternal family.

We have reached the end of the beginning. By God's grace, Judah has fought and won a battle over his own instinctive drive to protect and preserve himself, by offering himself as a substitute for his apparently guilty brother. He has chosen the path of self-sacrifice rather than self-service. The ball is now squarely in Joseph's court. How will he respond?

ELEVEN

FORGIVEN!

I was fifteen years old, and like most fifteen-year-olds, I could hardly wait for my sixteenth birthday—that great North American coming-of-age moment. I would then be eligible for a driver's license, enabling me to operate a car legally. However, some of my friends were already driving with their parents, under carefully monitored conditions, before they turned sixteen. So I began to pester my father for the same privilege. He resisted my pleas, but I was persistent, and for whatever reason—perhaps from sheer exhaustion—he finally relented. One Sunday after church, with no prior warning, Dad let me take the wheel for the drive home. It was less than a mile.

The trip was on side streets, and things went well until I had to make a right turn. I started to make the turn, but when I wasn't sure I was going to be successful, I panicked and tried to slam my foot on the brake. Only it wasn't the brake I hit, but the gas pedal! The car jumped forward, hitting a light pole head-on.

I vividly recall my tears and my sobbing declarations of regret—and the steam pouring from the ruptured radiator. I also recall my father's strange calm, his kind reassurance that it was only a mistake, and his gratitude that neither of us had been injured. As I repeatedly offered absolutely sincere apologies, Dad immediately declared that I was forgiven. Never again did I hear about that event—never a word about how much it had cost him, never a reminder of my incompetence, never a putdown. Dad paid the price and set me free. After I ultimately qualified for my license, he was consistently generous with his cars. It was a powerful lesson in forgiveness.

Years later, my wife had a similar misadventure, in a car borrowed from friends. We had been staying with them while I was doing doctoral studies in Dallas, Texas. One day, as I and the children were enjoying a water park, our hosts kindly allowed Elizabeth to use of one of their cars to go shopping. We don't believe the accident was Elizabeth's fault, but the police report laid the blame on her.

We needed to depart for home in Canada only two days later, and by the time we left, neither the repair costs nor the insurance issues had been settled. Immediately upon arriving home, my wife phoned our friends to ask what we owed them. The answer was somewhat evasive, but she did learn that the damage was so extensive that the car had been written off. More phone calls ensued, and each time our friends assured Elizabeth that they had taken care of the problem. The car was paid for, the bill was settled, Elizabeth's debt was completely cleared—and she was forgiven. Finding that hard to accept, Elizabeth kept phoning to ask how much she needed to pay. Finally, Alan reached his limit. "Elizabeth," he said firmly but kindly, "haven't you heard about grace?" She had, but it certainly meant more after this very tangible experience of it!

It is a hard thing to admit that we need to be forgiven. But it is a wonderful (if humbling) thing when we are truly forgiven, shown a grace that lifts the heavy weight of guilt. On the other hand, bestowing forgiveness is costly. In the case of damaged cars, they don't repair themselves—both my father and my friend had chosen to pay those costs themselves, setting me free from any need to repay.

Clearly, such forgiveness is a wonderful thing. But it is perhaps understandable when we are dealing with an accident, some unintended situation. Forgiveness reaches another level, though, when we are confronted with personal violations and sins that are deliberate and deeply hurtful. In those cases, we understand what C. S. Lewis meant when he wrote, "Everyone says forgiveness is a lovely idea, until they have something to forgive."[1]

Forgiveness, however, isn't just a *nice* thing for Christians to do; it is *commanded*. Forgiven people are to be forgiving people. The Lord Jesus taught us to pray, "Forgive us our sins, for we also forgive everyone who sins against us" (Luke 11:4 NIV). More directly He tells us, "If your brother sins, rebuke him, and if he repents forgive him" (Luke 17:3). In the words of the apostle Paul in Ephesians 4:32 (NIV), "Be kind and compassionate to one another, forgiving each other, just as in Christ God forgave you."[2]

All of us will encounter times when we need either to seek forgiveness or to grant it. How we respond will significantly shape both our character and our future, for good or for bad. There can be no doubt about the practical benefit of forgiveness—researchers have shown direct links between forgiveness and physical and emotional health. For Christ-followers, however, there are more compelling reasons to forgive than therapeutic personal benefits, valuable as they are. The supreme reason we should forgive is that our Lord and Savior both models and commands it. We, as His people, are called to follow the path of the One who has forgiven us at such great cost.

Mass shootings are a sad fact of modern American life. In one of the more shocking, a young white man entered a black church in South Carolina, and sat quietly in a midweek prayer meeting for more than an hour. Then, with no provocation, he pulled a gun and opened fire, leaving nine people dead in a horrific and grotesque act of racial terrorism. In startling contrast, the response of the victims' families was something of great beauty and power.

Just two days after the atrocity, many of the victims' relatives stood in a courtroom to confront the shooter at a bond hearing. Remarkably, though they were obviously grieving deeply, they chose not to lash out in anger. Instead they spoke of forgiveness toward the man who had killed their son, or mother, or grandmother or pastor. "I forgive you," one woman said. "You took something very precious from me. I will never talk to [my mother] again. I will never, ever hold her again. But I forgive you, and may God have mercy on your soul." Another said, "We have no room for hating, so we have to forgive." It was, as one secular reporter observed, "as if the Bible study never ended, as one after another, victims' family members offered lessons in forgiveness, testaments to a faith that is not compromised by violence or grief."[3]

This extraordinary display of grace confounded many people, caught up as they were in important, but typically inflamed, rhetoric about racism, systemic discrimination, and gun control. Clearly, these grieving church members spoke out of a desire to be faithful to their Lord. Predictably, some observers reacted negatively, complaining that the victims' words showed weakness and perpetuated injustice. But for far more people, these believers' words were, if incomprehensible, undeniably and deeply impressive. As one commentator observed, "I am a non-Christian, but I must say: This is a remarkable advertisement for Christianity."[4]

It must be said that an immediate response of "I forgive you" in many situations can cover over critical issues, such as the relationship between forgiveness and repentance, as well as the connection between justice and forgiveness. Such considerations, however, must not be allowed to cloud the beauty of the South Carolinians' response. They were not conducting an academic exercise; out of loyalty to their Lord, they committed themselves to walk the road of loving their enemy, rejecting a spirit of revenge and bitterness.

This issue of forgiveness lies at the very heart of the Joseph story. His brothers had done the unimaginable—they envied and hated Joseph to the point of selling him into slavery. Then, twenty-two years later, Joseph re-entered his brothers' lives, under very different conditions. Now he held all the power.

Jacob's sons had no idea that the Egyptian they stood before was the very brother they had once wanted to destroy. Joseph, for his part, had devised a carefully structured process to test and refine his brothers, a plan that culminated with Judah pleading to become his slave in place of his youngest brother, Benjamin. Judah said that was the only way to avoid causing the death of their aged father, a certainty if he were to lose the only surviving son of his late lamented wife, Rachel.

There are no obvious miracles in the Joseph story—no remarkable visions, supernatural appearances, or divine interventions such as occur in the lives of Abraham, Isaac, and Jacob. Yet his life allows us to witness perhaps the most significant miracle of all: how God transformed men's hearts and restored an irretrievably broken and dysfunctional family. Judah's declaration was a moment that Joseph had longed for and worked toward—but when it happened, he was stunned by its impact on him.

This self-sacrificing proposal revealed that Judah was now able to acknowledge his guilt publicly, and to accept—even respect—the special love his father had for Benjamin. Judah was willing to surrender his own future for the good of his youngest brother, if that would spare their father further heartbreak. Judah was a new man, interceding for his father and offering to lay down his own life as a substitute for the apparently guilty Benjamin. His was a love that thought first of his brother and father, not of himself—and in this holy moment, the dam of Joseph's steely self-control suddenly burst, leading to one of the most dramatic encounters in the Bible. In the process, it provides us with a very helpful case study in forgiveness.

Releasing the Past

Then Joseph could not control himself before all those who stood by him. He cried, "Make everyone go out from me." So no one stayed with him when Joseph made himself known to his brothers. And he wept aloud, so that the Egyptians heard it, and the household of Pharaoh heard it. And Joseph said to his brothers, "I am Joseph! Is my father still alive?" But his brothers could not answer him, for they were dismayed at his presence.

So Joseph said to his brothers, "Come near to me, please." And they came near. And he said, "I am your brother, Joseph, whom you sold into Egypt. And now do not be distressed or angry with yourselves because you sold me here, for God sent me before you to preserve life. For the famine has been in the land these two years, and there are yet five years in which there will be neither plowing nor harvest. And God sent me before you to preserve for you a remnant on earth, and to keep alive for you many survivors. So it was not you who sent me here, but God. He has made me a father to Pharaoh, and lord of all his house and ruler over all the land of Egypt."

Genesis 45:1–8

Unable to control himself, Joseph suddenly ordered everyone out of the room—everyone except his brothers. Judah's words had swept away any of Joseph's lingering reservations about the brothers' new mind-set, and he knew that the time for full disclosure had come at last. When the door shut behind all outsiders, the tension in the room must have felt oppressive.

At this time, Joseph had a double reason for privacy. First of all, this was an intimate, even sacred, moment, one reserved for family only. His own emotions were on a hair trigger, and he knew that he would likely lose control of himself. So many times he must have wondered how his brothers would respond when they discovered his true identity. Secondly, Joseph wanted to protect his brothers—there was no need for outsiders to know the deep evil they had perpetrated against him. By seeking privacy, he wasn't merely avoiding a public display of his own most personal feelings, he was safeguarding his brothers' reputations with the Egyptians. Their evil didn't need to become a matter of public record, because "love covers a multitude of sins" (1 Peter 4:8).

The pain and suffering of twenty-two years, the tears and sobs he had carefully kept hidden during earlier meetings (Genesis 42:24; 43:30) suddenly erupted from the depths of Joseph's soul: "He wept aloud, so that the Egyptians heard it, and the household of Pharaoh heard it" (45:2). Decades of pent-up hope and sorrow were in those sobs. The brothers would have stood silently, stunned and afraid, wondering what "the man's" emotional breakdown could mean for them.

Finally, between sobs, Joseph choked out the words he had longed to say for so long. Speaking for the first time in the brothers' language, he cried, "I am Joseph! Is my father still alive?" (45:3). If hearing Hebrew come from this Egyptian official's mouth surprised the brothers, the words he said would have shocked and overwhelmed them. Had he really said he was Joseph? How was that even possible? If it was really true, what would that mean for them?

But it must be true—how could this man know they had had a brother named Joseph? Their brother, who had vanished so long ago, had miraculously come back from the dead, materializing right before their eyes! Astounded by the very idea that this man was Joseph, they were immobilized by shock and paralyzed by fear: this had suddenly become the worst moment of their lives.

Jacob's sons were now in the hands not just of the great leader of Egypt, but of the very brother against whom they had sinned so atrociously. He must have been planning for years how he could pay them back.

What happened next would only have deepened their terror. Summoning the brothers closer, the man repeated his words with a terrifying addition: "I am your brother, Joseph, whom you sold into Egypt" (45:4). For twenty-two years, these men's actions had been a carefully guarded but guilt-inducing secret. Only Joseph knew what they had done, and his words made it clear that he remembered their betrayal vividly. Surely their doom was sealed.

But Joseph was not rebuking them; he was identifying himself. What followed was entirely unexpected: "Now do not be distressed or angry with yourselves because you sold me here, for God sent me before you to preserve life" (45:5). Those were words of life, words of forgiveness, words remarkably free of bitterness and vindictiveness, words of hope. Just as Judah's speech provided a helpful model of repentance, Joseph illustrates some powerful principles of forgiveness, in what is probably the most powerful scene of forgiveness in the Old Testament.

The essential truth is that only sins can and need to be forgiven. This is of fundamental importance: it means that the first requirement of forgiveness is that we *face the facts, honestly acknowledging the wrong that has been done.*

Joseph did not skirt the issue: "I am your brother, Joseph, whom *you sold* into Egypt. . . . *You sold me* here" (45:4–5, emphasis added). On a later occasion, Joseph would say clearly, "*You meant evil* against me" (Genesis 50:20, emphasis added). Joseph made no attempt to minimize the seriousness of the brothers' actions or downplay their malicious intentions. They intended and did evil.

Hurts, annoyances, and mistakes may be painful, but they don't require forgiveness. Rather, they need to be endured graciously, with patience and forbearance. Forgiveness is about releasing a person from true guilt brought about by real sin. Love calls us to look the offender in the eye and to name sin as sin. C. S. Lewis said it well:

"Real forgiveness means looking steadily at the sin, the sin that is left over without any excuse, after all allowances have been made, and seeing it in all its horror, dirt, meanness, and malice, and nevertheless being wholly reconciled to the man who has done that. That, and only that, is forgiveness."[5] Forgiveness, in words often attributed to G. K. Chesterton, "means pardoning the unpardonable, or it isn't forgiveness at all."

A second principle seen in Joseph's response is that, *to truly forgive, we need to feel it deep in our hearts.* Genuine forgiveness is a costly thing, and there is a great temptation to seal our hearts from the hurt of what was done by denying, minimizing, or suppressing the pain caused by the wrong. One way we do this is by turning our anger toward people other than the perpetrator. When that happens, people only distantly related to what happened become targets for our hostility, objects of the anger aroused by a real offender's wrongdoing. I recall one episode when a woman whose husband had been unfaithful chose to lash out at almost anyone within the circle of fallout of her husband's foolish and sinful choices. While she steadfastly "stood by her man," others felt the lash of her condemning tongue.

I suppose Joseph could have deflected his anger against the Midianites, who, after all, were involved in the wickedness of the slave trade. Or against Potiphar, who owned slaves. And certainly toward Potiphar's wife. But he did none of those things. Joseph allowed himself to feel again what his brothers had done, and his tears became an important way to lance the wounds in his soul. He chose to feel again the hurt of what his brothers had done, of all that their betrayal had cost him over the years. Joseph's tears are a reminder that no forgiveness takes place without great cost to the one doing the forgiving.

What is especially clear in Joseph's response is his choice to *frame the sin in a new way, by cultivating a divine perspective.* Three times he says it: "*God sent me* before you to preserve life" (45:5); "*God sent me* before you to preserve for you a remnant on earth" (45:7); "*It was not you who sent me here, but God*" (45:8). The brothers were not sovereign in Joseph's life, God was. He refused to see himself primarily as a victim of their sins, although he certainly had been victimized by them. Rather, Joseph knew himself to be God's servant.

Without in any way causing their sins, God himself had been mysteriously present in the brothers' mistreatment of Joseph, as much as He was in Pharaoh's subsequent elevation of Joseph. God's will and plan were the controlling realities of Joseph's life. The Lord had been at work in it all—the selling, the slavery, the unjust punishment, and the remarkable accession to undreamed heights of power, prestige, and possessions.

Those words, "You sold me . . . God sent me" (45:5), succinctly present us with the challenging question about the relationship between human responsibility and divine sovereignty. Joseph was not condoning his brothers' actions—they were sinful and evil. Yet God had been at work in and through those very actions, fulfilling His plan to preserve life on a broad scale during the famine, and, in a very particular way, to preserve for Jacob's family a remnant. As Iain Duguid observes, "For twenty years, Joseph couldn't see a single scrap of evidence that God was going to work his suffering for good. On the contrary, it must have seemed that any hope of reconciliation with his brothers was unthinkable."[6] But now the unthinkable was happening, and suddenly the light of God's faithfulness shone brightly into the darkness of his hard past.

When we ponder the relationship of God's sovereignty and our human experience of suffering, it is useful to make a distinction between mysteries and puzzles.[7] Puzzles are problems that are usually resolved by gathering more information. In fact, the books or movies that we label "mysteries" are, more precisely, puzzles. Throughout an unfolding story, we are led along a meandering path, seeking clues the author has scattered along the way. Finally, by sorting through the information and carefully putting pieces together, we are led to resolution—and discover who the real culprit is.

A mystery, on the other hand, lies beyond the realm of information and facts. A genuine mystery will not be solved merely by gathering more information, because it transcends the limits of our intelligence and our capacity to discern ultimate reality. To unravel a true cosmic mystery, we need either a mind as great as God's or a revelation from Him. As theologian and scholar Alister McGrath observes, "Our minds simply are not big enough to take in these mysteries. There are no slick and neat solutions here. We catch glimpses of possible solutions, but they always seem to lie beyond our reach. Puzzles lead to logical answers; mysteries often force us to stretch language to its limits in an attempt to describe a reality that is just too great to take in properly."[8]

Mysteries challenge us with ambiguity. Seen in that light, we must recognize that Joseph is confronting his brothers with a profound mystery that operates in our lives as well: "You sold me, but God sent me." That combination may be mysterious, though it is not irrational. We may not be able to "solve" the connection between the two, but wise believers rest in the truths that God has revealed about himself, especially in the person and work of our Lord Jesus Christ. The promises of God are sure, even when His immediate purpose in our lives is anything but clear.

For my wife and me, this became a precious truth. In the crucible of our suffering with our daughter, we often struggled to rest content in the wonderful truths of God's sovereignty and faithfulness. But we knew that, even in the darkest places, trusting a sovereign God isn't a retreat from reality. Rather, it is a laying hold of life-transforming, hope-sustaining truth.

This recognition—of the ultimate mystery of God's will as it applies to our lives, and to the way in which He weaves together human choices, the realities of a fallen world, and His active control of all things—has an importance far beyond the issue of forgiveness. As my wife and I walked through the valley of the shadow of death with our daughter, we constantly confronted, and continue to confront, the mystery of His will, especially with regard to the future of Janice's children. We occasionally catch glimpses of His purpose, though much remains hidden. But, while God's plan is a mystery, His character is not. He has revealed himself in His Word and, supremely, in His Son. We are not left to wonder about His goodness, His love, His power, or His wisdom.

We experience God's presence through His Spirit and in His people, as they come alongside us. We are confident that, although we do not perceive how, our suffering was and is accomplishing God's high and holy purpose. When He, the Good Shepherd, leads us into suffering, He is there with us. So in the midst of our pain and confusion, we can actively surrender ourselves into God's hands. As His Word tells us: "Let those who suffer according to God's will entrust their souls to a faithful Creator while doing good" (1 Peter 4:19).

Joseph had anchored himself in the character of his God. His children's names, which we saw in Genesis 41, stand as eloquent declarations that he had relinquished the past into God's hands. *Manasseh* made that clear: "God made me forget." Joseph had also embraced his present life in Egypt as God's gift, as *Ephraim* indicated: "God has made me fruitful" describes a life that was different from anything Joseph had expected as a young man.

Joseph was also deeply committed to God's work through him, in his position as a person held in the highest honor by Pharaoh himself. Joseph knew that his God had a purpose that transcended his own life-story: he had been called to preserve the lives of starving people. Most of all, he had been called to save his broken family, "to preserve *for you* a remnant on earth, and to keep alive *for you* many survivors" (45:7, emphasis added).

This personal mission was directly connected to the covenant that God had made with Joseph's great-grandfather Abraham back in Genesis 12:1–3. In the light of that covenant, Joseph was able to see his destiny in rather explicit ways. We as Christ-followers may not see our destiny in terms quite as specific as Joseph could, but we have the far richer and more complete provision of New Testament revelations of God's great plans for His people. Sometimes we look back at our lives in a kind of wonder, seeing how the Lord knit together so many apparently unrelated people and events to compose the quilt of our lives. For the present, however, "we see in a mirror dimly . . . [we] know in part" (1 Corinthians 13:12). One day, in the Lord's presence, we will know fully.

Joseph's fourth step was to *release those who sinned against him by declaring his forgiveness of them*. In the Bible account, Joseph never used the explicit words, "I forgive you." Nevertheless, he made it clear that the past had been forgiven both by his words ("Do not be distressed or angry with yourselves"), and his actions (embracing each brother while weeping on their shoulders). Forgiveness is a gift we give, not a reward someone earns.

Joseph was giving the gift to them, with no reservations or conditions; he had paid dearly for their sins against him, but now he required no payment in return. That is not to say the brothers found his forgiveness easy to receive, or even to believe—that kind of forgiveness seemed too good to be true! Decades later, they would revisit their old guilt (Genesis 50:15) and beseech Joseph's forgiveness. His response, as we will see, was to restate his words of chapter 45, comforting his brothers. They were still dragging the chains of the past; Joseph had released them long ago.

Free for a New Future

"Hurry and go up to my father and say to him, 'Thus says your son Joseph, God has made me lord of all Egypt. Come down to me; do not tarry. You shall dwell in the land of Goshen, and you shall be near me, you and your children and your children's children, and your flocks, your herds, and all that you have. There I will provide for you, for there are yet five years of famine to come, so that you and your household, and all that you have, do not come to poverty.' And now your eyes see, and the eyes of my brother Benjamin see, that it is my mouth that speaks to you. You must tell my father of all my honor in Egypt, and of all that you have seen. Hurry and bring my father down here." Then he fell upon his brother Benjamin's neck and wept, and Benjamin wept upon his neck. And he kissed all his brothers and wept upon them. After that his brothers talked with him.

When the report was heard in Pharaoh's house, "Joseph's brothers have come," it pleased Pharaoh and his servants. And Pharaoh said to Joseph, "Say to your brothers, 'Do this: load your beasts and go back to the land of Canaan, and take your father and your households, and come to me, and I will give you the best of the land of Egypt, and you shall eat the fat of the land.' And you, Joseph, are commanded to say, 'Do this: take wagons from the land of Egypt for your little ones and for your wives, and bring your father, and come. Have no concern for your goods, for the best of all the land of Egypt is yours.'"

Genesis 45:9–20

Joseph's goal involved far more than putting the past behind him. He had a God-given conviction that he needed to resolve the past for the purpose of establishing a new future for his entire family, including himself. So before he had even finished discussing the past, he began to talk about the immediate future—namely, the five remaining years of the famine. Joseph's family needed to recognize that God had elevated him to this position precisely for their well-being as a family. Looking beyond their failed past, he envisioned a new future: "Hurry and go up to my father and say to him, 'Thus says your son Joseph, God has made me lord of all Egypt. Come down to me; do not tarry'" (45:9).

Joseph's emphasis is once again obvious—his recognition of God's hand in all that has happened. When the brothers told their father that Joseph was alive, they would have much to answer for—the entire story of their hateful deed was bound to come to full light. But that wasn't Joseph's focus: his priority was that his father realize that his long-lost son was God's established agent for the family's deliverance from a life-threatening famine. Rather than dwelling on his brothers' evil, Joseph wanted to give them a vision of God's new possibilities.

It must be said that forgiveness does not always result in reconciliation, in the sense that some things, once done, cannot be undone. There are times when a violation has been so severe that there can be no return to a ruined marriage, friendship, or partnership. Trust, once broken, can take a long time to be rebuilt. Even when genuine reconciliation occurs, there must be the recognition that the old relationship can never return to what it once was. What happened has unalterably changed both parties, so to survive and thrive, the relationship must become something new, something better, something more honoring to God than it had ever been before.

Obviously, Joseph's family could not return to the way it had been twenty-two years earlier, nor should it. Joseph was no longer a pampered teenager; he was arguably the second most powerful man in the world, functionally the lord of all Egypt. His older brothers were no longer the family pacesetters, but they were also no longer men consumed by anger at their discriminating father and by jealousy toward their favored younger brother. The brothers needed Joseph now in a way that he didn't need them. Even Jacob was not only two decades older, he was now a man weathered by life's storms—especially the agonizing loss of a precious son. Yet he was about to experience what he had long given up hope of experiencing, the virtual resurrection of his long grieved son.

Joseph had certainly thought long and hard about what would follow his revelation of himself to his brothers. He had carefully chosen the precise part of the land where he would settle them, confident enough in his standing with Pharaoh to promise the family living space in the region of Goshen. That would be a place ideally suited to providing his family's needs, while also protecting them from the smothering cultural dominance of Egyptian society.

He was concerned that his family should survive the coming hard years: "I will provide for you . . . so that you and your household and all that you have, do not come to poverty" (45:11). However, Joseph wanted to build a *new* family to achieve its God-given destiny. Implicit in his invitation is a call to something new: in coming to Egypt, the brothers and even Jacob would embrace a different paradigm—Joseph would be the one in charge. In Egypt, they would submit to a life of dependence on him.

Would Joseph's family be willing to humbly submit to his dominance, or would they proudly insist on their self-sufficiency? Once again they were confronted with the dream and the dreamer they had hated years before. However, the "dreamer" has now shown himself to be a gracious, self-giving, servant leader. Would they fight him or see him as God's gracious provision for them?

Something more is at play here than even Joseph probably realized. Generations earlier, the Lord had promised to Abraham and his descendants the land of the Canaanites. Yet, in the course of giving that promise, God had told Abraham, "Know for certain that your offspring will be sojourners in a land that is not theirs and will be servants there, and they will be afflicted for four hundred years. But I will bring judgment on the nation that they serve, and afterward they shall come out with great possessions" (Genesis 15:13–14).

From our vantage point, we see that Joseph was the agent through whom God was bringing that part of His promise into fulfillment. What may have looked like a detour, as the family had to leave the place to which God had led them, was part of the divine purpose. Even the affliction that would eventually come to them in Egypt, when a generation of Egyptians arose "who did not know Joseph" (Exodus 1:8), was part of God's greater purpose. And so it is in our lives. As the familiar words of Psalm 23 remind us, the believer's confidence is that "even though I walk through the valley of the shadow of death, I will fear no evil, for you are with me" (v. 4). We can be certain of the Shepherd's presence, but the path on which He leads us often takes us into the hardest places in life.

Egypt would be, in God's good plan, a place of flourishing as well as suffering, of both prospering and testing. God's plans are always good, just as they are often deeply mysterious. In the story of Joseph, God's program of salvation is bound up with a scruffy, dysfunctional family, forced by famine to take seriously an offer of refuge in a foreign land. How could the hope of the world be represented by such an unlikely group? How could people such as these be the source of blessing to the world? Unlikely as it seems, that was precisely who they were and what God would do through them. So too today: the church of Christ all too often looks scruffy and dysfunctional, but it is God's chosen instrument for bringing blessing to the world through its proclamation and demonstration of the gospel.

Joseph, having spilled out a torrent of words that must have overwhelmed his stunned brothers, could say no more. With a last burst, urging the men to bring Jacob as quickly as possible to share in this astonishing turn of events, Joseph reiterated the amazing truth: "Now your eyes see, and the eyes of my brother Benjamin see, that it is my mouth that speaks to you" (45:12).

He then wept on his long-lost brother Benjamin, last seen and held as a small boy but now a grown man. As the guilty brothers observed the emotion-filled moment, it must have been a time of awkward tension, But Joseph turned to greet each of his former tormentors in turn, with a kiss full of forgiveness. Finally, we are told, "his brothers talked with him" (45:15). Wouldn't you love to watch a video of that discussion? As one commentator describes the scene, "The rift has been bridged; intimacy has been achieved."[9]

Earlier, when Joseph disclosed his identity with loud weeping, "the Egyptians heard it, and the household of Pharaoh heard it" (45:2).

Joseph's closest attendants probably pressed against the door he had shut on them, wondering whether they should rush in to rescue their sobbing master. They were able to hear enough to realize that these strange men, in whom Joseph had shown so much interest, were his own brothers. The servants would have learned little about the backstory of this overpoweringly emotional reunion, but it is no surprise that the word spread like wildfire through the Egyptian hierarchy. News like this was too remarkable to keep from Pharaoh himself, so they brought him the news that "Joseph's brothers have come" (45:16).

For Pharaoh, this was more than just interesting information. Perhaps he had always sensed there was a vacant place in Joseph's life, and the news "pleased Pharaoh and his servants" (45:16). Pharaoh appeared not merely to respect Joseph, but to love him. Without prompting, he ordered his second-in-command to do what Joseph had already purposed to do: to tell his brothers to return to Canaan with wagons that Pharaoh himself would provide, so they could pack up their households and come live in Egypt. They would thus enter the land not as marginalized refugees from a famine, but as honored guests with special status: "I will give you the best of the land of Egypt; and you shall eat the fat of the land" (45:18). Jacob's family would be given the very best of Egypt's creature comforts: "Have no concern for your goods, for the best of all the land of Egypt is yours" (45:20).

This provides us with a wonderful picture of the gospel. The brothers are accepted "for Joseph's sake," not their own; they are not simply allowed entrance into the land, they are loaded down with blessings. In a far greater way, we are accepted before God "for Jesus's sake," because of His saving death for us and on the basis of His merit and His righteousness, imputed to us by faith in Him. Further, God the Father "has blessed us in Christ with every spiritual blessing in the heavenly places" (Ephesians 1:3), "so that in the coming ages he might show the immeasurable riches of his grace in kindness toward us in Christ Jesus" (Ephesians 2:7).

A Door to New Blessings

The sons of Israel did so: and Joseph gave them wagons, according to the command of Pharaoh, and gave them provisions for the journey. To each and all of them he gave a change of clothes, but to Benjamin he gave three hundred shekels of silver and five changes of clothes. To his father he sent as follows: ten donkeys loaded with the good things of Egypt, and ten female donkeys loaded with grain, bread, and provision for his father on the journey. Then he sent his brothers away, and as they departed, he said to them, "Do not quarrel on the way."

So they went up out of Egypt and came to the land of Canaan to their father Jacob. And they told him, "Joseph is still alive, and he is ruler over all the land of Egypt." And his heart became numb, for he did not believe them. But when they told him all the words of Joseph, which he had said to them, and when he saw the wagons that Joseph had sent to carry him, the spirit of their father Jacob revived. And Israel said, "It is enough; Joseph my son is still alive. I will go and see him before I die."

Genesis 45:21–28

The eleven brothers now felt a great urgency to bring Jacob into this amazing story. Acting with the full authority of the Pharaoh, Joseph made complete provision not only for their journey back home, but also for their return and relocation in Egypt. And he went even further: Joseph provided a change of clothes for each of the men, almost certainly Egyptian in style, so they would be properly attired on their return when they would be presented to Pharaoh. We are not surprised to read that Joseph lavished special favors on his full brother Benjamin: five changes of clothing as well as a massive amount of money—three hundred shekels of silver. Remember that Joseph himself had been sold for twenty shekels (Genesis 37:28).

Benjamin's gift of clothing has a special significance. Many years earlier, Joseph's special robe had caused much trouble—the brothers had stripped it from him, then used it as a prop for Jacob to conclude that Joseph had been killed. This new clothing was therefore a fitting symbol of the family's reconciliation. Benjamin's arrest had caused the older brothers to tear their clothing, a symbol of new concern for the well-being of the favored son (44:13); now, the brother who had been stripped naked and sold as a commodity was providing clothing that would enable his sinful brothers to stand without shame before the king. Joseph's forgiven brothers were now dressed in Joseph's clothes.

There are fascinating echoes of the gospel in that transaction for those who know the truth of 2 Corinthians 5:21: "For our sake [God the Father] made [Jesus] to be sin who knew no sin, so that in him we might become the righteousness of God." By a great exchange in Christ, believers stand uncondemned, declared righteous before a holy God, and clothed in the righteousness of our Lord Jesus. He chose to take our sins on himself when He was crucified naked on the cross.

Joseph's most lavish gift, however, was the one intended for his father: ten donkeys loaded with the finest products of Egypt, and another ten female donkeys, loaded with provisions for the return journey. On one level, much of this gift makes little sense: if Jacob accepted Joseph's invitation, all of these things would just have to be transported back to Egypt. But on a higher level, the products were intended as an extravagant demonstration of Joseph's love and longing for his father—and they were a tangible demonstration of Joseph's wealth and status in Egypt. In a time of scarcity, only the richest and most powerful man could give such a gift—and that man was Jacob's beloved son Joseph.

It is impossible to read Joseph's parting warning to his brothers without a wry smile: "Do not quarrel on the way" (45:24). He knew his brothers only too well. Though they had changed significantly, they hadn't changed entirely! Joseph had already heard Reuben try to distance himself from responsibility for what had happened at the pit in Dothan (Genesis 42:22). Telling their father that Joseph was alive would be a double-edged sword: while it would bring the old man great joy, it would also uncover the brothers' terrible secret.

Human nature being what it is, Joseph knew that each brother would probably want to put himself in the best light before their father—and that would inevitably mean blaming the others. That could lead to a tumultuous journey full of arguments and the attempted rewriting of history. These men needed to stay humble and repentant, facing together the truth of what they had done. Joseph had forgiven them, but sin usually has an enlarging circle of victims—so seeking forgiveness is rarely a one-time event.[10] Now they had to face Jacob.

Some news seems too good to be true. When the old man heard that his beloved son was not only alive, but a man of enormous power in Egypt, "his heart became numb, for he did not believe them" (45:26).

No wonder! The brothers didn't have a sterling record of credibility when they had returned from Egypt earlier. Now was Jacob expected to believe not only that his son was alive, but that he was "the man" about whom he had heard so much, whose demand to bring Benjamin had been debated within the family?

Ironically, when Jacob's sons had come to him with their lie about Joseph's "death" (Genesis 37), he had believed them. Now, when they came with news that he was alive and very well in Egypt, Jacob simply could not accept it. The brothers had to tell their story in great detail, leading up to that remarkable moment when they had heard "the man" say, "I am Joseph! Is my father still alive?"

One wonders when and how the brothers confessed to Jacob the full story of how Joseph came to be in Egypt in the first place. It must have been excruciatingly difficult, both for them to tell and Jacob to hear. But, once again, Joseph's practical wisdom was revealed: if the brothers could not penetrate Jacob's mind with their words, the indisputable evidence of Joseph's lavish gift certainly could. These tangible evidences of Joseph's power and prosperity spoke loudly to Jacob, in a way that even the reappearance of Simeon and the safe return and testimony of Benjamin didn't. Jacob had to believe their words, because he couldn't doubt his eyes. "It is enough," he said. "Joseph my son is alive. I will go and see him before I die" (45:28).

Scripture tells us that "the spirit of Jacob revived" (45:27). A virtually dead man had come back to life, because his supposedly dead son was alive.

This is a story full of hope. It is far more dramatic than most, but it is a reminder that the living God is able to bring things once thought dead back to life. It foreshadows the story of the gospel, of how God in His forgiving grace—through the merit of His Son and our Savior—brings us from death to life, forgives us fully and freely, and invites us into a new relationship with Him. And in that relationship, He continues to lavish us with blessing!

Then, because forgiven people are to be forgiving people, this story brings hope in the midst of our broken, sin-filled relationships. Where there is genuine repentance, and where there is true forgiveness, there can be the beginning of new relationships profoundly richer than anything we have known before.

TWELVE

REUNION

Most of us are suckers for stories with happy endings. That explains why a small industry has developed to stage and film the reunions of military families, as service members return unexpectedly to their spouses and children. We are allowed to eavesdrop as soldiers startle and delight their unsuspecting children or spouses in remarkably creative ways—at school plays, sporting events, parades, church services, weddings, or a dozen other venues. The result is invariably a wonderful mixture of shock, tears, hugs, kisses, and smiles. No matter how many times I watch these scenes, I find myself touched and moved.

There may be reasons to question the wisdom of dealing with such intensely personal and emotional moments in such public ways. Regardless, we find these moments compelling because we readily identify with the cost of separation, the delight of reunion, and the enduring value of cherished relationships—especially family.

Some reunions, however, are more complicated than others. Separation is one thing, estrangement quite another. Geographical distance is infinitely easier to bridge than an estrangement caused by sinful and abusive behaviors. Reconciliation in such cases rarely occurs as a sentimental "Hallmark moment." If there is any reconciliation at all, it is the product of hard choices and deep repentance. And because of that, the fruit of reconciliation is bittersweet—it includes both the recognition of wasted times and the anticipation of better ones.

In the story that is probably our Lord's most loved parable, a father celebrates the return of his prodigal son with the declaration, "This my son was dead, and is alive again; he was lost, and is found" (Luke 15:24). How many grieving parents long to be able to repeat such words, if only their prodigal would come home at last!

Jacob had not been estranged from his much-loved son, Joseph. It was quite the opposite—he had been cruelly separated from Joseph, made to believe that he was dead and gone, no longer to be part of his life. Twenty-two years hadn't filled the vacuum caused by Joseph's absence. It was an aching hole in Jacob's heart, one that refused to be filled by anyone or anything.

Paradoxically, Joseph's absence was a never-absent fact of the family's life—the proverbial elephant in the room. The brothers' sin against Joseph made his a haunting presence, infecting the family's life. When they finally encountered him again in Egypt, their crime colored the entire exchange between the unrecognized Joseph and the guilt-ridden brothers.

Judah's repentance, shown by his willingness to be a self-sacrificing substitute for the apparently guilty Benjamin, changed everything. Joseph, certainly enabled by God's grace, finally found himself able to reveal his true identity to his brothers. He had chosen forgiveness and genuine reconciliation with his former tormentors, and the family schism had been bridged, making possible a new future for them all. But a giant step remained.

Jacob needed to be brought into the picture, and his response would be crucial. Obviously, he would be delighted to discover that his lost son was alive. But what would happen when he learned his other sons' guilt in Joseph's disappearance? Should he unleash an understandable fury on them, the new family relationship would be stillborn.

Jacob was far from perfect as a man and father. Almost every failing his sons had displayed can be traced back, in some degree, to Jacob's character and choices. His foolish favoritism had damaged the entire family and left a trail of brokenness. Then came his mysterious encounter with the Lord himself at the brook Jabbok, recorded in Genesis 32.

The Lord not only changed Jacob's name to Israel, His transforming grace began to slowly but surely change the man himself.

So when his sons set out to purchase food in Egypt and rescue Simeon, Jacob knew he was putting his beloved Benjamin at risk. Who could predict how that unreasonable Egyptian official would respond this time? He sent the men away with a prayer that was a mixture of grasping faith and fatalistic fear: "May God Almighty grant you mercy before the man, and may he send back your other brother and Benjamin. And as for me, if I am bereaved of my children, I am bereaved" (Genesis 43:14).

Jacob's waiting, alone in Canaan, must have been excruciating. He could not know that his prayer was about to be fulfilled beyond his wildest imaginings! He had shared the first seventeen years of Joseph's life, before the boy was cruelly torn from him. Now, Jacob was about to begin the last seventeen years of his own life—some of his very best—with that lost son restored and his broken family beginning to experience profound healing.

"Fear Not, for I Am with You"

So Israel took his journey with all that he had and came to Beersheba, and offered sacrifices to the God of his father Isaac. And God spoke to Israel in visions of the night and said, "Jacob, Jacob." And he said, "Here I am." Then he said, "I am God, the God of your father. Do not be afraid to go down to Egypt, for there I will make you into a great nation. I myself will go down with you to Egypt, and I will also bring you up again, and Joseph's hand shall close your eyes."

Genesis 46:1–4

Jacob was an old man, 130 years of age, when his sons returned from Egypt. We can imagine his mounting anxiety during their absence—counting the days, fearing the worst, hoping for the best. He probably had restless nights, struggling to find sleep, wondering whether he would ever again see any of his sons, especially Benjamin. Then, at the moment of their return, he felt sheer joy when eleven men—including Benjamin and Simeon—arrived safe and sound. That was what Jacob had longed for.

But there was more, far more. Jacob's sons tumbled over themselves, trying to tell him the incomprehensible news: his lost son Joseph was alive! And not only alive—he was, in fact, the mysterious man about whom Jacob had heard so much from his sons. Joseph was the ruler in Egypt, a man of unspeakable power and prestige!

There were no words for such a moment. Jacob's heart went numb at the news, almost stopped by a strange mixture of disbelief and delight (45:26). How could it possibly be true? For twenty-two years Jacob had grieved his son's death. But he was alive all this time? Leader of Egypt? That was too much for a sad old man to fathom. Yet, as he listened to his sons and saw the abundant provisions Joseph had sent with them, his shock began to turn to hope. Then joy sprang to life in his empty heart, and everything in him began to sing. Suddenly, nothing in life mattered more than getting to Egypt, as quickly as possible, to be with his lost and lamented son.

Seeing Joseph was an opportunity Jacob had no intention of missing. But this would be more than just a visit—it would be a family move to another country. That was a momentous task, so Jacob set in motion the travel plans as quickly as possible.

Leaving one's home country is never a small matter—having moved our small family from Canada to the United States, I am vividly aware of that. At least Jacob didn't have to deal with modern government bureaucracies that seem designed and determined to make such moves as difficult as possible! It would be a huge undertaking to move one's entire extended family, especially one as large as Jacob's, at any age. For a 130-year-old, this would be especially difficult, even with the help Joseph had sent. But Jacob was determined.

In leaving Canaan, more was involved than an extended journey to fulfill Jacob's fatherly desires. This was, after all, the Promised Land. Would this be a "famine length visit," extended but still temporary, or something more permanent? What about God's covenant with Jacob's grandfather Abraham, repeated to Abraham's son Isaac, and then to Jacob? How would leaving the very land God had promised to Abraham fit with God's promises about that land? What about God's purpose to bless Abraham's family in that land, making them a blessing to all the nations of the earth?

Where was God in all of this? Jacob needed to secure answers before he could freely head for Egypt and Joseph. It seemed logical and right to rush to his son, but a good idea isn't always God's idea. Was this trip really God's intention for Jacob's family?

To find answers, Jacob and his family made their way first to the settlement of Beersheba, about twenty-five miles south of where the family had lived near Hebron. Geography made Beersheba the functional southern boundary of the Promised Land: to the south was an increasingly severe desert, which stretches more than a hundred miles down to the Red Sea. It was a place that had played an important part in the Abraham family's life. Abraham himself had settled at Beersheba for a significant time (see Genesis 21:26–33; 22:19), even helping to give the town its name (21:31).

Years later, Jacob's father Isaac had also settled at Beersheba. It was the place where the Lord had appeared to Isaac with a great promise: "I am the God of Abraham your father. Fear not, for I am with you and will bless you and multiply your offspring for my servant Abraham's sake" (26:24). In response, Isaac had built an altar, pitched his tent, and raised his two sons—Esau and Jacob—in the region. And it was from the family home in Beersheba that Jacob had set out for Haran, seeking to escape the threats of his cheated and angry brother (28:10).

A host of family memories were tied up with Beersheba, making it a natural spot for Jacob to stop. But it was more than a place of nostalgia—it was for Jacob a sacred place, where he could seek direction from his God before leaving the Promised Land.

There was yet an even more compelling reason to stop at Beersheba. When Jacob was young, another famine had ravaged the region. His father Isaac had thought of going to Egypt for relief, the very thing Jacob was now planning to do. On that occasion, the Lord appeared to Isaac with both a warning and a promise: "Do not go down to Egypt; dwell in the land of which I shall tell you. Sojourn in this land, and I will be with you and bless you, for to you and to your offspring I will give all these lands, and I will establish the oath that I swore to Abraham your father" (26:2–3). Later, and more personally, the Lord had appeared directly to Jacob, when he returned to Canaan after his time with his uncle Laban in a region that is now part of eastern Turkey. The words he had heard from God himself must have resonated in Jacob's memory: "I am God Almighty: be fruitful and multiply. A nation and a company of nations shall come from you, and kings shall come from your own body. The land that I gave to Abraham and Isaac I will give to you, and I will give the land to your offspring after you" (35:11–12).

All of this history must have given Jacob pause. His father-heart longed to see his son, but would going to Egypt mean he was turning his back on God? Did the Lord's prohibition of Isaac's journey to Egypt also apply to Jacob? Or did God approve Jacob's travel? He needed to be sure he was being led by the Lord, not just by powerful parental longing emotions for a long-grieved son.

Jacob had sensed enough of the Lord's approval to have already set out to the south. Now, at the border of the Promised Land, he stopped to receive full confirmation. So we read that Jacob "came to Beersheba, and offered sacrifices to the God of his father Isaac" (Genesis 46:1). This was the act of a man making his relationship to the Lord his priority, seeking and following God's direction for his family, not merely his own interests and desires.[1]

The Lord honored Jacob's actions. It had been more than twenty-five years since Jacob had had a visionary encounter with the Lord.[2] As we have observed, Joseph is never said to have had such an experience, and the next time any Israelite would so directly encounter the living God would be 430 years later, when the Lord revealed himself to Moses at the burning bush (Exodus 3). There is an important observation here: we often misread the Bible, imagining that supernatural events were commonplace, that miracles and visions were regular occurrences. They were, in fact, rare. But on this night in Beersheba, "God spoke to Israel in visions of the night, and said, 'Jacob, Jacob'" (Genesis 46:2).

When he most needed confirmation of the Lord's direction, God in His grace came to this weak, sinful man with a great word of promise and hope: "I am God, the God of your father. Do not be afraid to go down to Egypt, for there I will make you into a great nation. I myself will go down with you to Egypt" (46:3–4). It is worth noting that God was even more concerned that Jacob be in His will than Jacob was. For some of us who worry and wonder about "finding God's will" for our lives, the promise that God graciously guides his people is a truth we need to remember.

———————————◼———————————

When God spoke to Jacob in Genesis 46, it is the fourth time in the book of Genesis that the Lord came to His people at a critical time to assure them that He is the ever-present, faithful and sufficient One (Genesis 15:1; 21:17; 26:24). This moment must have forced Jacob to recall his own earlier departure from the land, when he was desperately afraid of his brother Esau. At that time, the Lord had affirmed Jacob's role as the recipient of the promise to Abraham, and given him a great new promise: "Behold, I am with you and will keep you wherever you go, and will bring you back to this land. For I will not leave you until I have done what I have promised you" (Genesis 28:15). Jacob knew from experience how faithful God had been to that earlier promise. Now he was leaving the land again, once more with God's promise ringing in his ears. Jacob probably called to mind boyhood moments when his own father, Isaac, had spoken of hearing almost exactly the same words from God (Genesis 26:24). God had been completely faithful to Jacob's father. And God would be faithful to Jacob.

In Scripture, it is remarkable how often God comes to His people with words like these: "Fear not; I am with you." And in our times of deepest need, believers today find the Spirit speaking those same words through the Scriptures. The parting words of Jesus in Matthew 28:20 are His abiding promise: "I am with you always, to the end of the age." He is, as the psalmist says, "a very present help in trouble. Therefore we will not fear" (Psalm 46:1–2). When my daughter's life hung in the balance, words from Isaiah were a refuge for me:

"Fear not, for I have redeemed you;
I have called you by name, you are mine.
When you pass through the waters, I will be with you;
And through the rivers, they shall not overwhelm you;
when you walk through the fire you shall not be burned,
and the flames shall not consume you.

> For I am the LORD your God,
> the Holy One of Israel, your Savior."

Isaiah 43:1–3

Those were words of promise not just for me and Elizabeth, but for Janice and her children, Morgan and Connor. We can say that they are much more than a promise—they are a kept promise. "He who calls you is faithful; he will surely do it" (1 Thessalonians 5:24).

In Genesis 46:3, after assuring Jacob with a remarkable declaration, the Lord guaranteed that He would not only be with Jacob's family but would use Egypt as the place where He would fulfill His ancient promise to make "a great nation" from Abraham's line (Genesis 12:2). Jacob wasn't merely given permission to go, he was virtually commanded to.

Egypt was not a detour or dead end in God's purpose, it was a divinely-intended destination. There God would cause Abraham's seed to become a great nation, just as He had promised.[3] But, lest Jacob imagine that God's promises about the land had been forgotten, the Lord assured him, "I will also bring you up again" (46:4).

Jacob's return to the Promised Land would be a symbolic one, however. His body would be brought back to the land of his birth, the land of God's promise, in an anticipatory fulfillment of the "great nation's" return to its God-intended homeland. For that reason, we will see Jacob's dying insistence that he buried in the land of Canaan (49:29–33).

The words from God himself must have settled Jacob's heart. He was now ready to fully embrace the expectation of being reunited with Joseph.

"I Will Make You a Great Nation"

Then Jacob set out from Beersheba. The sons of Israel carried Jacob their father, their little ones, and their wives, in the wagons that Pharaoh had sent to carry him. They also took their livestock and their goods, which they had gained in the land of Canaan, and came into Egypt, Jacob and all his offspring with him, his sons, and his sons' sons with him, his daughters, and his sons' daughters. All his offspring he brought with him into Egypt.

Genesis 46:5–7

All the persons belonging to Jacob who came into Egypt, who were his own descendants, not including Jacob's sons' wives, were sixty-six persons in all. And the sons of Joseph, who were born to him in Egypt, were two. All the persons of the house of Jacob who came into Egypt were seventy.

Genesis 46:26–27

A number of years ago, my wife and I sensed strongly that the Lord was calling us to leave a ministry and a group of people we greatly loved. We felt we needed to accept an invitation we had not sought, but that seemed to be the Lord's will. The move also meant leaving Canada, "our home and native land" as our national anthem says. It was an enormously difficult move, because our roots go deep in Canada—and our future looked bright there.

Leaving was somewhat easier because all four of our parents had by that time graduated into the Lord's presence. But a change of countries is momentous for any family. Our choice to emigrate would have an impact on the future of our three children, each in high school or college and single at the time. They were most likely to meet their spouses in their new country, and raise future generations there. And so it has turned out—our eight grandchildren have all been born in the United States. Though we remind them that they are legally Canadian citizens, that identity completely underwhelms them. Our grandchildren are proudly and unrepentantly American!

Crossing the USA–Canada border doesn't really require many significant lifestyle changes. In contrast, the changes Jacob's family was about to face would be far-reaching indeed. Whatever hesitation Jacob felt would have been alleviated by the invitation of his highly-placed son, the affirmation of Pharaoh, and, most of all, by the clear promise of God himself. But Jacob's doubts and concerns would not have been completely erased, and the family's future held a host of unanswerable questions.

Jacob must have wondered at God's strange ways. His family was going to be a great nation with a secure homeland, but before they could receive that land, they needed to leave it—perhaps for a very long time! I doubt that Jacob was perceptive enough to realize that it would be four *centuries* before they would return, even though the Lord had revealed this to Abraham (Genesis 15:13). As the family wagons rolled south, however, Jacob would have known that life would never be the same, either for him or those with him.

The writer of Genesis underscores in two ways the fact that this family's time in Egypt wasn't intended to be a short visit but a prolonged stay. First, he describes the completeness of the entourage traveling with Jacob, making it clear that the family was moving "lock, stock and barrel"[4] to Egypt—no family was left behind to maintain a foothold in Canaan. The Promised Land was left entirely in God's hands. So we are told in summary, "All his offspring he brought with him into Egypt" (46:7). The writer then gives us, in verses 8–27, a list of Jacob's descendants, organized around his wives and concubines. Leah's line is described in verses 8–15, Zilpah's in 16–18, Rachel's in 19–22, and Bilhah's in verses 23–25, a total of seventy people in all.[5]

For most of us, long lists of names as found in Genesis 46:8–27 are an excuse to skip to the end of a chapter. In fact, I've chosen not to include the actual list of names in this book. However, we shouldn't skip over such passages without pondering their presence. While most of those names aren't important to us, they would have been very important to the first readers and hearers of the book of Genesis. When Moses wrote the book, he was addressing the descendants of these very people—their ancestors had long ago sought refuge in Egypt, the place they were now fleeing. The Israelites' destiny was as the "great nation" that God had promised they would become, a destiny that could only be realized in the face of immense obstacles. It was important for them to recognize the continuity of God's program for His people, and to understand their place in it.

This list of names should have moved the Israelites to awe and wonder at the faithfulness of God. The story of their family had begun with a childless, aged couple for whom parenthood was a biological impossibility. Yet, because Abraham trusted God, being "fully convinced that God was able to do what he had promised" (Romans 4:21), God had made Abraham's family grow to this considerable number only a few generations later.

The first readers of Genesis would have marveled even more, as they recognized that—in the intervening centuries between Jacob's journey to Egypt and their departure under Moses—the Abraham family had multiplied remarkably. So the book of Exodus begins with these words: "The people of Israel were fruitful and increased greatly; they multiplied and grew exceedingly strong, so that the land was filled with them" (Exodus 1:7). The list of names in Genesis 46:8–27 was vivid testimony to the fact that God's promises aren't ethereal or theoretical. He was doing exactly what He had promised, and that was grounds for the Exodus generation to believe that He would continue to do the same for them.

The Israelites of the Exodus needed the perspective Moses gave them as they heard Genesis for the first time. They, like their ancestors, were known to God by name—their family records, tracing the path of His faithfulness, should have been a source of great encouragement.

In the same way, the faithfulness of God was an anchor for us as a family, as we faced the implications of our daughter's aggressive cancer. Her children would experience significant parts of their lives without her special love and care. Elizabeth and I, as Morgan and Connor's grandparents, know that our time with them is limited, humanly speaking, by our age and health. But the record of God's enduring faithfulness to His people, etched not only in Scripture but also in church history and our own life experience, is an unending source of hope. God's promises, fulfilled in history and our own lives, call us to imitate the faith of Abraham, of whom Paul says, "No unbelief made him waver concerning the promises of God, but he grew strong in his faith" (Romans 4:20).

"This My Son Was Dead and Is Alive"

He had sent Judah ahead of him to Joseph to show the way before him in Goshen, and they came into the land of Goshen. Then Joseph prepared his chariot and went up to meet Israel his father in Goshen.

He presented himself to him and fell on his neck and wept on his neck a good while. Israel said to Joseph, "Now let me die, since I have seen your face and know that you are still alive." Joseph said to his brothers and to his father's household, "I will go up and tell Pharaoh and will say to him, 'My brothers and my father's household, who were in the land of Canaan, have come to me. And the men are shepherds, for they have been keepers of livestock, and they have brought their flocks and their herds and all that they have.' When Pharaoh calls you and says, 'What is your occupation?' you shall say, 'Your servants have been keepers of livestock from our youth even until now, both we and our fathers,' in order that you may dwell in the land of Goshen, for every shepherd is an abomination to the Egyptians."

Genesis 46:28–34

The journey was long, hard, and probably dangerous. The terrain was unforgiving, the heat unrelenting, and the travel monotonous. The wagon train, complete with women, children, and livestock, was far from an efficient or speedy means of travel, and it must have presented an attractive target for desperate people in a time of famine. For Jacob, whose heart was already running ahead to see Joseph, time must have dragged.

At one point, Jacob became impatient enough to send out Judah, by now the acknowledged leader of the brothers, to advise Joseph of the family's impending arrival and to be sure that all necessary arrangements were made. The choice was ironic—after all, it had been Judah whose suggestion had led to Joseph's enslavement in Egypt and, therefore, his separation from his father (Genesis 37:26–27). Now, Judah was to be the agent of Jacob and Joseph's reunion. This choice suggests that Jacob had made peace with the fact of the ten brothers' atrocious behavior toward his beloved son, and forgiven them to some degree.

When he revealed his identity to his brothers, Joseph had invited them to come to him with the promise, "You shall dwell in the land of Goshen" (45:10). So the family headed to that area, apparently in the eastern part of the Nile Delta, a region providing superb pastureland. When Judah told Joseph that the family was arriving, Joseph rushed in his chariot to meet them, "presented himself to [Jacob] and fell on his neck and wept on his neck a good while" (46:29).

He may have been the second in command of Egypt, but for that moment Joseph was once again a seventeen-year-old boy, sobbing with an overwhelming mixture of sadness and joy—sadness for all that had been lost, and joy for what was now possible. Tears could say what words couldn't. Earlier, Jacob had wept because he thought Joseph was dead (37:35); now Joseph could weep joyously because his father was alive (see 45:3).

Jacob's response was one of profound satisfaction: "Now let me die, since I have seen your face and know that you are still alive" (46:30). The words are strange to us, but Jacob wasn't really saying he wanted to die. (Genesis 47:28 indicates he would, in fact, live another seventeen years.) What Jacob meant was that the great question of his life had been solved, the unfinished business completed, the gaping hole filled. As one commentary puts it, "The man who feared his sons would bring him to Sheol in mourning now can die in peace."[6]

However, there was still practical business to attend to. The family's presence in Egypt (specifically in Goshen) needed to be ratified by Pharaoh himself. He had already made clear his approval of the family's move to Egypt (45:16–20). But, while Joseph was very important in Egypt, he wasn't the most important—so Jacob and his family would need to appear before Pharaoh himself to finalize their status.

Joseph carefully prepared the family, especially his brothers, for the meeting. The men were totally out of their depth, never having encountered anyone quite like an Egyptian pharaoh. Joseph would act as the family's advocate and mediator, but he wanted them to know exactly what he would say to Pharaoh and how they should respond to the ruler's inquiries. Much was at stake, since Joseph had a clear plan for his family's future. They needed to live in Egypt to prevent starvation, but at the same time, Joseph wanted them to live as a people apart, without becoming Egyptianized. They were, by God's gracious calling, a chosen family with a divine destiny, greater than anything Egypt had to offer. Joseph wanted to do more than provide for his family; he wanted to protect them.

Joseph's guidance was built on a simple premise: be who you are. Though it would have been tempting to trim their sails to the wind, to say the things Pharaoh might have expected or wanted them to say,

Joseph's approach was the opposite. He would describe things exactly as they were: "My brothers and my father's household, who were in the land of Canaan, have come to me. And the men are shepherds, for they have been keepers of livestock, and they have brought their flocks and herds and all that they have" (46:31–32). This was, of course, entirely true. But Joseph was insistent on the point: he knew that Pharaoh would certainly ask the men their occupation, pondering where they would best fit within his increasingly urban kingdom.

Joseph continued. "You shall say, 'Your servants have been keepers of livestock from our youth even until now, both we and our fathers'" (46:34). On one level, this doesn't seem the wisest answer, since shepherds and herdsmen weren't considered the most desirable immigrants. In fact, the Egyptians were deeply prejudiced against those professions, as Joseph made clear: "Every shepherd is an abomination to the Egyptians" (46:34).

The brothers had already had a taste of Egyptian exclusivism when they were seated by themselves at the banquet in Joseph's house, "because the Egyptians could not eat with the Hebrews, for that is an abomination to the Egyptians" (43:32). So why did Joseph insist on this? Why wouldn't he have the brothers trumpet some other skills and abilities they undoubtedly had? Why not try to make themselves less abominable and more attractive to Pharaoh and his officials?

Joseph knew that the family's status in Egypt wasn't dependent on who they were, but on who he was. They were being accepted on Joseph's merit, not their own—which is a wonderful picture of the gospel! Secondly, Joseph wanted to use the sinful prejudices of the Egyptians to further God's purposes for His people. He wanted to be sure that Pharaoh would direct them to the land of Goshen, an area where they would be set apart from the mainstream of Egyptian society. There, the family would be able to maintain their own identity and lifestyle, encountering far fewer temptations to intermarry and assimilate, temptations that had plagued them powerfully and constantly in Canaan.

Jacob's family had been called by God to be a blessing to the nations. Paradoxically, they could only become such a blessing when they were unlike the nations—a distinct, identifiable people modeling a better way, under the banner of the living and true God. Goshen, then, would become not only a place of physical provision, but also a place of moral, spiritual, and cultural protection. The family would have room to grow and space to be themselves.

When Neil Armstrong became the first human to walk on the moon, he famously said, "That's one small step for a man, one giant leap for mankind."[7] It was an enormous moment for Armstrong, but it had implications far beyond his personal accomplishment. In a similar way, the reunion of Jacob's family was a small but critical step in its history, especially for Jacob and Joseph themselves. But if we see the reunion in merely personal terms, we will miss its importance.

Because this reunion took place in Egypt, it changed the residence of God's covenant people for four centuries. This impacted the entire biblical story, which points to God's great deliverance of His people from Egypt as the proof and pattern of His saving power.

God is carrying out His great design. For the rest of the book of Genesis, Abraham's family will be in Egypt, just as the Lord had indicated in Genesis 15:13–14. The refuge would become a place of flourishing, but also a place where they would suffer, until "their cry for rescue from slavery came up to God. And God heard their groaning, and God remembered his covenant with Abraham, with Isaac, and with Jacob" (Exodus 2:23–24).

At that point, God's rescue operation—carried out by means of the Exodus from Egypt—would become a great foreshadowing of the far greater deliverance carried out through Judah's greatest descendant, our Lord Jesus Christ, through His death and resurrection.

THIRTEEN

ON THE TIGHTROPE

I have never been tempted to become a funambulist, or, as most of us would say, a tightrope walker. It's hard for me to see the "fun" part of walking on a thin wire at a ridiculous height, using a pole for balance. With no safety net or harness, even the slightest slip could mean, at best, a long stay in a hospital.

Skywalkers seem to be trying to outdo themselves in attempting the outrageous—walking between high rise office buildings or across Niagara Falls or part of the Grand Canyon—all the while dealing with treacherous winds and other dangerous elements. I stand in awe of their skills, but I have serious questions about their sanity.

I'm told that professional walkers are never quite on balance and never look down either at their feet or the wire. Rather, they constantly make small but critical compensating movements, feeling their way forward on the wire. They must resist the temptation to look down, keeping their head up with their eyes fixed on the goal, until they safely reach their destination.

I don't want to push the analogy too far, but a useful comparison can be drawn between walking a tightrope and living as a Christian in our present world. On one hand, we are called to follow Christ in every area of our lives, not being conformed to the world but living holy,

God-honoring lives distinct from whatever culture surrounds us. On the other hand, we are called to engage the world around us, serving the needs of its people, doing our jobs and loving our neighbors with a constant goal of gaining a hearing for the gospel from those who do not yet know and follow the Lord Jesus Christ.

It isn't hard to be distinct and separate if we don't care about being involved. We can form a kind of monastic community, a comfortable subculture where we can carefully protect ourselves from the pollution of the wider world. But we can also be so enamored of this world that we adapt ourselves to it—we can easily go with the flow by conforming our morals, beliefs, and behaviors to the culture, becoming indistinguishable from it, except in minor ways. Neither choice allows us to live in obedience to what our Lord Jesus called us to be: the salt of the earth and the light of the world (Matthew 5:13–16).

God's people have constantly faced two inseparable and inescapable questions: First, how do we establish our influence while maintaining our distinctiveness? And second, how do we keep our distinctiveness without forfeiting any meaningful influence on the world around us? These questions have become more urgent, because we find ourselves living in a time of almost unprecedented social change. Tectonic shifts in morality and technology have caused the cultural ground to move beneath our feet, changes that are reshaping society so dramatically and quickly that they only serve to make these perpetual questions more pressing.

Ours is a social environment increasingly hostile to biblical values. As a result, some Christians, in the name of relevance and cultural engagement, have removed long-held moral landmarks to accommodate the new reality. Others have reacted in anger, engaging the culture wars with zeal and passion, while others have chosen to withdraw from the battle, building a parallel set of institutions designed to minimize contact with the larger culture and protect their spiritual purity. Specifics change, but God's people have never been able to avoid the twin questions of influence and distinctiveness. Intriguingly, we see both at play in the next part of Joseph's story.

At Joseph's invitation, Jacob's family found itself in Egypt, surrounded by an imposing culture far more sophisticated than anything they had experienced in Canaan. Canaan was a tribal society, with numerous petty kingdoms and a relatively undeveloped culture. Egypt, in contrast, was a historic civilization, both technologically advanced and highly centralized, under the control of a very powerful single ruler—the Pharaoh. All people have a desire to fit it, to be accepted; now, in their new context, Joseph's family would have felt a powerful pull to "Egyptianize."

When she was a young girl, my mother emigrated from England to Canada with her parents. Quickly, she determined to shed any vestiges of "Englishness"—in her accent, her clothing, and whatever else made her un-Canadian. All her life, my mother bristled at the idea that she would be considered English rather than Canadian. Such a desire to fit in is both understandable and appropriate, but there are times in which the human desire to belong and to be accepted by the larger group or the inner circle becomes very dangerous. The cost of inclusion is inevitably assimilation to the new group's values.

Much was at stake for the Jacob family. As we have noted, they weren't just any family—they were God's covenant people, with a God-given identity and a God-given destiny. They were called to be a distinct people among the nations of the earth. Yet, at the same time, they were called to be a blessing to the nations, and that certainly included Egypt.

In considering his family's situation, Joseph would probably not have used terms such as "the tension between separation and engagement" or "maintaining distinctiveness and having influence." But whatever language he might have chosen, he found himself facing the challenge that God's people have always had to navigate. Here, it took the form of an extended family surrounded by an entirely pagan culture. At a later stage of their history, Israel would be called to be a holy people, a distinct nation set apart from all other nations (Exodus 19:5–6). Yet they were also divinely commissioned to be a light among and to those other nations.

With the birth of the church, the tension of "in but not of" the world took on a completely new relevance. God's church is not a distinct nation among the nations, but rather a community of Christ-followers scattered among the nations. They are citizens of an earthly kingdom, and they are simultaneously God's called-out people. Earthly kingdoms have their legitimate sphere of authority, but only God and His kingdom have ultimate authority.

The claims of those two kingdoms often clash head-on. In our own time, we find ourselves in a post-Christian culture, increasingly secular and with growing hostility to our claims of the exclusivity of Christ and biblical sexual standards. Finding the proper balance—between being engaged in God's mission in the world and being distinct from the world—often resembles life on a tightrope, with the ever-present danger of falling off one side or the other.

Joseph's time and cultural setting were very different than ours. He lived in a monolithic culture, held together by pagan religious values, while we live in a culture of "expressive individualism," dominated by an increasingly militant secular elite. Joseph instinctively recognized the need to insure his family's protection against a domineering culture, even as he modeled a life of engagement and influence in serving a pagan king at the very center of a pagan culture.

His precise problems certainly aren't ours. But his choices reveal underlying principles that prove helpful to us, many centuries later. We are to be, as the apostle Paul declares, "blameless and innocent, children of God without blemish in the midst of a crooked and twisted generation, among whom you shine as lights in the world" (Philippians 2:15).

A People Apart

So Joseph went in and told Pharaoh, "My father and my brothers, with their flocks and herds and all that they possess, have come from the land of Canaan. They are now in the land of Goshen." And from among his brothers he took five men and presented them to Pharaoh. Pharaoh said to his brothers, "What is your occupation?" And they said to Pharaoh, "Your servants are shepherds, as our fathers were." They said to Pharaoh, "We have come to sojourn in the land, for there is no pasture for your servants' flocks, for the famine is severe in the land of Canaan. And now, please let your servants dwell in the land of Goshen." Then Pharaoh said to Joseph, "Your father and your brothers have come to you. The land of Egypt is before you. Settle your father and your brothers in the best of the land. Let them settle in the land of Goshen, and if you know any able men among them, put them in charge of my livestock."

Then Joseph brought in Jacob his father and stood him before Pharaoh, and Jacob blessed Pharaoh. And Pharaoh said to Jacob, "How many are the days of the years of your life?" And Jacob said to Pharaoh, "The days of the years of my sojourning are 130 years. Few and evil have been the days of the years of my life, and they have not attained to the days of the years of the life of my fathers in the days of their sojourning." And Jacob blessed Pharaoh and went out from the presence of Pharaoh. Then Joseph settled his father and his brothers and gave them a possession in the land of Egypt, in the best of the land, in the land of Rameses, as Pharaoh had commanded. And Joseph provided his father, his brothers, and all his father's household with food, according to the number of their dependents.

Genesis 47:1–12

Had I been given the task of telling this story, I would have taken my time describing that great moment when Joseph and Jacob met after so many lost and wasted years. I would linger on them falling on one another's shoulders weeping—after all, that is one of the great emotional highlights of the entire book of Genesis. Moses, however, guided by God's Spirit, focuses our attention elsewhere, on Joseph's plan to secure the family a home of their own in the land of Goshen, the place that would be their dwelling place for the next four centuries.

From his first appearance to Abraham, the Lord had revealed His intention to make of Abraham's descendants "a great nation" (Genesis 12:1–3). Jacob, no doubt, had told his sons about the Lord's remarkable appearance to him at Beersheba, when God had explicitly said, "Do not be afraid to go down to Egypt, for there I will make you into a great nation" (Genesis 46:3). For that major relocation to be possible, the Israelites would need a place for their livestock, room to expand numerically, and protection geographically from the overpowering culture of Egypt. For all those reasons, Goshen was an ideal place for them to settle, and Joseph intended to do all he could to bring that about. As we have seen, Joseph had clearly thought out a strategy that he wanted his brothers to follow.

It is worth noting that Joseph's confidence in a sovereign, faithful God did not deter him from making plans and taking action. The opposite was, in fact, the case. Joseph knew that his God worked through human agents and personal choices. He also knew that God had sent him to Egypt "to preserve for you a remnant on earth and to keep alive for you many survivors. So it was not you who sent me here but God" (Genesis 45:7–8). *His conviction that the promises of God were unfailingly certain did not freeze him into passivity, but launched him into confident action.* Abraham had not only believed God's promise; he had left Ur in obedience to God's call. In his own generation, Joseph was not only trusting God's promises, he was doing his part to bring them into being.

So it should be with us. We show that we really believe God's promises when we act on them, not just when we memorize them. God's sovereignty is no excuse for apathy, nor does it render human activity meaningless. On the contrary, robust confidence in a sovereign God mobilizes our energy, challenges our creativity, and motivates our activity.

Hudson Taylor was a man of deep faith, called by God to take the gospel to China in the mid-nineteenth century, a time when that massive country was almost entirely unreached. He went, trusting God, and on the first part of his voyage he learned a life-changing truth. Sailing from England, Taylor's ship was caught in a terrible storm off the coast of Wales. The vessel was being driven onto the rocks by gale-force winds, and the captain ordered passengers to put on life jackets. At that moment, Taylor was convinced that to do so would be a sign of unbelief, dishonoring to his God. So he gave his own life jacket away and devoted himself to praying for God's intervention.

Providentially, just as the ship was about to be driven onto the rocks, the wind suddenly shifted. Hudson's vessel was able to tack away from danger into the open waters of the English Channel. He immediately recognized this as an answer to prayer, but he also came to another realization as he studied God's Word. "God gave me then to see my mistake; probably to deliver me from a great deal of trouble on similar occasions. . . . It would now appear to me to be as presumptuous and wrong to neglect the use of those measures which He himself has put within our reach, as to neglect to take daily food, and suppose that life and health might be maintained by prayer alone."[1]

Trusting God is fully compatible with wearing seatbelts in cars, going to doctors, saving for retirement, or making plans to settle your family in "the best of the land of Egypt" (Genesis 45:18). Joseph trusted God; he also strategized and acted diligently.

Joseph had made plans and Pharaoh had made promises. But Joseph needed Pharaoh to confirm those promises, so the family's status would be clear. Almost certainly, Jacob had brought household servants and other workers with him to Egypt, so the entire group probably numbered far more than seventy. Consider that, in Genesis 14:14, Abraham's extended household had been large enough for him to raise his own army of 318 trained men. So we should probably think of a group of two to three hundred people in all, a sizable number to arrive in a country that was undergoing a severe famine, when resources were already stretched.

To head off resentment against the new arrivals, Joseph chose not to make any unilateral decisions, for which he could be accused of favoritism. He intended to ensure that Pharaoh's direct authorization stood behind his family arrangements, even though as the de facto "ruler of the land" he could have done most anything he pleased. His goal was to have Pharaoh himself publicly validate Israel's special status in Egypt with land rights in Goshen.

As Genesis 46 closed, we saw Joseph carefully preparing his brothers for their audience with Pharaoh. Joseph was their means of access to Pharaoh, and he wanted his brothers to follow his own script for the occasion. Having told Pharaoh of their arrival, Joseph brought five of the men, along with their father, to the royal palace.

I'm sure there were good reasons for bringing only five of the eleven, as well as good reasons for the particular five he chose. We, however, are given no explanation for these actions. Was the number five part of Joseph's strategy, or did royal court protocol demand only a small number? Which brothers did he choose? The five most impressive, so Pharaoh would see them as desirable additions to his kingdom, or the five least impressive, so they wouldn't seem to be a threat? Perhaps, as Jewish rabbis suggested, he chose the weaker brothers so they wouldn't be recruited as Pharaoh's soldiers. But we have no way of knowing.

What we do know is that, somewhere during their audience, Pharaoh asked the inevitable question: "What is your occupation?" (47:3). Following Joseph's coaching, the brothers declared without hesitation that they were shepherds who had brought their flocks with them. That led to a direct request for permission to sojourn in the region of Goshen.[2] Rather than avoiding the stigma of being abominable shepherds (see 46:34), they embraced their profession. These men wanted to keep being shepherds, having no intention of changing their pastoral way of life.

Joseph's strategy was successful. Pharaoh had already been committed to do the family good for Joseph's sake. Now he gave them even more than they requested. Pharaoh's royal grant gave them entitlement to the best of the land in Goshen, where they would be able to retain their distinctiveness. Further, Joseph was commanded to select the best workers for positions in the royal administration, overseeing the care of Pharaoh's livestock. Four hundred years later, when Jacob's family of seventy people had swollen to perhaps two million, they would still reside, as a distinct, unassimilated people, in the land of Goshen (Exodus 8:22).

So far, so good, for Joseph's plan. I wonder if he held his breath, though, when he introduced his father to Pharaoh. Old men can be unpredictable, and Jacob more than most. Right away, Jacob acted against royal protocol. The rules are almost universal: Wait until the monarch speaks; speak when spoken to; don't touch the ruler. But Joseph's father seized the initiative. We are told that "Jacob blessed Pharaoh" (Genesis 47:7).

Jacob was standing before the enthroned Pharaoh, in Egyptian minds the representative of the gods and the most powerful man on earth. Cultural expectations made such situations clear: the greater blessed the lesser, not vice versa. The great Pharaoh was always the blessing giver, not the blessing receiver! Jacob was merely a refugee, a man without home, country, or standing apart from his status as Joseph's father. He was the petitioner, seeking Pharaoh's permission to bring his family into the country. But Jacob saw himself as something more: he was the representative of the living God, someone with a blessing to give.

Pharaoh had promoted Jacob's son to power and prominence, provided food during the family's battle with famine in Canaan, and granted the family's request for a place of refuge and residence in Goshen. Jacob was deeply grateful, and so, in this brief interview, he began and ended with words of blessing on the Egyptian ruler, all in the name of the living God.

Jacob was a remarkably old, yet active man, a fact that obviously impressed Pharaoh. The Egyptians believed the ideal life span was 110 years, a figure Jacob had already exceeded by twenty years. Jacob's age demanded respect, and Pharaoh's question, while strange to us, was perfectly reasonable: he essentially asked Jacob, "Just how old are you?"

Jacob's answer was respectful and honest, and he retained his dignity by not in any way groveling before Pharaoh. But his response was also disappointingly negative: "The days of the years of my sojourning are 130 years. Few and evil have been the days of the years of my life, and they have not attained to the days of the years of the life of my fathers in the days of their sojourning" (47:9).

His words may have been true overall, but the past few weeks had seen Jacob's life take a remarkable turn for the better, under the good hand of his God. He had been just reunited with his beloved son, who had reached levels of influence and affluence he could never have imagined. Further, Pharaoh himself had just solidified the family's status in Goshen. However, both his son's return and the thought of spending his dying days in Egypt, not Canaan, seem to have reminded Jacob that his life had been a long, hard struggle.

Jacob's answer was filled with a grumbling complaint. We could interpret his words like this: "I'm 130, pretty young compared to my father and my grandfather. And my life has been a long, hard uphill climb all the way." That was hardly seizing the opportunity to bear witness to his faithful God! Jacob's life had indeed been hard—he had been sinned against greatly, especially by family members, whether his father Isaac, his brother Esau, his uncle Laban, and his own sons. He had also been his own worst enemy more times than not. But God had been faithful throughout.

Hidden in Jacob's complaint, however, was a significant choice of words. Pharaoh had asked about "the days of the years of your life" (47:8); Jacob, in response, had spoken of "the days of the years of my sojourning" (47:9). *Sojourning* is a technical word, referring to living temporarily in a place as an outsider, without being a landowner, citizen, or permanent resident. That had indeed been Jacob's lot—sojourning as a boy with his parents in Canaan, "the land of his father's sojournings" (37:1); fleeing from his brother to Paddan-aram to sojourn with his uncle Laban; returning to the Promised Land with his family to sojourn there; and now ending his life as a sojourner once again, this time in Egypt (47:4).

This had been the life pattern of a man to whom God had declared, "The land on which you lie I will give to you and to your offspring" (28:13). As we shall see in the next chapter, Jacob still believed deeply in that promise, despite all that had happened to him. The Lord had assured him that the family's sojourn outside the Promised Land was only temporary (46:4).

So the Holy Spirit invites us to see more in Jacob's grumbling than we might otherwise see. Whether it was Egypt or even Canaan, Jacob had his eyes fixed on a better homeland, just as Abraham and Isaac had. The book of Hebrews speaks of a deeper insight that had captured their hearts:

> These all died in faith, not having received the things promised, but having seen them and greeted them from afar, and having acknowledged that they were strangers and exiles on the earth. For people who speak thus make it clear that they are seeking a homeland. If they had been thinking of that land from which they had gone out, they would have had opportunity to return. But as it is, they desire a better country, that is, a heavenly one. Therefore God is not ashamed to be called their God, for he has prepared for them a city.
>
> Hebrews 11:13–16

Legally, however, Jacob is no longer a sojourner. Pharaoh, through the intervention of Joseph, "gave them a possession in the land of

Egypt, in the best of the land, in the land of Rameses, as Pharaoh had commanded" (Genesis 47:11). They didn't merely have land-use rights; Pharaoh had bestowed ownership rights[3] by royal grant. Ironically, the first property the family owned, other than a burial plot in Hebron, was in the land of Egypt—not the God-promised land of Canaan.

We need to keep our eye on the larger issue in this encounter between Jacob and Pharaoh. Joseph had carefully sought to preserve the family's identity by enabling them to live "set apart." He was aware that his family's great danger was assimilation—if it had been a significant problem in Canaan, it was a much greater threat in the superpower that was Egypt, a nation of affluence, learning, and antiquity. Jacob's family was physically *in* Egypt; Joseph knew they would be in danger of becoming *of* Egypt. Joseph's plan for their living space would provide both provision and protection. In Goshen, they could not only survive but retain the hope of becoming "a great nation."

Geographic isolation—their remoteness from the powerful cultural pull of Egypt's great cities—enabled Jacob's sons to retain their identity as shepherds. When God's time came, they would be more likely to leave life in Egypt and head for the long-promised land than they would have been if their lives had been entangled in Egyptian business and culture. God was using the Egyptians' sinful prejudice to serve His purposes for His people. As the nineteenth-century writer Robert Candlish observed, "Egypt's frown is better for them than Egypt's flattery and fellowship."

In the course of time, that frown would turn into active persecution and attempted genocide. But even then, when times got hard on the Exodus journey, a substantial number of Israelites would hanker to return to "the good life" in Egypt.[4] Joseph's wisdom was more than substantiated by later events in the time of the Exodus.

This makes clear a fundamental spiritual principle: *we can only make a meaningful difference in the world if we are different from the world.* The New Testament speaks of us as "sojourners and exiles" (1 Peter 2:11), reminding us that we are never merely citizens of an earthly kingdom. We can only be a blessing to the world if we model a better way for the world. As Kent Hughes observes, "A worldly church cannot and will not reach the world. The church must be distinct from the world to reach the world. We must set ourselves apart to God if we hope to reach the world. In a word, the only hope for us and the lost world is a holy church."[5]

There is a major difference between Christ-followers and the Jacob family. They were set apart physically in Goshen; we are not to be separated physically from unbelievers, but morally and spiritually, by both our lifestyle and our contribution to the culture in which our Lord has placed us. We are not called to isolation but to penetration, as salt and light.

This affects our marriages, our families, our jobs and businesses, our morality, our business ethics, our use of money and possessions—the list goes on and on. Our marching orders are clear: "Do not be conformed to this world, but be transformed by the renewal of your mind" (Romans 12:2). "Live such good lives among the pagans that, though they accuse you of doing wrong, they may see your good deeds and glorify God on the day he visits us" (1 Peter 2:12 NIV).

Serving Pharaoh

Now there was no food in all the land, for the famine was very severe, so that the land of Egypt and the land of Canaan languished by reason of the famine. And Joseph gathered up all the money that was found in the land of Egypt and in the land of Canaan, in exchange for the grain that they bought. And Joseph brought the money into Pharaoh's house. And when the money was all spent in the land of Egypt and in the land of Canaan, all the Egyptians came to Joseph and said, "Give us food. Why should we die before your eyes? For our money is gone." And Joseph answered, "Give your livestock, and I will give you food in exchange for your livestock, if your money is gone." So they brought their livestock to Joseph, and Joseph gave them food in exchange for the horses, the flocks, the herds, and the donkeys. He supplied them with food in exchange for all their livestock that year. And when that year was ended, they came to him the following year and said to him, "We will not hide from my lord that our money is all spent. The herds of livestock are my lord's. There is nothing left in the sight of my lord but our bodies and our land. Why should we die before your eyes, both we and our land? Buy us and our land for food, and we with our land will be servants to Pharaoh. And give us seed that we may live and not die, and that the land may not be desolate."

So Joseph bought all the land of Egypt for Pharaoh, for all the Egyptians sold their fields, because the famine was severe on them. The land became Pharaoh's. As for the people, he made servants of them from one end of Egypt to the other. Only the land of the priests he did not buy, for the priests had a fixed allowance from Pharaoh and lived on the allowance that Pharaoh gave them; therefore they did not sell their land.

Then Joseph said to the people, "Behold, I have this day bought you and your land for Pharaoh. Now here is seed for you, and you shall sow the land. And at the harvests you shall give a fifth to Pharaoh, and four fifths shall be your own, as seed for the field and as food for yourselves and your households, and as food for your little ones." And they said, "You have saved our lives; may it please my lord, we will be servants to Pharaoh." So Joseph made it a statute concerning the land of Egypt, and it stands to this day, that Pharaoh should have the fifth; the land of the priests alone did not become Pharaoh's.

Genesis 47:13–26

For the first time, we are given a more complete account of the programs Joseph had instituted during the famine emergency. We enter into a very different world than our own, with a completely different governmental and economic structure. Almost none of us would be willing to trade Western democratic life, with all its flaws, for life in Egypt, either then or now.

It is tempting to measure Joseph's actions by our standards, and to blame him for a governmental regime over which he had no control. He may have had great power within Pharaoh's boundaries, but he was in no position to entirely change the rules of the game. Harsh as the program seems to us, we need to recognize that the people responded with great appreciation for Joseph: "You have saved our lives" (47:25).

Earlier, we read of Joseph's activity during the seven years of plenty, as he "stored up grain in great abundance, like the sand of the sea, until he ceased to measure it, for it could not be measured" (41:49).

The 20 percent tax during those years was onerous, but the bumper crops made it less painful—especially since so much food would have produced a glut in the market, thereby driving prices down. But the wisdom of Joseph's plan became evident when the famine set in, with all its life-threatening severity. As a result of Joseph's work, "There was famine in all lands, but in all the land of Egypt there was bread" (41:54).

Joseph's plan unfolded in three stages. In the first year, people bought Joseph's stored supplies, but the famine was so severe that peoples' funds were soon exhausted (47:13–14). The second stage involved bartering livestock for food (47:15–17). Cattle were an important capital asset, but in a time of famine they became a heavy liability—their owners couldn't afford to feed them, and no one else had the resources to buy them. That meant the herds would have to be slaughtered, but the lack of refrigeration meant that most of the meat would be wasted. This loss would be catastrophic after the famine ended. Joseph's plan thus saved the cattle from the butchers and their owners from bankruptcy.

The third stage was one of desperation. With money and livestock gone, the only assets the people possessed were their properties and the labor produced by their own bodies. However, the barren, drought-stricken land had no current value, while near starvation had weakened their bodies. So the people, with all other options gone, volunteered to trade both their land and their personal freedom for survival (47:18–19).

By the end of the famine, all the fields of Egypt, excluding only those belonging to the priests of the various gods, were owned by Pharaoh. In theory, he had always been regarded as owner of all the land in Egypt, but theory had now become hard reality. The people, in turn, are described as "servants" (47:25). The actuality, however, was not quite as harsh as that sounds. The people were tenant farmers, not welfare recipients or chattel slaves. They were given the right to remain on their land and to work it, with seed provided by the government, at the cost of a 20 percent harvest tax each year. From what we know of life in the ancient Near East, these were remarkably generous terms.

The average tax rate in the region was 33.3 percent. As one scholar observes, "In ancient societies slavery was the accepted way of bailing out the destitute, and under a benevolent master could be quite a comfortable status. . . . Ancient slavery at its best was like tenured employment, whereas the freeman was like someone who was self-employed. The latter may be freer but he faced more risks."[6] Distasteful as the result seems to us, the people's response was one of gratitude for Joseph: "You have saved our lives; may it please my lord, we will be servants to Pharaoh" (47:25). In their eyes, Joseph was not an opportunistic tyrant but a savior.

Some have wrestled with Joseph's actions, wondering whether this situation endorses political or economic practices that we today would find distasteful. Several observations help us put this in perspective.

First, Joseph's program was an emergency response to an unprecedented crisis—it is not a biblically mandated economic plan. The differences between this program and the later legislation given through Moses are profound. In God's law, the Torah, debts were canceled after the seventh year, and in the fiftieth (or Jubilee) year, slaves were to be set free and land returned to its original owners. Except in very limited circumstances, land could not be sold in perpetuity.

Second, state ownership of land was the norm, not the exception throughout Egypt's history. As we have observed, "the gods" owned the land, and Pharaoh was their living representative. The changes under Joseph, therefore, were probably not revolutionary.

Third, as we have noted, debt slavery was the ancient equivalent of bankruptcy. It was categorically different than the chattel slavery that so blighted American history. It was the way nearly all ancient societies dealt with those unable to pay their debts, apart from their own labor. It was their labor that was in bondage, not their persons. In Joseph's Egypt, people were not driven from their land and reduced to the status of homeless serfs.

In all of this, Joseph was a God-sent man with a God-given mission, both for the common good of Egypt ("to preserve life") and the specific good of his family ("to preserve for you a remnant on the earth"). He was called to serve in the "messy middle" of a sinful world—he didn't get to set the basic rules but he did get to bring the presence of God with him. Joseph modeled a life of "faithful presence," as we also should, in the various spheres of society in which the Lord has planted us.

For those of us called to be kingdom agents in the various spheres of our lives, several aspects of Joseph's life make it a model worth pondering. Joseph's was *a life of consistent faithfulness*. He served his father by going to his brothers; his slave master Potiphar in the administration of his affairs; the prison keeper, in the administration of his place of confinement; and Pharaoh himself, in a time of great national crisis.

His also was *a life of deep integrity*. Joseph refused the opportunity to frolic with Potiphar's wife, and there is no indication that he ever abused the privileges Pharaoh had granted him. Even as he settled his family in Goshen, something probably within his realm of authority, Joseph was careful not take advantage or act behind Pharaoh's back.

Further, he lived *a life of restrained power*. Joseph chose not to abuse his authority. We may wrestle with his efforts to bring his brothers to repentance, but even then, he used his position and privileges without abusing the men. One of the most important things that can be said about Joseph is that he was unspoiled by his success and uncorrupted by his power.

Finally, his was *a life of overflowing blessing*. He is the clearest example of God's promise to Abraham: "I will bless you and make your name great, so that you will be a blessing" (Genesis 12:2). So we read in Genesis 39:5, "The Lord blessed [Potiphar's] house for Joseph's sake." Joseph blessed Pharaoh by his wisdom, the entire nation of Egypt by his administration, and the surrounding nations who "came to Egypt to Joseph to buy grain" (41:57).

In the hardest of places, Joseph was a faithful presence, maintaining his integrity and meeting people's needs. Certainly he was a blessing to his own people, saving them not only from famine but from their sinful dysfunction and their descent into uselessness. Most of all, Joseph became a blessing to his father, whose special years were the first seventeen of Joseph's youth (37:2) and the final seventeen of his own (47:28). Joseph enabled Jacob to die with blessings for his sons rather than curses (49:28).

Joseph knew how to live on a tightrope, keeping his balance between distinctiveness and engagement. He was not a perfect man, and if God had so willed, the writer of Genesis could have exposed many of Joseph's flaws and weaknesses. But the Lord has spared him and us from that kind of exposure. Joseph is a model for us, living in a very different time and place, seeking that same balance, being distinctly Christian in our character and lifestyle while we faithfully engage our broken and needy world. Like Joseph we are called to live in the "messy middle," between our calling as God's people and a sinful world.

We have much to learn from Joseph's example, but we need more than simply an example. Instruction comes from viewing Joseph; empowerment comes when we fix our eyes on Jesus, our Lord and Savior.

FOURTEEN

PASSING THE BATON

At the 2008 Olympic Games in Beijing, both the American men's and women's 4x100 relay teams were overwhelming favorites to win gold medals. After all, their roster of runners had times faster than any other nation could boast.

But races are won and lost on the track, not in theory. Amazingly, neither team medaled—they didn't even make the finals because each team failed to pass the baton successfully. Distressed, the governing body of US Track commissioned a task force to evaluate the problem. Their conclusion was stated rather melodramatically: "The United States has made relay running a 400-meter enigma, wrapped in a conundrum, and shrouded in mystery."

The problem isn't unique to American relay teams, though. In fact, it's not even that uncommon. Studies show that at the elite level of the Olympics or the World Championships, almost 25 percent of competing teams have been disqualified, nearly always because of problems passing the baton. It is obviously important to have fast runners—but speed counts for nothing if the athletes can't make the handoff.

But it isn't just track athletes who need to "pass a baton" successfully. Years ago, Edith Schaeffer asked the question, "What is a family?" Part of her answer was that a family is "a perpetual relay of truth."[1] As she observes, "We are responsible for 'handing on the flag' and for being very careful not to drop it—or to drop out—because of our responsibility to the next generation. The primary place for the flag of truth to be handed on is in the family. The truth was meant to be given from generation to generation."[2]

This is a principle etched in Scripture from its earliest pages, bound into God's call of Abraham to bring blessing to the world. The way the Lord describes His priorities for Abraham is highly instructive: "*I have chosen him, that he may command his children and his household after him to keep the way of the LORD by doing righteousness and justice,* so that the LORD may bring to Abraham what he has promised him" (Genesis 18:19, emphasis added). Abraham's primary calling, like many of ours, was to be a parent, teaching truth to his children. By being faithful relayers of God's truth, both Abraham and his descendants after him would bring blessing to both themselves and also to the world.

There is, however, a huge difference between a running relay and our real-life race. On the track, once the baton is dropped, the race is over, for all intents and purposes. There is virtually no chance of winning, and just seeking to finish seems rather pointless. But Christ-followers live with the confidence that God, in His grace, can overrule our past failures and produce remarkable conclusions to unpromising beginnings. That is certainly the reality of Jacob's life.

He entered Egypt as a somewhat disillusioned old man, as his initial encounter with Pharaoh showed (Genesis 47:9). But in spite of Jacob's age and attitude, the Lord was not finished with him. Seventeen years later, as he drew near the end of his life, Jacob is seen as a God-focused man, concerned to arrange his affairs in a way that will make an indelible spiritual impression on his descendants. His greatest desire was to etch on their hearts—both his children's and grandchildren's—transcendent truths that would far outlive him. As he felt the time of his death drawing near, it is hardly surprising that Jacob turned to his son Joseph to help him accomplish those important and increasingly urgent goals.

Visible Trust

Thus Israel settled in the land of Egypt, in the land of Goshen. And they gained possessions in it, and were fruitful and multiplied greatly.

And Jacob lived in the land of Egypt seventeen years. So the days of Jacob, the years of his life, were 147 years.

And when the time drew near that Israel must die, he called his son Joseph and said to him, "If now I have found favor in your sight, put your hand under my thigh and promise to deal kindly and truly with me. Do not bury me in Egypt, but let me lie with my fathers. Carry me out of Egypt and bury me in their burying place." He answered, "I will do as you have said." And he said, "Swear to me"; and he swore to him. Then Israel bowed himself upon the head of his bed.

Genesis 47:27–31

At the age of ninety-two, after a long and richly blessed ministry, Billy Graham began a book of reflections on his advancing years with a confession: "I never thought I'd live to be this old. All my life I was taught how to die as a Christian, but no one ever taught me how to live in the years before I die. I wish they had, because I am an old man now, and believe me, it's not easy. Whoever said it first was right: old age is not for sissies."[3] I suspect Jacob, at this point more than fifty years older than Billy Graham, would have wholeheartedly agreed.

That is not to say everything in Jacob's life was bad. The last seventeen years had been good ones, in many ways the best and easiest of his life. Family concerns and responsibilities had been taken off his shoulders by Joseph. Jacob and his descendants were settled in a good place, having entered Egypt during the last five years of a devastating famine, when even the Egyptians were being pushed to the edge. Ordinary citizens had been forced to take desperate measures to survive, reducing themselves to tenant farmers under Pharaoh, stripped of most of their personal possessions; for the Jacob family, however, things had been very different. Joseph had "provided his father, his brothers, and all his father's household with food, according to the number of their dependents" (47:12). The Israelites had been uniquely free of the anxieties that raked their contemporaries, secure in their property and provision for their daily needs. After the famine, things became even better. Goshen was a desirable place to live—the "best of the land," Pharaoh had called it (47:6), and the family flourished: "they gained possessions in it, and were fruitful and multiplied greatly" (47:27).

Easy as life in Egypt might be, Jacob knew it would never be the family's true home. Canaan was much more than Jacob's birthplace and the region where he had spent most of his life. It was the Promised Land, the territory God had specifically and repeatedly promised to Jacob's grandfather Abraham and his father, Isaac (Genesis 12:7; 13:15; 15:7, 18; 17:8; 26:3). Moreover, Jacob himself was the recipient of that promise, directly from the Lord (Genesis 28:13; 35:12). Through all the ups and downs of his life, Jacob had never lost sight of that divine pledge, unfulfilled though it remained. So it is hardly surprising that one of his primary concerns, as death approached and as his descendants became increasingly at home in Goshen, was that they never lost sight of their true homeland. Jacob wanted his approaching death to be a means of making his hope their hope.

Aware of his growing weakness, Jacob summoned Joseph to his deathbed. Joseph was now the acting leader of the family, the one through whom all the family's needs were provided and the one his father most trusted to willingly and faithfully carry out his wishes. Joseph was also the family member most likely to see Egypt, not Canaan, as his true homeland. After all, for Joseph, Canaan was part of a distant and painful past, perhaps best forgotten.

Egypt, on the other hand, was the land in which Joseph had flourished, where he had enjoyed a lifestyle of unimaginable prominence, prestige, power, and privilege. His wife was Egyptian, probably thoroughly at home in her native culture. His children, though half Hebrew and bearing Hebrew names, were certainly surrounded by a dominant Egyptian culture. By any normal way of predicting, the destiny of Joseph and his sons lay in Egypt, not faraway and primitive Canaan.

But that was not God's purpose, and Jacob intended to impress this reality upon his son. The arrangements he put in place for the disposition of his inheritance (and his body) were designed to underline a major truth: Egypt is not our promised land, Canaan is. By his manner of dying and his place of burial, Jacob intended to make that point, establishing family memories that would become perpetual reminders. His greatest concern, as death drew near, was for his descendants' spiritual well-being, that they would not forget their true identity as God's special people.[4]

As we read Genesis, it is important to remember that Moses was first of all writing for the Exodus generation. As they left behind all that was familiar in Egypt to make a long and difficult trek through the wilderness, they particularly needed to know that their destiny did not lie behind them. They were the recipients of a God-given covenant, made with their ancestors, and this covenant God was now leading them to take possession of the land He had promised them. Knowing their family history would help the Israelites understand their present situation as refugees, as well as their destiny as citizens of the nation of Israel, when they would live as owners of the old family home of Canaan.

When Joseph came to his father's bedside, Jacob made a request that strikes us as bizarre and uncomfortable: Joseph was asked to place his hand under Jacob's thigh. In that time and place, Joseph would have understood this action as the symbolic prelude to taking a very sacred oath (as in Genesis 24:2, 9). Its highly intimate nature made it a solemn and sacred act, a symbol more potent even than our modern practice of having a witness place his hand on a Bible.[5] Without telling Joseph what he was going to request, Jacob was signaling to his son that he was requesting an inviolable promise of the most binding kind. When Joseph complied, Jacob made his plea: "Do not bury me in Egypt, but let me lie with my fathers. Carry me out of Egypt and bury me in their burying place" (47:29–30).

Joseph would have known that his father was speaking about the family burial plot in Hebron, the cave of Machpelah. Abraham had purchased it to bury his wife Sarah (23:1–20), and in turn, Abraham himself, Isaac and his wife Rebekah, and Jacob's wife Leah, mother of six of his sons, had been buried there (25:9–11; 49:29–32). The desire to be surrounded by one's loved ones in death is natural, but Jacob almost certainly had something more in mind than sharing space with his relatives' bones. This reunion at burial was to be a symbolic statement about the family's continuing fellowship after physical death, in the presence of their covenant God.

Jacob wouldn't allow Joseph merely to nod his agreement to this request. "Swear to me," he insisted (47:31). Joseph did so, thus making the fulfilling of his father's wishes a matter of sacred duty for him. He was now honor-bound before both his father and his God.[6]

This was a request of such enormous importance to Jacob that he was careful to repeat it to his other sons, with virtually his dying words, as recorded in Genesis 49:28–32. He was leaving nothing to chance: burial in Canaan went beyond merely an emotional and sentimental desire—it was a deeply personal spiritual statement of his faith in the sure promises of God. Jacob believed that the Lord had meant what He had promised in His covenant, and that, therefore, the Promised Land would one day become the "Possessed Land" for his descendants. This was an act of faith and confidence that the Lord would fully keep His promise made when Jacob left the land to reunite with Joseph: "I will also bring you up again" (46:4).

Jacob's burial was to be a visible object lesson in faith for his entire family, arousing them to a similar faith in God's promises, one that would prevent them from ever seeing Egypt as their true home. Goshen may be "the best of the land of Egypt," but it was not, and never would be, the Promised Land. So when Joseph made his vow to carry out his father's request, "Israel bowed himself upon the head of his bed" (47:31). This was a quiet moment of worship, as he acknowledged his gratitude to his faithful Lord.

Leaving his father's bedside, Joseph carried both a vow he fully intended to keep and a perspective he would come to fully share. Years later, as we shall see, when it came time for him to die, Joseph's instructions to his own family were modeled on those of his father: to bury his bones in Canaan (see Genesis 50:24–25). *He not only understood precisely what his father had intended, he had embraced his father's true homeland as his own—by faith in God's promises.*

A Deathbed Adoption

After this, Joseph was told, "Behold, your father is ill." So he took with him his two sons, Manasseh and Ephraim. And it was told to Jacob, "Your son Joseph has come to you." Then Israel summoned his strength and sat up in bed. And Jacob said to Joseph, "God Almighty appeared to me at Luz in the land of Canaan and blessed me, and said to me, 'Behold, I will make you fruitful and multiply you, and I will make of you a company of peoples and will give this land to your offspring after you for an everlasting possession.' And now your two sons, who were born to you in the land of Egypt before I came to you in Egypt, are mine; Ephraim and Manasseh shall be mine, as Reuben and Simeon are. And the children that you fathered after them shall be yours. They shall be called by the name of their brothers in their inheritance. As for me, when I came from Paddan, to my sorrow Rachel died in the land of Canaan on the way, when there was still some distance to go to Ephrath, and I buried her there on the way to Ephrath (that is, Bethlehem)."

Genesis 48:1–7

We are not told how much time elapses between Joseph's visit, recorded at the end of chapter 47, and this visit, but it was probably relatively short. Already aware of his father's increasing frailty, Joseph received word that Jacob's condition was rapidly deteriorating. Immediately, Joseph rushed to his father's side, this time bringing with him his two oldest two sons, Manasseh and Ephraim.

Joseph wanted his sons to see their grandfather, perhaps for the last time, but he also had another motive: he wanted his father to pronounce his blessing over them. Joseph's Egyptian-born sons needed to know that they came under the promise and the blessing of the covenant God. The priority of this idea of "blessing" becomes clear when we observe that the word "bless" or "blessing" is used six times in this chapter. Joseph was coming to have his sons blessed, but what his father did before he blessed the boys took him entirely off guard.

Jacob's worsening health made it an effort just to sit up in his bed. But, told that Joseph and his sons had arrived, he struggled into a sitting position. Whatever was on Joseph's mind, it immediately became apparent that Jacob had an agenda of his own—and he quickly seized the initiative. Though he was fragile of body, he was still very clear of mind.

Like many an old man, Jacob began to speak of the past. Specifically, he talked about one of the great moments of his life, a time when the covenant God had revealed himself to Jacob. I wonder how often Joseph and his sons had heard such stories before. But this was far more than an old man reminiscing about the past—this was about

God and His plans and purposes for the whole family. Jacob wanted Joseph and his sons to understand their place in the covenant promise God had made to their forefather Abraham.

The specific event Jacob had in mind isn't entirely clear, since the Lord had twice appeared to him at Luz, also known as Bethel. The first time was that famous occasion when, fleeing to his uncle Laban away from Esau's threats, he saw "Jacob's ladder" (28:10–22). The second time was when he returned from Laban to Canaan (35:1–15). The events are similar, and both are related to God's covenant. It is more likely the latter occasion is the one in view, since the wording of Genesis 48:4 is very similar to what we read in Genesis 35:11–12. Jacob wanted his son and his grandsons to understand their legacy in light of the divine promise: "The land that I gave to Abraham and Isaac I will give to you, and I will give the land to your offspring after you" (35:12).

Joseph and his boys were heirs of that promise, and they must never forget that truth. As Jacob recounted God's Word to him at that time, he also was careful to emphasize that the source of the promise was El Shaddai, "God Almighty."[7] Manasseh and Ephraim, Jacob's Egyptian offspring, raised as they were in a land abounding in gods of all kinds, needed to know there was only one "God Almighty." He alone was completely able to do all that He said, however unlikely that might seem at the present time.

El Shaddai's promise was not grounded in the family's worth or achievement, in any human effort or merit. Rather it was based on God's utterly reliable character, on the truthfulness of His word which He had made so emphatic: "*I will make* you fruitful . . . *I will make* of you a company of people . . . *I will give* this land to your offspring." God's promise was grounded in who He was, not on how Jacob or his family performed. Those promises, and the God who made them, were precious to Jacob— and he longed for them to be equally precious to Joseph and his sons.

For all his many failures as a father, Jacob was right on track at this time. He longed for his descendants to know the defining spiritual moments of his life, as well as its undergirding spiritual principles. He yearned for them to value such things for themselves. (It is worth pondering whether our children or grandchildren could relay to others the spiritually defining moments of our lives and the spiritual promises that have shaped our choices and values. They should hear us speak of those things regularly and passionately.)

At this point, Jacob did something that almost certainly shocked Joseph. Looking at his grandsons, Jacob declared that he was adopting them as his own sons: "Your two sons, who were born to you in the land of Egypt before I came to you in Egypt, are mine; Ephraim and Manasseh shall be mine, as Reuben and Simeon are" (48:5). The custom of adopting grandchildren as sons is foreign to us, but apparently it could and did occur in the ancient world.[8]

Behind Jacob's action were legal issues such as the rights of inheritance and the position of the firstborn, who, by the custom of the times, was granted a "double portion" of the division of the family inheritance (Deuteronomy 21:17). By definition, the word firstborn indicates the oldest. But, as will become evident, Reuben had forfeited that position by his sin against his father. The patriarch of a family had the power to appoint a successor, the next family leader. Now, by giving Joseph's two oldest sons equal status with Jacob's two oldest sons, Reuben and Simeon, Jacob was giving Joseph himself the double portion, the family's birthright.[9] He was also placing Ephraim and Manasseh among the ancestors of the twelve tribes that would constitute the future nation of Israel.

This deathbed adoption explains why, throughout the rest of the Old Testament, we read of the tribes of Manasseh and Ephraim, but almost never of "the tribe of Joseph." Joseph, in fact, was deemed as present in his two sons, since Jacob had bestowed on Joseph the firstborn's "double portion." That these three had a special place in Jacob's heart was also revealed by the way he spoke of his loss of Rachel, his beloved wife and Joseph's mother. Joseph, Ephraim, and Manasseh represented her abiding legacy as well as his.

Jacob was old, but he wasn't senile. He knew that, if Joseph was the son most likely to see his destiny as lying in Egypt, his grandsons were even more likely to think of themselves that way. Jacob was acting to reshape their view of the future in light of God's promises. Joseph's sons needed to identify themselves with Israel, not Egypt, as their people. Canaan, not Egypt, is their true home. Once again, he was directing his family to God's great promises.

Bound for the Promised Land

When Israel saw Joseph's sons, he said, "Who are these?" Joseph said to his father, "They are my sons, whom God has given me here." And he said, "Bring them to me, please, that I may bless them." Now the eyes of Israel were dim with age, so that he could not see. So Joseph brought them near him, and he kissed them and embraced them. And Israel said to Joseph, "I never expected to see your face; and behold, God has let me see your offspring also." Then Joseph removed them from his knees, and he bowed himself with his face to the earth. And Joseph took them both, Ephraim in his right hand toward Israel's left hand, and Manasseh in his left hand toward Israel's right hand, and brought them near him. And Israel stretched out his right hand and laid it on the head of Ephraim, who was the younger, and his left hand on the head of Manasseh, crossing his hands (for Manasseh was the firstborn).

And he blessed Joseph and said, "The God before whom my fathers Abraham and Isaac walked, the God who has been my shepherd all my life long to this day, the angel who has redeemed me from all evil, bless the boys; and in them let my name be carried on, and the name of my fathers Abraham and Isaac; and let them grow into a multitude in the midst of the earth."

When Joseph saw that his father laid his right hand on the head of Ephraim, it displeased him, and he took his father's hand to move it from Ephraim's head to Manasseh's head. And Joseph said to his father, "Not this way, my father; since this one is the firstborn, put your right hand on his head." But his father refused and said, "I know, my son, I know. He also shall become a people, and he also shall be great. Nevertheless, his younger brother shall be greater than he, and his offspring shall become a multitude of nations." So he blessed them that day, saying, "By you Israel will pronounce blessings, saying, 'God make you as Ephraim and as Manasseh.'" Thus he put Ephraim before Manasseh.

Then Israel said to Joseph, "Behold, I am about to die, but God will be with you and will bring you again to the land of your fathers. Moreover, I have given to you rather than to your brothers one mountain slope that I took from the hand of the Amorites with my sword and with my bow."

Genesis 48:8–22

Joseph had brought his sons to see his dying father, not simply to pay a visit, but to receive a blessing from him. It is hard for us to enter into all that this meant, since a "blessing" in the book of Genesis went far beyond a prayer for God's favor upon on an individual. It was far more than an expression of good wishes or a positive affirmation from a parent to a child. While these things have their own importance, the essence of blessing in the book of Genesis is very different.

Here, the goodness of God is made evident in any and every aspect of life, in tangible ways—crops, family, protection from enemies, or good health. Blessings could be spoken with great power by a responsible person, because they were the result of God's promise. As Gordon Wenham observes, "Where modern man speaks of success, Old Testament man talked of blessing."[10] To be blessed by someone who had received God's covenant promises was more of a prophecy than a prayer, since the "blesser" was viewed as speaking in God's name and guided by God's Spirit. Jacob was such a person. No wonder this moment was important to Joseph!

Jacob's initial question seems strange. Why, as he looked at his grandsons, did he suddenly ask, "Who are these?" (48:8). We will be told shortly that his eyes "were dim with age" (48:9), so it may be that he genuinely was unable to identify Joseph's sons. This seems unlikely, however, in light of verse 5.

It has been suggested, more plausibly, that this was a ceremonial statement rather than a genuine question. For example, when the minister asks, in many marriage ceremonies, "Who gives this woman in marriage to this man?" it is a ritual statement, rather than an actual question. In response to Jacob's query, Joseph identified the two as his sons, and Jacob asked him to bring the young men to him, "that I may bless them" (48:9). As Wenham observes, "Jacob, who was so anxious at his father's deathbed to acquire blessing for himself, is now just as keen to pass it on to his descendants before he dies."[11]

The next moments were filled with deep emotion for Jacob. Having hugged and kissed his grandsons, who would by this time be about twenty years old, he turned to Joseph and declared, "I never expected to see your face; and, behold, God has let me see your offspring also" (48:11). Joseph then carefully arranged the young men, apparently on their knees before Jacob's bed, with Manasseh, the oldest, opposite Jacob's right hand, and Ephraim in front of Jacob's left hand. Joseph fully expected Jacob to follow the conventional order, giving the oldest son the primary blessing, signified by his right hand.

But Jacob confounded Joseph, crossing his hands so that Ephraim was under his right hand as he pronounced the blessing. Right after he finished, Joseph objected, perhaps seeing in this action the confusion of a senile old man. Joseph tried to switch his father's hands to the conventional order, and have his father replay the bestowal of blessing. But Jacob refused. His hand-crossing had not been an example of carelessness, but the prophetic action of a spiritually sensitive man. As was so often the case, God had plans that went against cultural customs and the conventional ordering of things.

Before Jacob's birth, the Lord had made it clear to his mother Rebekah that she was carrying twins—but contrary to expectations, "the older shall serve the younger" (Genesis 25:23). This had proven to be the case, when Jacob received the promise. The pattern of "birth order reversal" occurs regularly in Genesis: the firstborn is passed by (as in the cases of Cain and Ishmael, for example), and will be repeated in Jacob's blessing of his sons in Genesis 49, when Reuben, the oldest, is denied firstborn status (1 Chronicles 5:1–2).

Led by the Lord, Jacob recognized that it was God's purpose that "his younger brother shall be greater than he" (Genesis 48:19). As biblical scholar Victor Hamilton observes, "Jacob may be losing his sight, but he is not losing his insight."[12] In the course of events, Ephraim did become the more important and numerous of the two tribes, at times the major rival to the tribe of Judah. For example, Joshua, Israel's leader after the death of Moses, the man who leads the people into the Promised Land, will be a man from Ephraim (1 Chronicles 7:20–27).

In Jacob's act of blessing Ephraim, the writer of Hebrews sees the primary display of genuine faith in Jacob's life: "By faith, Jacob, when dying, blessed the sons of Joseph, bowing in worship over the head of his staff" (Hebrews 11:21). Jacob had certainly spoken about the past, about Rachel's death and the loss of Joseph, but he was not delving into nostalgia as aging people often do. Rather, he had his eyes on God's future, showing his descendants that they were called to be merely sojourners in Egypt, ready to set out when God called them to go. That spirit of forward-looking faith was embodied in the words of blessing with which Jacob had blessed Joseph and, through him, his sons in Genesis 48:15–16.

These are words of a man who has spiritually matured, a man quite different than one who had chosen to grumble about the hardship of his life when he first stood before Pharaoh in Genesis 47:9. His words now convey a testimony of faith worth pondering:

> "The God before whom my fathers Abraham and Isaac walked, the God who has been my shepherd all my life long to this day, the angel who has redeemed me from all evil, bless the boys; and in them let my name be carried on, and the name of my fathers Abraham and Isaac; and let them grow into a multitude in the midst of the earth."

Jacob was not content simply to pronounce a blessing. For Joseph's sons to have the spoken blessing without knowledge of the One from whom it came would be a tragedy, not a gift. So Jacob bore witness to what he had learned about the living God, who was the source and basis of the blessing, and into whose hands he was entrusting the young men.

First, Jacob indicated that *God is the promise-keeping God*, who keeps His covenant across the generations, "the God before whom my fathers Abraham and Isaac walked." Jacob was looking back on the time the Lord had appeared to the ninety-nine-year-old Abraham with the command, "I am God Almighty; walk before me, and be blameless, that I may make my covenant between me and you" (Genesis 17:1–2). Clearly, this is not a call to live sinlessly, for neither Abraham nor Isaac came close to such a standard. But it was a call to "orient one's entire life to his presence, promises, and demands."[13]

The patriarchs were weak men, but the Lord had enabled them to live faithful lifestyles. Jacob's own path had hardly been without spectacular failures, yet he had consistently returned to the place of living before God. Jacob wanted his descendants to know that they were recipients of a double legacy, that of the kept promises of their covenant God and the faithful lifestyle of their ancestors. Since the Lord had been the faithful God of Abraham, Isaac, and

Jacob, he would also be the faithful God of Joseph, Ephraim, and Manasseh—as well as the trustworthy God of all the generations that would follow.

More personally, Jacob wanted Joseph's sons to know that *our God is a faithful shepherd*, "the God who has been my shepherd all my life long to this day" (48:15). Jacob had lived all his life around sheep—he knew only too well their straying ways and their constant need of provision and protection. Jacob himself had been proven to be remarkably sheep-like in his wandering, yet he had been given the divine promise, "I am with you and will keep you wherever you go" (28:15).

Time and again, this shepherd had reached into Jacob's life to rescue, protect, discipline, or provide for him. To call the Lord his shepherd, as Jacob looked back over the long sweep of his life, was to confess both his own "sheep-ness" and to celebrate the Lord's provision for him. This is the first time in Scripture that God is given the name "shepherd," a metaphor that will capture the imagination of a much later shepherd, King David, who celebrated in Psalm 23 that "the LORD is my shepherd" (v. 1). Even more significantly, the Lord Jesus would take this title to new heights when He declared to His people, "I am the good shepherd. The good shepherd lays down his life for the sheep. . . . I am the good shepherd. I know my own, and my own know me" (John 10:11, 14).

Those are truths about our triune God that sustain us through the hardest of times. Sometimes well-meaning Christians tell us, in our suffering or confusion, "God will never give you more than you can handle." With all due respect, that is pious sounding nonsense.[14] The great apostle Paul declared of himself, "We were so utterly burdened beyond our strength that we despaired of life itself" (2 Corinthians 1:8). However, his deep sense of insecurity and insufficiency was accompanied by an even greater recognition: "That was to make us rely not on ourselves but on God who raises the dead. He delivered us from such a deadly peril, and He will deliver us" (2 Corinthians 1:9–10). Paul's secret was not that *he* had the strength, but that he had a reliable, available, and more-than-adequate Shepherd.

God's promise, Jacob had come to know, was not that we will never face a problem we can't handle, but that "even though I walk through the valley of the shadow of death, I will fear no evil, for you [the shepherd] are with me" (Psalm 23:4). I cannot say how much that promise, which I memorized as a little boy, came to mean to me and my entire family—Janice most of all—as we walked through death's shadowy valley with her. It was both the promise and the presence of the Good Shepherd, through both the indwelling Holy Spirit and the love and care of His people, that sustained us. And now Janice is dwelling in the house of the Lord forever, just as He promised (Psalm 23:6)!

A third great truth Jacob wanted his boys to know is that *our God is a redeeming God*: "the angel who has redeemed me from all evil" (48:16). Calling God an "angel" seems strange, until we remember that it was as the angel of the Lord that God had appeared to Jacob (see Genesis 31:11–13).

Clearly, Jacob does not mean that the Lord had protected him from all evil or hardship. He had been the victim of his father's favoritism, his brother's Esau's murderous anger, his uncle Laban's deceptions, and his own sons' treachery. He had suffered both the loss of his beloved wife and her beloved son, and he had managed to bring down on himself innumerable difficulties caused by his own sinful actions. No, Jacob was speaking a greater truth—that the Lord had been at work to redeem those very evils and hardships.[15]

Standing in front of Jacob was the clearest evidence of God's sovereign power over even the worst of evils—Joseph, the lost son, the victim of his brothers' wickedness, who had become the savior of the family and the nations around Egypt. It is important to note, however, that only time could reveal how God was redeeming Jacob from the evil done to Joseph—it had seemed anything but redemptive for twenty-two long years.

So it is with us. Sometimes we can look back and see the mysterious way God's tapestry has become beautiful in spite of some very dark threads. Even now, we can see evidence of the Lord bringing good out of the bad of Janice's suffering. But, more often than not, only eternity will reveal how God has redeemed every evil we have known. In the interim, we walk by faith, not sight, because we know that He is unfailingly with us and for us in Christ.

Jacob has spoken from his heart, bearing witness to his son and grandsons about the majestic character of his God. The fact that we have these words recorded for us in Scripture is evidence that Jacob's descendants not only remembered them, they repeated them to others. There is an important message here for me as I advance into my senior years: I don't want those who come after me to remember my complaints and criticisms about life and people. My hope is rather that they will remember my declarations of praise to my gracious God, and the satisfaction of having trusted His promises and experienced His faithfulness.

When Jacob pronounced his blessings on Joseph and his boys, he was not thinking about their success and status in Egypt. His focus was on the privilege of their participation in the great covenant promises God had first made to Abraham, which would lead to the Jacob family growing "into a multitude in the midst of the earth" (Genesis 48:16). Even more importantly, that blessing would lead to the Good Shepherd, the Redeemer who would pay the price of sin and evil by His death on the cross.

Jacob had one final piece of business as the end of Joseph's visit drew near. Once again, he had eyes on the future and on the promises of God, so he would not let Joseph himself believe that Egypt was the family's destiny. By this time, Joseph had lived for thirty-nine years in Egypt. He had had his family there, and made his fame, fortune, and career there. Humanly speaking, the good life for Joseph and his sons would be Egyptian. But with all of the force and solemnity of a dying man, Jacob pressed the point on Joseph and his sons: "Behold, I am about to die, but God will be with you and will bring you again to the land of your fathers." (48:21; the word *you* here is plural). Jacob's descendants must never allow this vision of their destiny to die.

There is one final word for Joseph himself, Jacob's last will and testament: "I have given to you rather than to your brothers one mountain slope that I took from the hand of the Amorites with my sword and with my bow" (48:22). There is a mystery about this bequest—we know nothing of the events by which Jacob came into ownership of the mountain ridge of which he speaks, or even which ridge it is. The fact that Joseph was eventually buried at Shechem (Joshua 24:32) suggests it was located there.

But Joseph was a rich man—he hardly needed a "place" in Canaan, when the riches of Egypt were at his disposal. *The purpose of this gift wasn't to enrich Joseph, but to implant in his mind Jacob's absolute certainty that God could be trusted to keep His promises.* Many families have keepsakes, passed from generation to generation, to remind them of who they are and where they came from. That small plot of land was Jacob's keepsake, entrusted to his son, to keep alive the hope that God would do just what He said He would.

Jacob's bedroom was holy ground for Joseph. For years he had yearned to be with his father, and now the Lord had granted him the privilege of hearing Jacob speak of the most precious and personal things in his life. I remember a car ride with my father, not long before he died, when he spoke more personally and intimately than I had ever experienced, about his love for his Lord, his wife, and his family. Moments like that shape a man and his values.

My father had passed the baton to me years earlier, but that car ride was a significant time of confirming that I was now the one holding the baton for the next generation. Jacob's life had been full of ups and downs, but beyond question he knew the calling of God on his life—he was part of the Abraham family, and he knew the God who had called him, the Shepherd-Redeemer who would be with him even as he entered the "valley of the shadow of death." Now it was Joseph's turn, as God's runner, carrying the baton of the Abrahamic covenant toward generations yet to come.

FIFTEEN

GOD'S MYSTERIOUS WAYS

The sixteenth century was a difficult and dangerous time for Christians in England.

In the 1530s, King Henry VIII had a king-sized problem. He longed for a male heir that his present wife had proven unable to give him. But the pope, representing the Catholic church, refused to grant the king a divorce. Driven by anger and his adulterous lust for Anne Boleyn, Henry declared himself head of the Church in England, severing all ties with the pope. He still held to Catholic doctrines, but this split allowed believers captured by the truth of the Reformation to gain increasing influence in the country.

When Henry died, his nine-year-old son Edward (born of the third of Henry's six wives) came to the throne, and during his time, the church moved in a strongly Protestant direction. It was a short breath of spring, though. Edward survived only six years, followed on the throne by his half-sister, Mary, a devoted Catholic determined to return England to submission to Rome and the Pope. She unleashed a reign of terror which resulted in more than three hundred Protestant clergymen being burned at the stake for their loyalty to Christ and His gospel, while hundreds of others fled to the Continent seeking refuge.

One of the men caught up in this persecution was Bernard Gilpin, a pastor in northern England. He had begun as dogmatically Catholic himself, but through study of God's Word and interactions with those who had discovered the truth of the gospel, came to saving faith in Christ. No part of God's Word was more important to Gilpin than the apostle Paul's great declaration in Romans 8:28, "And we know that for those who love God all things work together for good." That truth so gripped Gilpin that he became known for his characteristic response to even the most difficult circumstances: "God's will be done; all is for the best."

One day a detachment of soldiers arrived at Gilpin's church, carrying orders to arrest him and take him to London to stand trial. It was a process certain to result in his death. As the soldiers arrested Gilpin, they taunted him with his own words: "I suppose this is for the best, too." He responded that he was sure that it would be. When townspeople heard the news, scores gathered tearfully at the church to bid him farewell, convinced they would never again see him alive. "Don't be afraid for me," Gilpin told them. "The will of God be done. All is for the best."

Over the next two days, sneering soldiers threw the pastor's words into his face with every opportunity, and on the second night, their derision soared when Gilpin's horse bolted as he was dismounting. His foot caught in the stirrup, Gilpin was dragged a considerable distance and seriously injured. A doctor diagnosed a broken leg, a condition requiring Gilpin to have the fracture set and then to be immobilized for a period of time. Looking at the minister as he writhed in pain, the soldiers' captain said with a smirk, "I suppose this is all for the best too." To which Gilpin again answered, "I have no doubt but that it is."

Recuperation took several weeks, but the inevitable day came when the doctor declared Gilpin well enough to travel. The captain announced that Gilpin would leave for London the next morning; within days, the pastor would make his long-delayed appearance before the court. But at daybreak, just as they were preparing to leave, riders brought the message that Queen Mary had died. A new monarch, Elizabeth, had come to the throne, decreeing that there should be no more burnings of Protestants and no further restrictions on their message.[1] Gilpin was suddenly free, a turn of events that would have led a less godly man to say, "I told you so!"

There are only a few times in life when the connection between our suffering and God's purposes becomes quite so clear! More often, God's purposes are shrouded in mystery. Afterward, looking back, we may be able to detect a pattern and purpose in what transpired. The trouble is, of course, that we need to live our lives looking forward, so we continually find ourselves walking into the fog of mystery, not clarity. Or, to put it in biblical language, we walk by faith, not by sight (2 Corinthians 5:7).

I don't know the reason for my daughter's brain cancer or why it took her from her children far too early. I don't know why some of my friends have had to go through terrible experiences of rape, betrayal, physical abuse, infertility, or the loss of a loved one. I don't understand why people I care about are enduring heartbreaking diagnoses, crippling disabilities, terrible illnesses, and financial perils. But I do know the One who is the Good Shepherd, who entered into our world of brokenness, sin, and suffering to demonstrate both His love and His power.

An old proverb observes, "The same sun that hardens the clay melts the wax." That is a vivid way of saying what we have all seen: experiences that break some people make others. Some become grim; others become gracious. Some grow; others shrivel. A closer look shows that the difference isn't so much about what is happening *to* us, as it is about what is happening *in* us.

All of us will at various times undergo hardships and problems, but there is no necessary connection between the intensity of our difficulties and the outcome in our lives. Over the years, I have been humbled and challenged by the special beauty of people who have endured long seasons in the school of deep suffering. While many people would become rigid and resentful, these have come through resilient and refreshing. Life makes some people wise; others just become weary.

What a long and winding road we have traveled with Joseph, a journey that has taken us quite literally from the pit to the palace.

Through it all he stands out as one of the most attractive figures in the Bible, a man who overcame traumatic circumstances that would have crushed, or at least crippled, most people.

Joseph lived a remarkably healthy and attractive life, one that certainly wasn't due to a warm, nurturing environment. Born into a badly broken, dysfunctional family; deprived of his mother's love through her untimely death when he was a young teenager; hated with murderous jealousy by his brothers; kidnapped, falsely accused, and imprisoned—all of these things could have made Joseph a prime candidate for brokenness and bitterness. Instead, he emerged as a healthy, godly, and productive man.

God's hand was clearly on Joseph, protecting and preserving him through those troubled times. At the very lowest points of his life, recorded in Genesis 39, we read four times that "the LORD was with" Joseph (vv. 2, 3, 21, 23). God's presence was a potent part of Joseph's survival, but he himself had a critical role to play. Perhaps the most important characteristic of the man was the God-centered, God-trusting perspective we see him cultivating at every stage of his journey. He allowed God to be God in his life, even though there was no way Joseph could have deduced how the Lord would construct something good out of all those broken pieces and fragments.

To see both God's mysterious ways and what it means to live with a God-centered perspective, let's turn to two events, separated by about fifty years, at the very end of the account of Joseph's life.

"God Meant It for Good"

Thus his sons did for him as he had commanded them, for his sons carried him to the land of Canaan and buried him in the cave of the field at Machpelah, to the east of Mamre, which Abraham bought with the field from Ephron the Hittite to possess as a burying place. After he had buried his father, Joseph returned to Egypt with his brothers and all who had gone up with him to bury his father.

When Joseph's brothers saw that their father was dead, they said, "It may be that Joseph will hate us and pay us back for all the evil that we did to him." So they sent a message to Joseph, saying, "Your father gave this command before he died: 'Say to Joseph, "Please forgive the transgression of your brothers and their sin, because they did evil to you.'" And now, please forgive the transgression of the servants of the God of your father." Joseph wept when they spoke to him. His brothers also came and fell down before him and said, "Behold, we are your servants." But Joseph said to them, "Do not fear, for am I in the place of God? As for you, you meant evil against me, but God meant it for good, to bring it about that many people should be kept alive, as they are today. So do not fear; I will provide for you and your little ones." Thus he comforted them and spoke kindly to them.

Genesis 50:12–21

Jacob was determined to be buried in Canaan, not Egypt. He had stated that desire very clearly, first to Joseph (Genesis 47:29–31), then later to all his sons. On his deathbed, Jacob issued a command, not a request: "I am to be gathered to my people; bury me with my fathers in the cave that is in the field of Ephron the Hittite, in the cave that is in the field at Machpelah, to the east of Mamre, in the land of Canaan, which Abraham bought with the field from Ephron the Hittite to possess as a burying place" (49:29–30). This was a dying statement of faith, a declaration of his confidence that the promise-making, covenant-keeping God would bring his descendants back to the Promised Land.

God would also grant that land to the children of Israel as their national possession, so Jacob's burial wishes were a powerful incentive for his descendants to trust those same promises and that same faithful God for themselves. Egypt may have become the land of prosperity for his family; it would never be the land of promise.

Care for the dead, especially people of importance, was a state industry in Egypt, one to which pyramids and mummies continue to bear witness. Although Jacob was a foreign refugee, the fact that he was the father of Joseph made his death a state occasion. In contrast to the Egyptians, Israelites simply wrapped their dead in a shroud and placed them in a grave or cave.[2] But, given Jacob's request and Joseph's importance, this body was given special care: Joseph ordered physicians to embalm Jacob's body, something done only for those of special status because the process required forty days to complete.

Concurrent with the embalming was a public period of mourning, one that lasted seventy days. This indicates something of the enormously high regard in which Jacob, as Joseph's father, was held. Pharaohs were mourned publicly for seventy-two days! When the period of state mourning concluded, Joseph led a huge funeral entourage north to Canaan. Accompanied by "a very great company" of state officials (50:9), Joseph made his way to Hebron to entomb Jacob's body with his family, in careful compliance with his wishes.

Those who have gone through times of mourning know that, immediately following death, there are a multitude of details to be addressed, work that numbs us from feeling the full force of bereavement. Then, after all the funeral events have finished and friends return to their routines, the reality of the "new normal" rushes in. Something like that seems to have happened to Joseph's brothers.

On their return from Hebron to Goshen, they grew nervous about the possibility of Joseph taking revenge for their betrayal of him forty years earlier. Joseph had done nothing to deserve such suspicion, but the brothers feared that Jacob's passing had removed a buffer between them and Joseph. This is not uncommon—my pastoral experience over four decades tells me that the death of a parent who was the glue of a family often exposes weaknesses, cracks and fissures that lie hidden very close to the surface of the family's life.

There is a huge difference between knowing one's guilt and confessing that guilt to the offended party. Joseph's brothers had spoken about their guilt to one another, but there is no record that they ever openly acknowledged to Joseph himself what they had done—or directly asked for his forgiveness. (There is also an immense difference between being forgiven and personally accepting and embracing such forgiveness.)

So, once again, the old elephant of their sin against Joseph filled the room. Without Jacob's mediation, the brothers felt helpless before the powerful Joseph. His treatment of them had always seemed too good to be true; surely now, they imagined, he would retaliate. As they said to one another, "It may be that Joseph will hate us and pay us back for all the evil that we did to him" (50:15).

Their father was dead and gone, their guilt wasn't. Jacob's oldest sons had no doubt about the nature of their actions against their brother; they had been evil. Their guilty consciences were replaying their instinctive response years earlier, a time they had found themselves in a difficult situation: "In truth we are guilty concerning our brother" (42:21).

For seventeen years Joseph had treated his brothers with great grace, without the slightest evidence of hatred or retaliation. Their guilty consciences, however, made it impossible for them to accept his many kindnesses at face value. Now full of fear, they fell back on the pattern of years before when they had blatantly deceived their father.

Afraid to approach Joseph directly, they sent him a contrived message, claiming it was a command their father issued on his deathbed: "Say to Joseph, 'Please forgive the transgression of your brothers, and their sin, because they did evil to you.' And now, please forgive the transgressions of the servants of the God of your father" (50:17). Beyond question, this is a despicable fabrication born of cowardice. If Jacob had felt a need to say any such thing, he would certainly have said it directly to Joseph, not indirectly through the brothers.[3] And the claim to be "the servants of the God of your father" was an attempt to cloak their deception with piety.

But, while the story itself was an invention, their description of their treatment of Joseph was honest and true. What they had done was indeed transgression, sin, and evil. They had finally admitted—without excuse or rationalization—the shameful wrong they had suppressed for forty years.

Joseph wept as he heard their message, his grief compounded when the brothers bowed down before him in humility and presented themselves as his servants. (Again the old dream emerges!) Undoubtedly, Joseph's tears flowed from a variety of sources—places in his heart made newly tender by reliving their cruelty; frustration over their openly expressed doubt of his honesty and integrity after he had said he'd forgiven them; anguish over their continued distrust as well as the pain and fear that they were still needlessly carrying. They had been dragging this corpse of their guilt for so many years.

We learn some important lessons here. Genuine forgiveness—the kind that produces real reconciliation—requires honest and heartfelt acknowledgment by both parties of the sin that has occurred. This had only happened in part years before. Judah had modeled repentance, but apparently hadn't confessed his guilt explicitly. For true healing, such an admission needs to be direct and clear.

A famous athlete, notorious for attempting to cover his use of performance-enhancing drugs, released a written apology saying he took "full responsibility for the mistakes that led to my suspension." As I read that, I inwardly groaned. The man hadn't merely made mistakes—he had engaged in prolonged, intentional, and extensive violations of the rules of his sport. And labeling these violations as "mistakes" circumvented the central issue: What had he actually done? What exactly were those mysterious "mistakes" this man claimed to take responsibility for? He was still covering and hiding, using weasel words and legalese.

It is much harder to speak the truth: "I sinned when I committed this act." But only such honest confession will enable the offended to really forgive and the offender to embrace that forgiveness.

In light of some modern ideas, it is important to note that the brothers' problem wasn't that they couldn't "forgive themselves." The problem was that they wouldn't and didn't believe Joseph, the one against whom they had sinned, when he had forgiven them and treated them with amazing grace. If this is important on the horizontal level, it is even more significant in our vertical relationship with God.

Joseph's response to his brothers was full of grace and theological insight, as relevant for us as it was for them. Rather than reacting to their fears and foolishness, he responded with mature, godly wisdom.

First, *Joseph calmed their fears*: "Do not fear" (50:19). This is more than a cliché, since he repeats it in verse 21, and the writer of Genesis goes on to tell us that "he comforted them and spoke kindly to them." Though Joseph was in a position of absolute power over his brothers, he chose to be a servant leader, not a self-gratifying one. Since the reunion, all of Joseph's actions had been guided by the conviction that "God sent me before you to preserve for you a remnant on earth" (Genesis 45:7). He knew himself to be called by God to serve God's purposes, not to indulge his resentments or seek revenge for his grievances.

Second, *Joseph refused to play God*: "Am I in the place of God?" (50:19). Joseph truly knew what it was to live *coram Deo*, a Latin expression meaning "before the face of God" or "in the presence of

God," under His authority and for His glory. We saw Joseph doing that when he resisted the seduction of Potiphar's wife, and later when he was summoned before Pharaoh. Now he takes the same posture as he deals with his brothers. As a renowned pastor of an earlier time, Griffith Thomas, observed, "The name of God was often on his lips, but still better, the presence of God and the fear of God were always in his heart."[4]

Joseph had undeniable power over Egypt and also over his brothers. In human terms, he was almost beyond accountability, standing only before Pharaoh to give an account for his actions. But Joseph knew himself to be constantly standing and acting before the living and true God. Because he was both accountable to God and confident in Him, Joseph was fully able to leave the righting of wrongs in the Lord's hands, not to take vengeance into his own (Romans 12:19).

Third, *Joseph rested in the mysterious sovereignty of God*: "As for you, you meant evil against me, but God meant it for good, to bring it about that many people should be kept alive, as they are today" (50:20). This remarkable statement is the great biblical example of what theologians call *concursus*,[5] the mysterious way in which human choices and God's sovereign purposes work together in the outworking of events to God's appointed ends.

Joseph was forthright about the brothers' complicity in what had happened: "You meant evil against me." He did not back away from their description of what they had done—it had indeed been transgression, sin, and evil. They had not been coerced into acting badly; they had done it eagerly, willingly, actively. It was fully their sin, flowing out of their sinful hearts. Yet, remarkably, the very events the brothers intended for evil, God was intending for good. Through and in it all, He had been invisibly at work, bringing about exactly what He wanted, so that Joseph was elevated to the highest position in Egypt. God had not merely permitted the brothers' sin—He had acted in and through it, and the result was blessing for the nations, with human lives saved during a disastrous famine.

On a larger scale, all these things had transpired so that God's people, who would become the nation of Israel, might be physically kept alive, transferred to Egypt as He had indicated to Abraham years before (15:13–16). There He would begin to fulfill the promise of making Abraham's family the great nation He intended them to become (46:3–4). Joseph saw the hand of God at work all along the twisting pathway of his life. As one commentator has said, "What became of Joseph in Egypt was the handiwork of God, too great for him to have accomplished alone. Evil succumbs to God's gracious purposes."[6]

This mysterious weaving of human evil into God's purposes, so that He alone is sovereign, is vividly seen in other places in Scripture. Satan intended the evils he brought against Job for evil, to cause him to curse God; God intended those very things for Job's ultimate good (Job 1:2–2:10; 42:10–17). Paul describes a painful physical problem as "a messenger of Satan," obviously intended by Satan for evil effects in Paul's life. But Paul also recognized it as God's gracious gift, to keep him humble and deepen his confidence that God's grace was sufficient for any and every situation (2 Corinthians 12:7–10). Most of all, evil men and Satan conspired to crucify the Lord Jesus, yet at the same time He was "delivered up according to the definite plan and foreknowledge of God" to bring about our salvation (Acts 2:23; 4:27–28). In none of these cases should we minimize the evil or the pain involved, but neither should we deny the sovereignty of our gracious God.

At times, our experience may resemble that of Joseph's, so that we can look back and seek the outworking of God's purpose. The Lord allowed Joseph to live long enough to see how many of the puzzle pieces of his life fit together in God's plan. More often, however, our experience will resemble Job's. When we read his story, we know exactly why those catastrophic disasters kept falling upon him, though Job was never given that privilege. It was not until Job finally entered the Lord's presence that he would have seen how, in all things, God was at work for good in his life (Romans 8:28).

Most of us will need to wait for heaven to see how the tapestry of our lives, with all its dark and bright threads, was woven. We read Romans 8:28 with hope, but at present we cling to the majestic verses that follow that great statement: "If God is for us, who can be against us?" (8:31); "Nothing in all creation will be able to separate us from the love of God in Christ Jesus our Lord" (8:39).

Finally, *Joseph continued to love his brothers graciously and generously*: "So do not fear; I will provide for you and your little ones" (Genesis 50:21). He had been caring for his extended family for the past seventeen years. The death of his father would not change anything in his family relationship. Joseph had forgiven, fully and deeply, and because of that he was able to look forward, without reopening old wounds.

Joseph and His Bones

> So Joseph remained in Egypt, he and his father's house. Joseph lived 110 years. And Joseph saw Ephraim's children of the third generation. The children also of Machir the son of Manasseh were counted as Joseph's own. And Joseph said to his brothers, "I am about to die, but God will visit you and bring you up out of this land to the land that he swore to Abraham, to Isaac, and to Jacob." Then Joseph made the sons of Israel swear, saying, "God will surely visit you, and you shall carry up my bones from here." So Joseph died, being 110 years old. They embalmed him, and he was put in a coffin in Egypt.
>
> Genesis 50:22–26

We are given no information about the remaining fifty years of Joseph's life, until we come to this deathbed scene. He had been seventeen when he entered the country as a slave; thirty when his life had been transformed by Pharaoh's remarkable elevation; thirty-nine when his brothers had reentered his life and the family had moved to Egypt; and fifty-six at the time of his father's death. Then the Bible account goes silent until Joseph was 110, the ideal lifespan in Egyptian culture.

Joseph was, in many ways, deeply Egyptianized. He had lived in the country for more than ninety years, and possessed an Egyptian name, an Egyptian wife, Egyptian descendants, an Egyptian title, and an Egyptian lifestyle. But those were external things—at the core of his being, Joseph knew himself to be part of God's people. The defining truth of his life was God's call upon him, a call that made him see himself as a citizen of another kingdom, a recipient of different and better promises than anything Pharaoh could provide.

We are told that Joseph ultimately lived to see three generations of his son Ephraim's descendants, as well as those of Manasseh, an

259

indicator of the flourishing of the family numerically (Exodus 1:1–7). Aware that death was drawing near, Joseph summoned his family to him.[7] His goal was not merely to express his last wishes, but to make a statement of faith, pointing his family one last time to God and his promises: "I am about to die, but God will visit you and bring you up out of this land to the land that he swore to Abraham, to Isaac, and to Jacob" (Genesis 50:24).

Having lived his own life *coram Deo*, he longed for his family to live the same way—in the presence of their covenant God, trusting His promises. The expression "God will visit you" conveys the idea that He would take care of and pay special attention to the family, and would intervene to bring them to the land that He had promised. The same word *visit* will reappear in the book of Exodus as its great events began to unfold (Exodus 4:31).

The promise was based not on the family's merits, but on their God's unconditional and gracious promise. From all appearances, Joseph had been the family's protector and provider in Egypt. But their true protector and provider, El Shaddai, would remain long after Joseph's departure. Joseph would have agreed with the inscription on the tomb of John and Charles Wesley in Westminster Abbey: "God buries his workmen, but carries on his work."

Joseph had a specific request to make of his family, one similar to that made by his father. And, like Jacob, he considered the request so sacred that he insisted his family take an oath to fulfill it: "God will surely visit you, and you shall carry up my bones from here" (Genesis 50:25). This was a remarkable request, since Joseph was almost certainly due an extravagant state funeral in Egypt, followed by interment in a monument of great public prestige. Instead, "they embalmed him, and he was put in a coffin in Egypt" (50:26), apparently unburied, at least in a normal way.

To the very end, Joseph remained completely convinced that Egypt was not his true homeland, no matter how much he had prospered there. Nor was Egypt his family's ultimate destiny. God would certainly keep His promises regarding His people's own land. It is understandable, then, that the writer of Hebrews saw Joseph's final request as the epitome of his faith: "By faith Joseph, at the end of his life, made mention of the exodus of the Israelites and gave directions concerning his bones" (Hebrews 11:22). His dying words were the product of an undying faith.

That simple request planted a seed deep in the hearts of the children of Israel, one that endured down through the centuries. Joseph's coffin must have been located somewhere in their Egyptian homeland of Goshen, where everyone could see it and be reminded of its significance for their future. It served not as a symbol of death, but as a beacon of hope—even amid the troubles that came upon Joseph's descendants, as Egyptian policy reduced them from favored residents to distrusted slaves.

On the first Passover night, despite all the urgent preparations and endless details to address to get the Israelites out of Egypt before Pharaoh changed his mind, we are told that "Moses took the bones of Joseph with him, for Joseph had made the sons of Israel solemnly swear" (Exodus 13:19). Then, for more than forty years, the Israelites carried that coffin through the wilderness and finally into the Promised Land, under the leadership of Joshua.

At the very end of the book that bears Joshua's name we are told, "As for the bones of Joseph, which the people of Israel brought up from Egypt, they buried them at Shechem, in the piece of land that Jacob bought from the sons of Hamor the father of Shechem for a hundred pieces of money. It became an inheritance of the descendants of Joseph" (Joshua 24:32). Joseph's body was home at last.

But he had reached his true homeland much earlier. The Old Testament throws a veil over death, giving only glimpses of what precisely happened when an Old Testament believer died. That veil was removed by the Lord Jesus, "who abolished death and brought life and immortality to light through the gospel" (2 Timothy 1:10). The writer of Hebrews makes it clear that the true longing of Joseph, as well as the other patriarchs, wasn't just for earthly homeland: "They desire a better country, that is, a heavenly one. Therefore God is not ashamed to be called their God, for he has prepared for them a city" (Hebrews 11:16).

When he died, Joseph entered "the city that has foundations, whose designer and builder is God" (Hebrews 11:10). That was by God's grace, and through the substitutionary death of Joseph's greatest descendant, the Lord Jesus.

Our daughter Janice died at home. After her second surgery, with its devastating side effects, she spent a month in a rehabilitation hospital, then came back to our house, where she had been since her first operation. This time was different. Within a few weeks, it became evident that her cancer was growing rapidly, and we made the difficult decision to put Janice under hospice care.

Her last weeks were simultaneously precious and heartbreaking. Leaving her children was agonizing for Janice, but at the same time, she had a robust faith in the Lord. As she put it, "I haven't always loved Christians, but I've always loved Jesus!" Caring for our daughter in her dying weakness was something Elizabeth and I had certainly never expected to do. But when it became necessary, we experienced the enormous privilege of surrounding her with our love and care, doing our best to meet her needs.

Janice was slipping away from us as the brain tumor impacted more and more of her faculties. It is common to speak about "dying with dignity," but there is, in one sense, no dignity in death—it is the great enemy. Yet the Lord Jesus has made the death of Christians qualitatively different, through His death and resurrection. So, amid the sadness and the suffering, there were moments of exquisite beauty and amazing grace which the Lord gave to her and to us. Overriding everything was the certainty that for Janice, absence from the body would mean presence with the Lord in her new home (2 Corinthians 5:8). Had we been unable to share those last moments with Janice, we would have missed so much.

The night before she passed, Janice rallied her strength for a time. Her children, her sister, and her mother and I gathered around the bed to sing, pray, and express our love. With her last words she responded to her daughter's "I love you" with a faintly whispered "Love you too." Then she lapsed into unconsciousness.

I sat by her bed, praying, singing and reading God's Word to her. Then her mother and sister took their turns, sharing their love and our shared hope in Christ, deep into the night. When I awoke very early, I discovered that only moments before the Lord had taken Janice to her eternal home.

The Heidelberg Confession begins with a question which has special relevance for such a time: "What is your only comfort in life and in death?" The answer is both wonderful and biblical: "That I am not my own, but belong—body and soul, in life and in death—to my faithful Savior, Jesus Christ. He has fully paid for all my sins with His precious blood. . . . Because I belong to Him, Christ, by His Holy Spirit, assures me of eternal life." That is the confidence we have in Christ, and, in the presence of death, it is a great comfort indeed. Janice died in her earthly father's house; she now lives in her eternal Father's house, where her Lord and Savior Jesus Christ had already prepared a place for her.

We do not think often enough about heaven. The busyness of life, the demands of daily living, and the enticements of this world distract us from raising our eyes to think about "what God has prepared for those who love Him" (1 Corinthians 2:9). But life's hard times—especially the times when death knocks on our door—shift our focus.

Hope has been described as "oxygen for the soul," and there are times that we need a hope far more substantial than an optimistic longing, some feeling that our wishes and desires could somehow come to pass. There is, Paul tells believers in Christ, a "hope laid up for you in heaven" (Colossians 1:5), a hope that "does not put us to shame" (Romans 5:5), because it is inseparably connected to God's sure promises and His love, "poured into our hearts through the Holy Spirit" (Romans 5:5). Therefore, Paul writes, "I consider that the sufferings of this present time are not worth comparing to the glory that is to be revealed to us" (Romans 8:18).

Because our union with Christ is stronger than the power of death, our immediate experience is "to depart and to be with Christ, for that is far better" (Philippians 1:23). For now, we are given only a glimpse of that immediate experience of God's presence. It is, the Lord Jesus tells us, being in "my Father's house" (John 14:2), a picture of safety, security, provision, and pleasure. As well, God's Word assures us, "Blessed are the dead who die in the Lord from now on . . . that they may rest from their labors" (Revelation 14:13).

That beatitude does not set before us a prospect of boring inactivity, but rather the promise of rest from our burdens, of relief from our weaknesses, and of rejoicing in our perfect surroundings, all while we actively serve our Lord. And even those things are only a prelude to our eternal experience, after we have received our resurrection bodies at the Lord's return, bodies perfectly designed to enjoy all the richness of "new heavens and a new earth in which righteousness dwells" (2 Peter 3:13). When I fill my heart with those truths, and think of all that my daughter is enjoying before me, my sadness at her absence is tinged with a new joy.

The book of Genesis begins with God's people in a garden in Paradise (Genesis 2–3); it ends with God's man in a coffin in Egypt. The book starts with the beauty of God's life; it ends with the ugly reality of death in a fallen world. But paradoxically, the coffin is a symbol of hope, a reminder of God's promises, a sign of redemption and deliverance. It is both a reminder of the reign of death brought into God's creation by sin, and a signal that death will not have the final word—that God's promise to Abraham will be fulfilled, along with the greater promise to Eve that a deliverer would come from her seed to crush the seducing serpent's head (Genesis 3:15).

The story of Joseph is a reminder that, although it may look like sin and death have had their way with God's world and people, God always has the final word. Great as Joseph was, there is a greater Joseph, born in fulfillment of the promise to Judah, and who, through death, would conquer death.

CONCLUSION

In his famous allegory of the Christian life, *The Pilgrim's Progress*, John Bunyan depicts death as the crossing of a river. I love his description of the death of a faithful believer named Valiant-for-Truth: "So he passed over, and all the trumpets sounded for him on the other side." Almost certainly Bunyan was thinking of the wonderful promise of 2 Peter 1:11 (NIV), "You will receive a rich welcome into the eternal kingdom of our Lord and Savior Jesus Christ."

The last verse of Genesis tells us that Joseph's body had been embalmed and placed in a coffin in Egypt—but we know that he himself had entered into the presence of his Lord. And I love to think of all the trumpets sounding for Joseph as the Lord greeted His faithful servant.

By any standard of measurement, Joseph lived a remarkable life. Born into the relational snake's nest of a polygamous family, he had begun life as the favored son of a powerful but misguided father. Then, when his mother died giving birth to his much younger brother, Joseph found himself the all-too-convenient target of his brothers' jealous hatred, an animosity inflamed by their father's foolish favoritism and Joseph's recounting of some rather startling dreams. On the brink of murdering Joseph, the brothers chose instead to sell him to some passing Bedouin traders, knowing he would end up in the slave markets of

Egypt. His future seemed hopeless—he would be a defenseless slave in an entirely alien culture.

But Joseph's obvious gifts and his remarkable character soon made him indispensable to his Egyptian owner. Unfortunately, they also made him irresistible to his master's wife. When her seductions failed, she retaliated by accusing him of trying to rape her. So Joseph found himself unjustly imprisoned, with thirteen years of his life stolen from him and no foreseeable way to a happy and meaningful future.

Then, overnight, everything changed. In an incredible reversal of fortunes, Joseph was elevated by the Pharaoh himself into the highest non-royal position in Egypt—one of the most powerful positions in the ancient world. Power, wealth, and prestige were now his in abundance. And in an even more remarkable change of events, the rejected brother became the agent of his entire family's deliverance from impending death, the means whereby they were resettled into a productive and prosperous existence in Egypt.

Joseph's life was far from ordinary. But what made it truly extraordinary was that, despite all external appearances, the hand of God had been constantly causing and controlling all that transpired. Joseph's was far more than a rags-to-riches story—while the story is his, it was written by God himself, with Joseph as a strategic figure in God's program of history that would one day culminate in the coming of God's Son, the Lord Jesus. So, while Joseph is front and center, offering us much to learn from the example of his life, the far more important lessons point us to the Lord himself.

As we look back over the Joseph story with all its bewildering twists and turns, what stands out is *the enduring faithfulness of a faithful and sovereign God*. It has been said that, while life must be lived going forward, it will be understood only when we look backward, after our journey is done. Knowing that our God is both faithful and sovereign enables us to keep moving forward, even when our pathway takes us through the darkest and hardest of places.

Suffering is an ever-present reality in a fallen world. Sometimes we suffer because we don't have what we want—something that seems precious is denied or taken from us. Other times, we have what we don't want—illnesses, bills, loneliness. Viewed one way, suffering isolates us, as we must bear it alone. In another way, it connects us in a profound way to others. If we are wise, we will allow suffering to push us closer to our gracious, all-wise God.

In my family's experience, the Lord was with us every step of the way as we journeyed with Janice into and through "the valley of the shadow of death" (Psalm 23:4), and into the new world on the other side. Sometimes His presence was almost tangible. Other times, we had an anchoring confidence from clinging to His promises. Very often, God met us through the kindness and care of His people as they loved and served us. Always, He was there—and we knew that he would never, ever forsake us (Hebrews 13:5).

Throughout Scripture, God's people see a continuing principle most succinctly declared in 2 Corinthians 5:7: "We walk by faith, not by sight." This is easier to say than it is to do. After all, we go to an uncertain destination on an unfamiliar path following an unseen Lord. But we are not following an unknown Lord—He has made himself known to us, in ways far beyond anything Joseph could have experienced. Supremely, He has made himself known by taking on our humanity, living among people, and leaving us His completed Word and indwelling Spirit. His ways and means may at times seem mysterious to us, but He himself is not a mystery. He is for His people, and "if God is for us, who can be against us?" (Romans 8:31).

That leads us to a second truth: *our eyes are fixed on One greater than Joseph*. For centuries, Bible scholars have pointed to ways in which the story of Joseph seems to anticipate our Lord Jesus Christ. The one chosen by God is despised and rejected by his own family, who plot to take his life. Yet, in God's plan, the victim, sold by his brothers and falsely accused, becomes the deliverer who saves the very ones who rejected him. Such parallels seem to have been in the mind of Stephen as he recounted the Joseph story as a foreshadowing of the Jewish people's resistance to the Lord Jesus, and their complicity in His crucifixion (Acts 7:9–16).

Joseph was a great hero for his people—so much so that they would not leave their bondage in Egypt until they made sure that his bones accompanied them on their journey to the Promised Land (Exodus 13:19; Joshua 24:32). Today, though, we have something much better than a dead hero—we have a living Savior, seated at the right hand of the Father in heaven, watching over and caring for His people on earth. So, as Christ-followers, we journey on, "looking to Jesus, the founder and perfecter of our faith" (Hebrews 12:2). He doesn't simply inspire us, He empowers us to live faithfully—all the way home.

And the promise of that home means *we have a far better hope than Joseph did.* We cannot be sure how much he and the earlier patriarchs knew of what awaited them on the other side of death. Much of their hope focused on the prospect of a land of their own in Canaan, the Promised Land. We, in contrast, have the sure promise that death will bring us instantly into the presence of Christ (Philippians 1:23; 2 Corinthians 5:8).

There, in the Father's house (John 14:1–4) and ultimately in the "new heavens and a new earth in which righteousness dwells" (2 Peter 3:13), we will experience all that our triune God has prepared for those who love Him. Joseph has begun to enjoy that promise, and so has my Janice. One day I, and hopefully you, will as well.

NOTES

Chapter One

1. The copy my mother had said that the author was unknown. Some credit the author as Malachi Franklin (1882–1965), though several other possibilities have been suggested.

Chapter Two

1. Natalie Angier, "The Changing American Family," *New York Times*, Nov. 23, 2013, www.nytimes.com/2013/11/26/health/families.html?pagewanted=all, accessed Nov. 14, 2014.

2. Chap Clark, *Hurt: Inside the World of Today's Teenagers* (Grand Rapids, MI: Baker, 2004), p. 34.

3. The stories are told in Genesis 12:10–20 and 20:1–18. Abraham's behavior is indefensible.

4. See Genesis 13. Abraham's graciousness is seen in his unselfish response to Lot, and in the way he came to his rescue in the events recorded in Genesis 14.

5. The story is found in Genesis 29.

6. Lamin Sanneh, *Summoned from the Margin: Homecoming of an African* (Grand Rapids, MI: William B. Eerdmans, 2012), p. 28.

7. Sanneh, p. 24.

8. Sanneh, p. 29.

9. The Hebrew expression is ambiguous, used elsewhere only in 2 Samuel 13:18–19 where it refers to the garment of the princess Tamar, David's daughter. The Hebrew text suggests "a robe to the palms (of the hands)," thus "long-sleeved." The rendering "many colored" comes from the Septuagint. Note that the New International Version uses the phrase "an ornate robe."

10. We read of dreams in the experience of Abimelech, a pagan king (Genesis 20:3–7); Jacob (28:12–17; 31:10–13); Laban (31:24); Pharaoh's servants (40:5–22) and Pharaoh himself (41:1–36). In each case, there was immediate recognition that this was not an ordinary dream, but one sent by God.

11. There is a mystery here. The moon perhaps refers to Joseph's mother, Rachel, who was dead. It could conceivably refer to Rachel's concubine, Bilhah, who may have become his surrogate mother upon Rachel's death. It is also possible that it refers to Leah, who is Jacob's official wife, and thus the recognized mother of the family. Nothing significant rests on the precise woman referred to.

Chapter Three

1. In verses 25 and 28 we are told that the caravan is a group of Ishmaelites; in vv. 28 and 36 they are described as Midianites. The term *Ishmaelite* (a descendant of Ishmael) appears rarely in the Old Testament, and in Judges 8:24, it is used as a synonym for Midianite. The most likely explanation is that Ishmaelite is a more general term, meaning "nomadic trader" or "Bedouin," while Midianite is geographical, indicating that they came from the region of Midian, roughly describing the southern part of today's country of Jordan.

2. It is possible, even likely, that there is an echo in Judah's memory of the guilt of Cain for killing his brother Abel. On that occasion the Lord had declared, "The voice of your brother's blood is crying to me from the ground" (Genesis 4:10).

3. "'Twenty shekels' was the typical price of male slaves between five and twenty years old, both in the old Babylonian period and in Israel according to Lev. 27:5. . . . For shepherds who might expect to earn, if employed by others, about eight shekels a year, the sale of Joseph represented a handy bonus." Gordon J. Wenham, *Genesis 16–50*, Word Biblical Commentary Volume 2, (Dallas: Word Books, 1994), 356.

4. It is most likely that "Sheol" here simply refers to the grave, as it does later in Genesis (42:38; 44:29, 31). In the light of the New Testament, life after death brings the hope of reunion with loved ones. However, it seems likely that Jacob here means that death alone will terminate his mourning—not that death will bring reunion with his son. Thankfully, the Lord Jesus "abolished death and brought life and immortality to light through the gospel" (2 Timothy 1:10).

5. Iain M. Duguid and Matthew P. Harmon, *Living in the Light of Inextinguishable Hope* (Philipsburg, NJ: P&R Publishing, 2013), 22.

Chapter Four

1. John S. Feinberg, *The Many Faces of Evil: Theological Systems and the Problems of Evil*, rev. ed. (Wheaton, IL: Crossway Books, 2005).

2. John S. Feinberg, "A Journey in Suffering," in Christopher W. Morgan and Robert A. Peterson, editors, *Suffering and the Goodness of God* (Wheaton, IL: Crossway Books, 2008), 219.

3. Ibid., 219.

4. Ibid., 225.

5. Warren Wiersbe, *Why Us? When Bad Things Happen to God's People* (Old Tappan, NJ: Fleming H. Revell, 1984), 115.

6. John R. W. Stott, *The Cross of Christ* (Downers Grove, IL: InterVarsity Press, 1986), 335–36.

7. I owe this illustration to one given by Vince Vitale in the book he authored with Ravi Zacharias, *Why Suffering? Finding Meaning and Comfort When Life Doesn't Make Sense* (New York: Faith Words, 2014), 84–85.

8. Ibid., 86.

9. The Hebrew name rendered LORD (in distinction from "Lord") in most English translations involves the four letter name YHWH. Its precise pronunciation is debated, since the Jewish people believed it too sacred to pronounce. Scholars agree that Yahweh is the most appropriate English rendering.

10. Jerry Bridges, *Trusting God: Even When Life Hurts* (Colorado Springs, CO: NavPress, 1988, 2008), 54.

11. John J. Davis, *Paradise to Prison: Studies in Genesis* (Grand Rapids, MI: Baker, 1975), p. 269.

12. Jerry Sittser, *A Grace Disguised: How the Soul Grows through Loss—Expanded Edition* (Grand Rapids, MI: Zondervan, 2004), 29.

13. Ibid., 17–18.

Chapter Five

1. In following the story of Joseph, we have passed over Genesis 38, moving directly from Genesis 37 to 39. Genesis 38 is one of the most sordid stories of the OT, revolving around Judah's sexual dalliance with a prostitute, who turned out to be his daughter-in-law Tamar in disguise. Judah is seen acting in totally disreputable ways, but there is a turning point in the story, and in his life, that will prove significant later in the Joseph story. Our focus on Joseph leads us to pass over that story for the present, but we will return to it in Chapter 10. It is important to notice that Moses is putting Judah and Joseph in stark contrast in Genesis 38 and 39. Judah "sees and takes" the prostitute (38:6); Joseph refuses and flees his seductress.

2. The word rendered "laugh" in the ESV is rendered "make sport of" in the NIV. The term has sexual overtones in Genesis 26:8, while in 21:6, it connotes insulting behavior. This is probably the sense it has here, while in verse 17 it clearly has sexual overtones.

3. Gordon J. Wenham, *Genesis 16–50. The Word Bible Commentary* (Dallas, TX: Word Books, 1994), 378.

4. Russell Moore, *Tempted and Tried: Temptation and the Triumph of Christ* (Wheaton: Crossway Books, 2011), 48.

Chapter Six

1. This is from a transcript of one of Elisabeth Elliot's *Gateway to Joy* radio broadcasts, and was originally posted on the Back to the Bible website. It can now be found at http://everlypleasant.com/do-the-next-thing-by-elisabeth-elliot/ Accessed May 20, 2016.

2. J. Vergote, cited by John Wenham, *Genesis 16–50, Word Biblical Commentary* (Dallas, TX: Word Books, 1994), 382.

3. Victor P. Hamilton, *The Book of Genesis, Chapters 18–50*. The New International Commentary on the Old Testament (Grand Rapids, MI: Eerdmans, 1995), 476.

4. Iain Duguid and Matthew Harmon, *Living in the Light of Inextinguishable Hope* (Phillipsburg, NJ: P&R Publishing, 2013), 69.

5. A. W. Tozer, *The Knowledge of the Holy* (New York: Harper and Row, 1961), 9.

6. Ibid., 12.

7. Malcolm Muggeridge, *Jesus Rediscovered* (New York: Doubleday, 1969), 77.

8. Malcolm Muggeridge, *A Twentieth Century Testimony* (New York: Thomas Nelson, 1978), 72.

Chapter Seven

1. Richard Halverson, *Between Sundays* (Grand Rapids, MI: Zondervan, 1965), 30–31.

2. Bruce K. Waltke with Cathi J. Fredricks, *Genesis: a Commentary* (Grand Rapids, MI: Zondervan, 2001), 536.

3. "He did not need to promote himself, even after so many disappointments, because his trust remained in God to protect him and provide for him." Iain Duguid and Matthew Harmon, *Living in the Light of Inextinguishable Hope* (Phillipsburg, NJ: P&R Publishing, 2013), 77.

4. Science of Us. "Holding a Grudge May Literally Weigh You Down" by Melissa Dahl, January 9, 2015, http://nymag.com/scienceofus/2015/01/holding-a-grudge-may-literally -weigh-you-down.html, accessed May 13, 2016.

5. Richard Halverson, *No Greater Power* (Portland, OR: Multnomah Press, 1986), 213.

6. J. Oswald Sanders, *Robust in Faith* (Chicago: Moody Press, 1965), 44.

7. GraceGems.org. "The Lord's Prayer" by Thomas Watson. http://www.gracegems.org /Watson/lords_prayer6.htm, accessed May 13, 2016. Watson wrote in the late seventeenth century; the words quoted are presented in updated language.

Chapter Eight

1. Dwight D. Eisenhower, *At Ease: Stories I Tell to Friends* (Garden City, NY: Doubleday, 1967), 52.

2. "Fear of a hostile infiltration of the land is a very genuine characteristic of ancient Egyptian life. The northeast frontier was one of the vulnerable places of the Egyptian empire." Gerhard von Rad, *Genesis: a Commentary*, Revised Edition (Philadelphia: Westminster Press, 1972), 382.

3. See also Genesis 43:30; 45:2, 46:29; 50:1, 17.

4. Gordon Wenham, *Genesis 16–50, Word Biblical Commentary* (Dallas, TX: Word Books, 1994), 409.

Chapter Nine

1. BBC Sport Cycling. "Lance Armstrong Interview: An Abridged Transcript" by Dan Roan, January 26, 2015, http://www.bbc.com/sport/cycling/30955902, accessed January 27, 2015. All Armstrong quotations are from this transcript.

2. Bruce K. Waltke with Cathi J. Fredricks, *Genesis: a Commentary* (Grand Rapids, MI: Zondervan, 2001), 552.

3. Victor P. Hamilton, *The Book of Genesis, Chapters 18–50.* The New International Commentary on the Old Testament (Grand Rapids, MI: Eerdmans, 1995), 554.

4. Waltke, 556.

Chapter Ten

1. The practice of divination is explicitly condemned elsewhere in the Torah (Leviticus 19:26; Numbers 23:23; Deut. 18:10). While the use of divining cups was probably common in Egypt, such a practice seems contrary to Joseph's conviction that God himself revealed dreams and hidden truths (Gen. 48:8; 41:16). It is probably more likely that this is part of Joseph's ploy, to increase the seriousness of the act by suggesting that it was not only a personal object, but a sacred one.

2. "He cannot be referring to the goblet, for he has just asserted their innocence. He may be referring to guilt in general, but more probably to their crime against Joseph." Bruce K. Waltke with Cathi J. Fredricks, *Genesis: a Commentary* (Grand Rapids, MI: Zondervan, 2001), 561.

3. "It is Judah's moving speech of self-sacrifice, of his love for his father and family . . . that incites Joseph to move the family beyond its pain of the past to a new beginning." Kenneth A. Mathews, *Genesis 11:27–50:26, The New American Commentary, Volume 1b* (Nashville, TN: Broadman and Holman, 2005), 807.

4. C. S. Lewis, *The Problem of Pain* (New York: Macmillan, 1962), 109.

Chapter Eleven

1. C. S. Lewis, *Mere Christianity* (New York: Scribners, 1952), 89.

2. I have considered the subject of forgiveness at length in my book *Forgiveness: Discovering the Power and Reality of Authentic Christian Forgiveness* (Grand Rapids, MI: Discovery House, 2005).

3. Boston Globe. "At Roof bond hearing, victims' relatives speak of pain, forgiveness" by Nikita Stewart and Richard Perez-Pena, June 19, 2015, http://www.bostonglobe.com/news/nation/2015/06/19/church-shooting-suspect-thought-blacks-were-taking-over-world/IOuZIsIzXdOvdTQFF0jhEP/story.html, accessed September 9, 2015.

4. USA Today. "Christians forgive the unspeakable" by Kristin Powers, quoting Charles C. W. Cooke, June 24, 2015, http://www.usatoday.com/story/opinion/2015/06/23/charleston-families-forgive-dylann-roof-columns/29113573/, accessed September 9, 2015.

5. C. S. Lewis, *The Weight of Glory* (New York: HarperCollins, 1949), 182.

6. Iain Duguid and Matthew P. Harmon, *Living in the Light of Inextinguishable Hope* (Harrisburg, NJ: P&R Publishing, 2013), 121.

7. Alister McGrath discusses this distinction, which he attributes to Austin Farrar, in *If I Had Lunch with C. S. Lewis* (Carol Stream, IL: Tyndale House, 2014), 176–77. In a very different context, it also occurs in Malcolm Gladwell, *What the Dog Saw, and Other Adventures* (New York: Little Brown and Company, 2009), 153–54.

8. McGrath, 176–77.

9. Bruce K. Waltke with Cathi J. Fredricks, *Genesis: a Commentary* (Grand Rapids, MI: Zondervan, 2001), 564.

10. Some at this point suggest that Joseph is "encouraging them not to have second thoughts about returning to Egypt for fear of how they may be treated in the future" (Gordon J. Wenham, *Genesis 16–50, Word Biblical Commentary* [Dallas, TX: Word Books, 1994], 430). This is possible, but the suggestion in the text seems to me to be more likely.

Chapter Twelve

1. "Providential guidance had seemed so clear when Joseph's message came to Hebron that Jacob got underway for Egypt at once. At the southern extremity of the land of promise, the momentous character of such a step came home to him with greater clearness. God had not yet spoken directly. . . . The decisive step was not to be taken without clear divine direction." Herbert C. Leupold, *Exposition of Genesis Volume 2* (Grand Rapids, MI: Baker, 1942), 1107.

2. There are five other times in Jacob's life when he had a supernatural encounter with God: at Bethel as he fled Canaan in fear of Esau (Genesis 28:10–22); in Haran (Genesis

31:10–16); at Mahanaim (Genesis 32:1–2); at the brook Jabbok (Genesis 32:22–33); and at Bethel (Genesis 35:9–15).

3. This promise of the Covenant is repeated often, in the face of the slow growth of the Abrahamic family. See Genesis 12:2 and 18:18, as well as here.

4. Using that expression made me wonder where it came from. It apparently dates back several centuries, and describes the various working parts of an ancient rifle, thus, collectively, "everything, the totality."

5. Verse 26 says that 66 traveled with Jacob, while verse says that 70 came into Egypt. The larger number probably comes by adding Jacob, Joseph, and Joseph's two sons to the 66 descendants who made the trip.

6. Bruce K. Waltke with Cathi J. Fredricks, *Genesis: a Commentary* (Grand Rapids, MI: Zondervan, 2001), 585.

7. This is the way Armstrong insisted he said it, not as it is often remembered, "one small step for man."

Chapter Thirteen

1. Dr. and Mrs. Howard Taylor, *Biography of James Hudson Taylor* (London: Hodder and Stoughton, 1965), 86–87.

2. The term "sojourn" is significant, since it refers to a temporary, not a permanent, status. In our context, they are asking for work permits, not immigrant papers.

3. The word translated *possession* "refers to inalienable property received from a sovereign, or at least from one who has the power to release or retain land." Victor Hamilton, *The Book of Genesis Chapters 18–50* (Grand Rapids, MI: Eerdmans, 1995), 613. They thus receive far more than they asked for.

4. This is seen preeminently in the famous events recorded in Numbers 14:1–4; see also Numbers 11:4–6.

5. Kent Hughes, *Set Apart: Calling a Worldly Church to a Godly Life* (Wheaton, IL: Crossway Books, 2003), 17.

6. Gordon J. Wenham, *Genesis 16–50, Word Biblical Commentary* (Dallas, TX: Word Books, 1994), 449.

Chapter Fourteen

1. Edith Schaeffer, *What Is a Family?* (Grand Rapids, MI: Baker, 1997), 105.

2. Schaeffer, 107.

3. Billy Graham, *Nearing Home: Life, Faith and Finishing Well* (Nashville, TN: Thomas Nelson, 2011), vii.

4. "His concern was that there should be nothing done in respect to his death whereby Israel's hopes should be blunted or blurred. This could occur if he should be buried in Egypt." Harold Stigers, *A Commentary on Genesis* (Grand Rapids, MI: Zondervan, 1976), 322.

5. The specifics are debated. The word refers either to the thigh or the sexual organs, and it is interesting that both in Genesis 24 and here in Genesis 46 the oath is related to family matters.

6. "Joseph, in taking the oath, makes himself directly accountable to God and places himself under God's wrath if he reneges on his promise." Victor P. Hamilton, *The Book of Genesis, Chapters 18–50*. The New International Commentary on the Old Testament (Grand Rapids, MI: Eerdmans, 1995), 625.

7. This name occurs six times in Genesis. "It tends to be matched to situations where God's servants are hard pressed and needing assurance." Derek Kidner, *Genesis: An Introduction and Commentary* (London: Tyndale Press, 1967), 129.

8. "Texts found at Nuzi indicate that adoption of this kind was not uncommon in the Middle East of the time." Leon Wood, *Genesis: A Study Guide Commentary* (Grand Rapids, MI: Zondervan, 1976), 144.

9. That Joseph received the birthright, rather than Reuben, is spelled out in 1 Chronicles 5:1–2: "The sons of Reuben the firstborn of Israel (for he was the firstborn, but because he defiled his father's couch, his birthright was given to the sons of Joseph the son of Israel, so that he could not be enrolled as the oldest son; though Judah became strong among his brothers and a chief came from him, yet the birthright belonged to Joseph)."

10. Gordon Wenham, *Genesis 1–15. Word Biblical Commentary* (Dallas, TX: Word Books, 1987), 24.

11. Gordon Wenham, *Genesis 16–50. Word Biblical Commentary* (Dallas, TX: Word Books, 1994), 464.

12. Hamilton, 636.

13. Bruce K. Waltke with Cathi J. Fredricks, *Genesis: A Commentary* (Grand Rapids, MI: Zondervan, 2001), 259.

14. 1 Corinthians 10:13 is often claimed to say this, but it doesn't. It is speaking specifically of temptation and promising a way of escape. But imagine a Christian being threatened with beheading by ISIS terrorists. There is humanly "no way of escape," and only God's mysterious presence through his indwelling Spirit can enable such a believer to handle martyrdom. The strength certainly won't come from clichés or personal resources!

15. "What Jacob was affirming was that his God had redeemed all of that evil. It is not that bad things never happened to him, but rather that those bad things were worked by God into something that was good." Iain Duguid and Matthew P. Harmon, *Living in the Light of Inextinguishable Hope* (Harrisburg, NJ: P&R Publishing, 2013), 166.

Chapter Fifteen

1. I first came across the story of Bernard Gilpin in Ajith Fernando, *The Call to Joy and Pain* (Wheaton, IL: Crossway, 2007), 39–40. This version reflects further details gleaned from the Internet.

2. Egyptians embalmed bodies so as to assist their journey in the afterlife.

3. "If they misstate the truth at the beginning to Jacob (ch. 37), what is to prevent them from misstating the truth about Jacob at the end? And why would Jacob share this with them and not directly with Joseph? . . . The best one can say is that the brothers' quotation of their father's earlier words is unverifiable." Victor P. Hamilton, *The Book of Genesis, Chapters 18–50*. The New International Commentary on the Old Testament (Grand Rapids, MI: Eerdmans, 1995), 703.

4. W. H. Griffith Thomas, *Genesis: A Devotional Commentary* (Grand Rapids, MI: Eerdmans, 1946), 498.

5. "God's actions and human action run along together. God's action and God's control happen in addition to and alongside human action and influence. We have abundant examples in the Bible of such divine action. But it remains mysterious to us exactly *how* God's action relates to human action in such a way that God is fully in control and human agents are at the same time fully responsible." Vern S. Poythress, *Chance and the Sovereignty of God* (Wheaton: Crossway, 2014), 57.

6. Kenneth A. Mathews, *Genesis 11:27–50:26, The New American Commentary, Volume 1b* (Nashville, TN: Broadman and Holman, 2005), 928.

7. The text says that he "said to his brothers" (Genesis 50:24). Joseph was the second youngest of Jacob's twelve sons, and it seems very unlikely that, when he was 110, all of the others were still alive. The term probably is intended to include any surviving brothers, and the children of the others.

NOTE TO THE READER

The publisher invites you to share your response to the message of this book by writing Discovery House, P.O. Box 3566, Grand Rapids, MI 49501, USA. For information about other Discovery House books, music, or DVDs, contact us at the same address or call 1-800-653-8333. Find us online at dhp.org or send e-mail to books@dhp.org.